# Alternative Publishers of Books in North America

## 6<sup>th</sup> Edition

# Alternative Publishers of Books in North America

## 6th Edition

By Byron Anderson

Under the auspices of:
The Alternatives in Publication Task Force
of the Social Responsibilities Round Table
of the American Library Association

Library Juice Press, LLC
Duluth, Minnesota

Library Juice Press, LLC
Duluth, Minnesota
http://libraryjuicepress.com/

ISBN-10: 0-9778617-2-4
ISBN-13: 978-0-9778617-2-9

Anderson, Byron, 1944-

Alternative publishers of books in North America / by Byron Anderson
under the auspices of The Alternatives in Publication Task Force of the
Social Responsibilities Round Table of the American Library Association. 6th edition. -- Duluth, Minnesota : Library Juice Press LLC, copy-
right 2006.

Preface by Nancy Kranich.
Includes bibliography on alternative publishing and subject index.

1. Alternative presses--United States--Directories. 2. Alternative
presses--Canada--Directories. 3. Little presses--United States--
Directories. 4. Little presses--Canada--Directories. 5. Underground
press--United States--Directories. 6. Underground press--Canada--
Directories. I. Kranich, Nancy C., 1950- II. American Library Association. Social Responsibilities Round Table. Alternatives in Publication
Task Force. III. Library Juice Press.

# Table of Contents

themselves as multi-media information, entertainment, and shopping giants, controlling both the transmission and the content of information. To many, newly converging technologies and industries promised abundant open access to an infinite array of resources that could foster political participation and enrich people's lives. Indeed, the arrival of the information age inspired dreams of a utopia where people could access myriad ideas, no longer constrained by location, format, cost, or other barriers. But instead of increased competition and more diversity, deregulation sparked mega mergers with companies such as Viacom absorbing Simon and Schuster Publishers and the CBS television network, General Electric buying NBC, and Capital Cities/ABC purchasing Disney. With the arrival of these new media giants, public concern aronse once more; but this time discourse focused mostly on the technological rather than content and cultural implications.

In the early 1990's, media industries intensified their efforts to influence public policy, culminating in the passage of Telecommunications Act of 1996--the first wholesale revision of communications law since 1934. The 1996 Act further relaxed already loose limits on how many radio or TV stations a single company could own, and eliminated barriers to cross-ownership of broadcast, cable television, and newspapers as well as local and long distance telephone services. New activist organizations like Computer Professionals for Social Responsibility, the Center for Media Education, the Electronic Frontier Foundation, and the Internet Free Expression Alliance concentrated on various components of the law, ranging from deregulation to communications decency to ownership limits. These and other groups joined progressive activists who mobilized against a new media landscape that they perceived as threatening to the future of democratic discourse. To contemplate how to free the media from corporate control, many of these activists convened congresses to express their outrage.

But not until the FCC decided to loosen its already relaxed media consolidation and cross-ownership rules in 2003 did widespread opposition boil over. Outcry came spontaneously from both the political right and left, who feared that further reductions in the number of media owners would result in less diversity and more concentrated control over ideas and information. Although a federal appeals court issued a preliminary injunction blocking the FCC's rule changes in September 2003, mainstream media elbowed each other in a gold rush to acquire and merge without so much as a nod to their public interest obligations. The result: a monoculture where the United States has become the "best entertained,

# Preface

Millions of Americans spoke out in 2003 when the Federal Communications Commission (FCC) announced changes in media ownership rules that allowed more consolidation and cross-ownership of media. They accused the FCC of undermining a viable democracy and weakening the ability of broadcasters to ensure "the widest possible dissemination of information from diverse and antagonistic sources." (*Associated Press v. United States*, 326 U.S. 1, 20 (1945). This grassroots activism arose from years of frustration with a U.S. media system unresponsive to the need for diversity and localism.

Public concern about the impact of media consolidation on "the widest possible dissemination of information from diverse and antagonistic sources" dates back several decades before the Associated Press decision to the days when a broadcast reform movement emerged that opposed the commercialism taking hold of radio and encouraged the establishment of a non-profit, noncommercial sector. The Communications Act of 1934, which created the Federal Communications Commission (the FCC), signaled a recognition that government has a role to play in making information available, and set forth a "public interest, convenience, and necessity" standard for licensing and regulating radio and later TV broadcasting over the public airwaves. This regulatory framework for ensuring competition over a scarce number of channels defused reformers' efforts to promote a non-profit alternative for the next thirty years. By the early 1960s, dissatisfaction with the airwaves re-surfaced following the 1959 quiz show scandals and Newton Minow's 1961 speech describing television as a "vast wasteland." In 1967, Congress passed the Public Broadcasting Act, which ushered in new opportunities for airing unprofitable cultural, educational, and public affairs programming—a move that was to level the playing field for a fair and balanced airing of diverse voices. Over the next few decades, increased penetration of cable television gave rise to an alternative television movement focused on public access and guerilla television that was produced by an engaged public armed with portable video cameras who could show their work on channels reserved for public, government and educational purposes.

The breakup of AT&T and the emergence of new information and communication technologies shaped both the information marketplace and the nation's policy agenda. No longer limited to highly regulated telephone or television services, communication conglomerates repositioned least informed society in the world." (Neal Postman, *Amusing Ourselves to Death: Public Discourse in the Age of Show Business*, Penguin Books, New York, 1995.)

When Ben Bagdikian published his first exposé in *The Media Monopoly* in 1983, he warned against the chilling effects that control by fifty media companies could have over the free flow of diverse ideas and information. Critics at the time called Bagdikian "alarmist." Today, the number of corporations controlling most of America's magazines, radio and TV stations, books, movies, and daily mass-circulation newspapers has dropped from fifty to five, with those conglomerates amassing unprecedented influence over what Americans see, hear, and read. Activists like Robert McChesney have joined Bagdikian by documenting the debilitating impact of mergers, acquisitions, and legislative "de-regulation" on a functioning democracy and healthy culture. In addition, they have channeled public fury into a media reform movement aiming to increase popular participation in policy making; and ultimately, to invigorate independent media.

So how can this catalytic reform movement against the mainstream media also become an opportunity to elevate alternatives, particularly alternative book publishing? For media conglomerates have grown ever more massive and powerful, many reputable and independent book publishers, distributors, and booksellers have disappeared; and, once absorbed into conglomerates, financial and marketing people dominate editorial processes. If a book does not look as if it will sell a certain number of copies—and that number increases every year—the "numbers" people argue that the company simply cannot afford to undertake the project. Market censorship is increasingly in force in a decision-making process now based on whether there is a pre-existing audience for a particular title. Books by well-known authors or obvious successes are preferred; whereas new authors and critical viewpoints increasingly face rejection by the major houses. As a result, the playing field tilts toward larger firms with vast advertising budgets, publicity networks, and sales forces. The result, in the words of Project Censored's Peter Phillips, is a U.S. media that "has lost its diversity and its ability to present different points of view."("Building Media Democracy," in *Censored, 1999: The News That Didn't Make the News*, by Peter Phillips and Project Censored, Seven Stories Press, New York, 1999, p. 129.)

While small, independent presses provide an alternative to counter balance the corporate media, their share of the market is estimated at less than 1% of total book sales. Unable to compete on equal footing, they do not have the strength or resources of the major firms, and they do not have anywhere near as ready access to bookstores and libraries. These presses are often absent from the review media, standard bibliographic tools, and conference exhibits. Furthermore, little money, influence or prestige backs alternative publishers. They are small, their authors and editors rarely known. Often, Library of Congress cataloging is minimal or non-existent for their publications. Book distributors omit them from approval plans, making it difficult for libraries and bookstores to acquire their titles efficiently. They are also outside the mainstream of other traditional distribution channels and the peripheral vision of wholesale book buyers like librarians and independent bookstore owners. Some are even unaware of the potential of selling to these markets or confused as to how to do it. This is unfortunate.

If the public is to benefit from a full range of relevant facts and opinions, authors and readers must make an extra effort to support independent, alternative producers. In the book publishing arena, they must pursue those presses that provide more obscure, diverse perspectives as well as vital information about their communities. Alternative publishers are on the cutting edge of important literature and issues. Their books may not make the bestseller list, but they have a vast, untapped audience that must be reached. Their important cultural and literary contribution is an essential part of the community of publishers with whom authors and readers must interact.

As of late, the frightening pace of media consolidation and disappearance of trusted publishers has dismayed many activists. Nevertheless, they have reason for hope. Over the last few years, book production in the U.S. has skyrocketed, driven largely by small publishers, with the output of the larger houses increasing only minimally since 2003. While overall revenues are barely rising, the outlook for alternative publishing is promising. As Americans seek new political visions and reject corporate control of the media, many look to progressive publications as an antidote. And it is within alternative books that new arguments and inquiries are examined at length and in depth. Moreover, these books are now more likely to find new audiences thanks to what *Wired* editor Chris Anderson calls "The Long Tail" of the Internet—a tail that makes it easier for consumers to find and buy niche products because of the net's "infinite shelf-space effect." (*Wired Magazine*, Issue 12.10, October 2004, http://www.wired.com/wired/archive/12.10/tail.html)

New distribution mechanisms can break through the bottlenecks of traditional retail, offering enhanced opportunities to draw attention to such niche products as alternative books. To take advantage of a more promising political and economic environment, activists must harness the same technological vehicles they have successfully deployed to mobilize political action--vehicles such as blogs and online customer reviews to showcase lesser known voices in the alternative press. An essential tool for identifying those meaningful voices is *Alternative Publishers of Books in North America*. Today, public participation and freedom of expression are at stake in the battle to control the flow of information and ideas. By promoting access to alternative book publishers, this Directory will help independent presses beat the odds in the marketplace for ideas, thereby ensuring access to the diversity of opinion so essential to the future of democracy.

Nancy Kranich
Past President of the American Library Association
June 5, 2006

# Introduction

"Our culture needs to snap out of the trance we're lulled into by corporate dominance of the way we learn, live, and get our news and entertainment. We authors, publishers, and journalists need to realize just how important our roles as watchdogs and whistle-blowers are."
Jim Barnes, Editor and Publisher. Editor commentary, *Independent Publisher Online*, vol. 6, no. 1 (January 2006)

"Throughout the twentieth century, oppositional and minority movements, including workers, welfare mothers, people of color, gays and lesbians, and disabled persons have used the alternative press to develop the vision and power their struggles have required"
Chuck D'Adamo, Editorial Collective, Alternative Press Center. "Some Alternative Press History," American Library Association, Annual Conference, Toronto, 2003

The presses profiled in this directory were culled from hundreds of small, active independent presses. This effort builds on the previous five editions of this directory. In total, one will find 126 U.S. presses, nineteen Canadian, and eighteen international presses having either a North American address or distributor. Thirty-three presses are new to this edition. To be included required minimum at least five titles in print and on average the publication of one new title per year. The presses that remained after all the culling and limiting were the 163 active alternative presses found in this directory.

Alternative press as a term is nearly inexplicable. Everything is alternative to something else, meaning that one could theoretically define "alternative" as one would wish. Yet, in social and political arenas, "alternative" is a term generally associated with the political left. The 102 headings found in the subject index further help to define the presses by assigning them publication interests in the areas of, for example, sustainable development, punk, social justice, gender studies, human rights, anarchism, and globalization. The presses provide a platform to spread progressive ideas to activists and ordinary citizens alike, and the publications help the ideas find a place in our culture.

Alternative publishers counter the concentration of media ownership, which for the publishing industry amounts to six conglomerates that dominate in book sales and marketing. In this competitive arena, small alternative presses lack resources to compete and for the most part are marginalized. This business environment is a form of market censorship which makes media consolidation an intellectual freedom issue. Alternative presses struggle to get their publications into libraries and the hands of readers, and have limited resources to do so.

The presses profiled are, first, independent, that is, independent of corporate ownership. Exceptions are a few imprints of larger presses; however, there is every reason to believe that these alternative presses have editorial control over their publications. Second, the presses are small, averaging approximately one to 100 new titles per year. Third, alternative publishers are generally not driven by profit or the bottom line, though breaking even is essential for survival and profit is important for expanding the press's mission and output. They often have to rely on grants and donations to survive, and many have a 501(c)(3) not-for-profit status. Fourth, the publishers are individuals often dedicated to a cause or movement and are frequently driven with a desire to get certain titles into print regardless of their "saleability." Fifth, these publishers take risks that mainstream publishers rarely take. They take risks on bringing to print voices of minorities, new authors, experimental writing, controversial and radical subjects, translations, and reprints of classic older titles. Also, the titles are kept in print much longer that those of the mainstream press, sometimes for the life of the press. Finally, small presses are increasing in number, currently numbering over 73,000 in the U.S. that publish between one and ten titles per year. At the same time, a number of these presses are very vulnerable—many will not make it beyond their first title. Some of the directory's presses have a questionable survival, including Rising Tide Press, Sister Vision Press, and Third Woman Press. The turnover of presses in the directory since 1998 has been approximately 50 percent.

Not found in this directory are small presses that are clearly alternative in some way, but do not fall within the defining characteristics found above. This would include publishers in subject areas such as spirituality, New Age, alternative medicine, paranormal, and conspiracy theory. While some presses having titles in erotica are included, others with a focus on pornography are not. Publishers of alternative comics are included if they also publish in other alternative subject areas. Not found are the many independent presses that have alternative titles, but not enough to be considered an alternative press. There is a major difference between alternative publishers of books and publishers of alternative books. Even corporate presses occasionally publish alternative titles, but missing is the level of dedication and compassion that so many of the alternative publishers embrace. Corporate presses are not out to change the world, rather they're in business to profit from publishing. Academic presses are not included, though included are a few presses associated with a college or university, usually in the form of working space or affiliation with a department. Also missing are self-published alternative books and presses where a large majority of books were authored by the publisher. This latter would include, for example, Henry Rollins's 2.13.61's punk-advocate press, and Marvin X's Black Bird Press.

The directory is a unique reference tool that gathers information on significant alternative presses and places this under one cover. The information attempts to educate and bring more awareness of alternative presses to librarians and others interested in these publications. Librarians can clearly benefit from the directory when the publications are incorporated into the library's collection as well as its collection development procedures. The titles would readily expand the diversity of the collection and fill-in gaps. For library purchases, many of the publishers work with trade distributors, particularly Consortium, Small Press Distribution, AK Press Distribution, and Publishers Group West. Other presses require buyers to purchase directly from the press, a sometimes burdensome process for acquisitions units. Still, librarians are encouraged to do so, and should always inquire about a library discount as many provide this.

For individuals interested in purchasing a title from one of the presses in this directory, buying direct from the publisher is the most beneficial for the press. Most have a website and purchasing options are listed with many having a secure bookcart feature and/or an optional online order form that can then be mailed. If purchasing from a bookstore, go to an independent bookstore. If you lack an independent bookstore in your area, purchase from Booksense, http://www.booksense.com, a website of independent bookstores. Make a political statement: support independent publishers and independent bookstores.

The directory is an on-going project of the Alternatives in Publication Task Force (AIP), a section of the Social Responsibilities Round Table of the American Library Association. The authority for this directory comes from the collective expertise of the AIP members and its long-term involvement with the alternative press. The unsung hero award in getting early editions published goes to Charles Willett, founder and editor of CRISES Press. Without his efforts, the directory likely would not exist. He had the foresight to see its value and the dedication to bring the title into print through the first five editions, 1994-2002. The directory now continues through Library Juice Press. Finally, I would personally like to thank Nancy Kranich, long-time advocate of media diversity, for her willingness to write the preface.

The directory's editor makes no pretense that the profiles represent a complete, comprehensive list of alternative publishers. The publishing industry changes too fast to assume comprehensiveness, and as a result, a few presses may have been missed. Yet, there is every reason to believe that these publishers at least represent both the core and "lion's share" of alternative publishers active today. For additional resources, go to the "Bibliographic and Web Tools for Alternative Publishers" webpage at http://www.libr.org/AIP/bibtools.html. Also related to this directory is a counterpart for alternative periodicals, *Annotations: guide to the independent critical press*, edited by Marie Jones (Baltimore, MD: Alternative Press Center, 2004). Future editions of *Alternative Publishers of Books in North* America are planned. The editor welcomes recommendations for inclusion in future editions at any time.

Byron Anderson,
Editor and Compiler
Alternatives in
Publication Task Force

banderson@niu.edu

# Directory of Publishers

## AK PRESS

674A 23rd St.
Oakland, CA 94612-1163
(510) 208-1700 Fax: (510) 208-1701
Email: akpress@akpress.org Web: www.akpress.org

**Editor**: Collective editing
**Associated with**: AK Press, Edinburg/London; AK Press Distribution; AK Press Audio
**ISBN prefix**: 1-873176, 1-9022593
**Average number of titles published per year**: 25
**Number of titles in print**: 150
**Other materials produced**: Audio CDs
**Distributors**: publisher direct via the website's; AK Press Distribution, Consortium, and Small Press Distribution
**Publication interests**: Activism, Alternative Culture, Anarchism, Critical Theory, Cultural Studies, International Issues/Relations, Music, Politics, Punk, Social Justice, Surrealism
**Motto**: "Purveyor of radical literature."

Founded in 1991, AK Press and Distribution is a worker-owned run book publisher and distributor whose goal is to make available radical books and other materials published independently which can make a positive change. AK Press is known for anarchist, anti-authoritarian and alternative culture books, and is a major publishing outlet for the punk and surrealist movements. Top sellers include *Philosophy of Punk* now in its second edition and *SCUM Manifesto*. Examples of other titles include: Ward Churchill's *Reflections on the Justice of Roosting Chickens: the consequences of U. S. imperial arrogance and criminality*; Noam Chomsky's *Language and Politics*, 2nd ed., on the political aspects of language; Joel Andreas' *Addicted to War: why the U.S. can't kick militarism*, a revealing account of why the U. S. has been involved in more wars in recent years than any other country; and Rudolf Rocker's *Anarcho-Syndicalism: theory and practice*, written a half century ago, it still has relevance for people who are concerned with problems of liberty and justice.

## THE ADVOCADO PRESS
P.O. Box 145
Louisville, KY 40201
(502) 894-9492  Fax: (502) 899-9562
Email: office@advocadopress.org  Web: www.advocadopress.org

**Editor**: Mary Johnson
**ISBN prefix**: 0-9721189, 0-9627064
**Average number of new titles published per year**: 1
**Number of titles in print**: 8
**Other materials produced**: periodical *The Disability Rag Reader* (also called *Ragged Edge*) and diskettes for braille and speech readers
**Distributors**: publisher direct via the website
**Publication interests**: Activism, Civil Liberties, Disabilities, Discrimination, Law/Legal Studies, Social Issues

Founded in 1981, Advocado Press publishes books and periodicals on disability rights and the disability experience. Examples of titles include: Julie Shaw Cole's *Getting Life*, a fictional account of the pains and triumphs of a seventeen-year nursing home resident; *The Ragged Edge Anthology*, the disability experience from the pages of *The Disability Rag*; and *To Ride the Public's Buses: the fight that built a movement*, edited by Mary Johnson and Barrett Shaw, how the effort to get lifts on buses became a movement.

## AFRICA WORLD PRESS
541 West Ingham Ave., Suite B
Trenton, NJ 08638
(609) 695-3200  Fax: (609) 695-6466
Web: writers.aalbc.com/africaworldpress.htm

**Editor:** Kassahun Checole
**Affiliated press names**: The Red Sea Press, Inc.
**ISBN prefix**: 0-865439, 1-59221 (Africa World) and 0-932415, 1-56902 (Red Sea)
**Average number of new titles published per year**: 80
**Number of titles in print**: 530
**Distributors**: Red Sea and Agora Publishing
**Publication interests**: Africa, African American, Anthropology, Art, Children/Juvenile, Cultural Studies, Development Studies, Economics, Health, History, Human Rights, Latin American Studies, Literary, Poetry, Politics,

Race/Race Relations, Religion, Sociology, Third World Studies, Women's Issues/Studies
**Motto**: "Our books define your world."

Founded in 1983, African World Press is dedicated to the publication of books on the African world. It is a premier publisher of books on Africa, African-American, Caribbean and Latin American issues. As of mid-2005, the press's main web address and phone was not working (the above is a substitute) and emails have not been returned. The Red Sea Press was founded in 1985 and has since become a premier distribution network, distributing the books of over 250 publishing companies, with a special focus on and about people of African descent in the United States, Europe, the Caribbean and Latin America. Red Sea has become one of the world's foremost publishers on the Horn of Africa. Examples of titles include: *Ogun's Children: the literature and politics of Wole Soyinka since the Nobel*, edited by Onookome Okome; *Race, Gender and Culture Conflict: debating the African condition*, edited by Alamin Mazuri and Willy Mutunga; Clenora Hudson-Weems' *Africana Womanist Literary Theory*; and Tanya Lyons' *Guns and Guerilla Girls: women in the Zimbabwean liberation struggle (1965-1980)*.

## AFRICAN AMERICAN IMAGES
1909 W. 95th St.
Chicago, IL 60643
(800) 552-1991 (773) 445-0322  Fax: (773) 445-9844
Email: customer@AfricanAmericanImages.com
Web: www.africanamericanimages.com

**Editor**: Dr. Jawanza Kunjufu
**Associated with**: African American Images Bookstore
**ISBN prefix**: 0-913543; 09749000
**Average number of new titles published per year**: 10
**Number of titles in print**: 199
**Other materials produced**: Africentric multicultural curriculum material designed for today's youth
**Distributors**: publisher direct via the website; Independent Publishers Group
**Publication interests**: African-American, Biography, Discrimination, Economics, Education, Men's Issues/Studies, Minorities, Race/Race Relations, Religion, Women's Issues/Studies

Founded in 1980, African American Images publishes and distributes books of an Africentric nature that promote self-esteem, collective values, liberation, and skill development. The children's and young adult books provide a celebration of blackness, and offer guidance through a black perspective. All books are nonfiction and numerous titles are authored by the editor. Examples of titles include: Carter G. Woodson's *The Miseducation of the Negro*; Jimmy Dumas' *24 Reasons Why Black People Suffe*; Lawson Bush, V's *Can Black Mothers Raise Our Sons?*; Felix Ehui's *What if Blacks Didn't Exist?*, a historical and political analysis of the contributions made by Africans and African Americans; and *Countering the Conspiracy to Destroy Black Boys*, vols. 1-4, a multi-volume set that offers suggestions to correct the dehumanization of African American children and how to ensure that African American boys grow up to be strong, committed and responsible African American men.

## AKASHIC BOOKS
P.O. Box 1456
New York, NY 10009
(212) 433-1875 Fax: (212) 414-3199
Email: akashic7@aol.com   Web: www.akashicbooks.com

**Editor**: Johnny Temple
**Affiliated press names**: Punk Planet Books and RDV Books (imprints)
**ISBN prefix**: 1-888451; 0-9719206
**Average number of new titles published per year**: 12
**Number of titles in print**: 75
**Other materials produced**: Distributes music CDs
**Distributors**: publisher direct via the website (uses PayPal); Consortium, Small Press Distribution, AK Press and Marginal (Canada)
**Publication interests**: Alternative Culture, Gay, Lesbian, Literary, Music, Politics, Punk
**Motto**: "Reverse-gentrification of the literary world."

Founded in 1997, Akashic Books is a New York City-based independent company dedicated to publishing urban literary fiction and political nonfiction by authors who are either ignored by the mainstream or who have no interest in working within the ever consolidating ranks of the major corporate publishers. The press was awarded the 2005 Temple Miriam Bass Award for Creativity in Publishing by the American Association of Publishers. Publishes material on the punk movement, not only about its passionate music, but also about punk's politics and do-it-yourself culture. Example of titles include Joe Meno's

*Hairstyles of the Damned* (debut novel from the Punk Planet Books imprint), about teenage outcast experience, and Krist Hovoselics's *Of Grunge and Government: let's fix this broken democracy*, a personal and political memoir from a founding member of the rock band Nirvana.

## ALICE JAMES BOOKS
238 Main St.
Farmington, ME 04983
(207) 778-7071  Fax: (207) 778-7071
Email: AJB@umf.maine.edu  Web: www.umf.maine.edu/~ajb

**Editor**: April Ossmann, Program Director
**Associated with**: University of Maine at Farmington since 1994, and the Alice James Poetry Cooperative, Inc.
**ISBN prefix**: 0-914086, 1-882295
**Average number of new titles published per year**: 5
**Number of titles in print**: 118
**Distributors**: Consortium, Small Press Distribution
**Publication interests**: Literary, Poetry

Founded in 1973, Alice James Books represents an alternative way to run a press and generate books ignored by the mainstream. The seven founding members decided to take control, formed a shared work cooperative, and published their own books. The shared work cooperative brought into print high quality poetry. The emphasis was on publishing poetry by women, and every book published was to remain in print as long as the press existed. Poets become active members of the Alice James Poetry Cooperative when their manuscripts are selected through both regional and national competitions. The process ensures that poets have a great deal of control over the final appearance of their finished books. The books are non-mainstream more than alternative, though some cover feminism and gender studies. The press published a 1998 National Book Award Finalist, B.H. Fairchild's *The Art of the Lathe*, poems on the working-class world of the Midwest.

**ALYSON PUBLICATIONS**
6922 Hollywood Blvd., 10th fl.
Los Angeles, CA 90028
(800) 525-9766  Fax: (323) 467-0173
Email: mail@alyson.com  Web: www.alyson.com

**Editor**: Greg Constante
**Affiliated press names**: Advocate Books (imprint), Alyson Wonderland (imprint)
**ISBN prefix**: 0932870, 155583, 1-59350
**Average number of new titles published per year**: 30
**Number of titles in print**: 130+
**Distributor**: publisher direct via the website; Consortium
**Publication interests**: Adolescents, Biography/Memoir, Children/Juvenile, Erotica, Gay, Lesbian, Mysteries, Romance, Sexuality, Travel
**Motto**: "Publications reflecting the rich diversity of gay life in America."

Founded in 1980, Alyson Books publishes materials for gay teens and men, lesbians, and their children. The books explore the political, legal, financial, medical, spiritual, social and sexual aspects of gay and lesbian life. Alyson Classics Library is dedicated to keeping lesbian and gay literary heritage alive. Alyson Wonderland is a publisher of children's books, including *Daddy's Roommate* (1990) and *Heather Has Two Mommies* (1999) that are among the most challenged and censored books in libraries. Advocate Books showcase *The Advocate* magazine's rich historical perspective as well as the heroes who are shaping the future for gay men and lesbians. Examples of titles include: Michael Kort's *Dinah! 3 decades of sex, golf and rock and roll*, a history of the lesbian phenomenon known as the Dinah Shore weekend; *Best Lesbian Love Stories* and *Best Gay Love Stories*, both annual publications; Frank Sanello's *Tweakers: how crystal meth is ravaging gay America*; and Blair Mastbaum's *Clay's Way*, winner of the 2005 Lambda Literary Award's Trustee's Award for Debut Gay Men's Fiction.

**AMNESTY INTERNATIONAL (USA)**
5 Penn Plaza, 124th fl.
New York, NY 10001
(212) 807-8400; Fax: (212) 627-1451
email: admin-us@aiusa.org  Web: www.amnestyusa.org
www.amnesty.ca (Canada English), www.amnistie.qc.ca (Canada French)
**Editor**: William F. Schulz, USA Executive Director
**ISBN prefix**: 0-939994, 1-887204, 0-900058 (Great Britain)

**Average number of new titles published per year**: 10 monographs, 8 reports
**Other materials produced**: *Amnesty Now*, quarterly magazine, brochures, calendars
**Distributor**: Publisher direct via the website or by phone, (800) AMNESTY
**Publication interests**: Africa/African Studies, Asia/Asian Studies, Europe, Globalization, Human Rights, Immigration, International Issues/Relations, Latin American Studies, Mental Health, Middle East Studies, Political, Prison/Prisoners, Refugees, Religion, Social Justice, Third World, Women's Issues/Studies
**Motto**: "Defend human rights and protect lives."

Founded in 1961 in London, England and the United States in 1966, Amnesty International was founded on the principal that people have fundamental rights that transcend national, cultural, religious and ideological boundaries. The organization works to free all prisoners of conscience detained anywhere for their beliefs or because of their ethnic origin, sex, color, or language, who have not used or advocated violence; ensure fair and prompt trials for political prisoners; abolish the death penalty, torture and other cruel treatment of prisoners; and end extrajudicial executions and "disappearances." AI does not accept any governmental funding. As part of its campaign to protect fundamental human rights, AI regularly publishes country reports and other documents on human rights issues around the world. AI reports from 1996 on can be downloaded from the Web site. Examples of publications include: *Threat and Humiliation: racial profiling, domestic security, and human rights in the United States*, AI's first report on racial profiling by law enforcement; *Shattered Lives: the case for tough international arms control* (published with Oxfam and International Action Network on Small Arms); and *Why am I Here? Children in immigration detention*, details of the fate of over 5,000 unaccompanied children arriving to the U.S. each year.

**ANNICK PRESS**
15 Patricia Ave.
Toronto, Ontario M2M 1H9 Canada
(416) 221-4802 Fax: (416) 221-8400
Email: use website's email form Web: www.annickpress.com

**Editor**: Rick Wilks, Publisher
**ISBN prefix**: 0-920236, 0-920303, 1-55037
**Average number of new titles published per year**: 30

**Number of titles in print**: 344
**Distributors**: Firefly Books (Canada and USA)
**Publication interests**: Adolescents, Children/Juvenile, Cultural Studies, Hispanics/Latinos, Minorities, Multiculturalism
**Motto**: "Excellence and innovation in children's literature"

Founded in 1975 and originally called Books by Kids, Annick Press produces books that mirror reality honestly, reassure and support, and build self-esteem in children. The books portray children who respect themselves and others and who accept differences without fear. The books share fantasy and stimulate imagination, while encouraging children to trust their own judgment and abilities. They try to give children faith in their own and the world's survival, and offers to minority children a chance to see their lives reflected on the printed page. Most emphasis is on nonfiction titles, but in 2000 the press moved into young adult fiction. A select number of books are published in French and Spanish editions. Among the press's best-selling authors is Canada's Robert Munsch, including his modern classic, *The Paper Bag Princess*. Examples of titles include Shari Graydon's *In Your Face: the culture of beauty and you*, a critical look at the culture of beauty, and Fran Fearnley's *I Wrote On All Four Walls: teens speak out on violence*. Allan Stratton's *Chandra's Secret* won the 2004 IPPY Award in the Juvenile/ Young Adult Fiction category.

**THE APEX PRESS**
777 United Nations Plaza, Suite 3C
New York, NY 10017
(914) 271-6500  Fax: (800) 316-2739
Email: cipany@ipg.org  Web: www.cipa-apex.org/

**Editor**: Ward Morehouse
**Affiliated press names**: Bootstrap Press, an imprint of the Intermediate Technology Development Group, and other Council on International and Public Affairs publishing programs: Center for International Training and Education, CITE World Cultures Series, Policy Studies Associates, Real World Social Studies, and Development Group of North America
**Associated with**: The Council on International and Public Affairs, founded 1954 as a nonprofit research, education, and publishing group
**ISBN prefix**: 0-945257, 1-891843, 0-929859 (Bootstrap), 0-942850 (Bootstrap)
**Average number of new titles published per year**: 5

Number of titles in print: **50+**
**Other materials produced**: *Too Much*, a quarterly newsletter devoted to capping excess income and wealth in the United States
**Distributors**: Publisher direct via the website or by phone, (800) 316-2739; Fernwood Books (Canada)
**Publication interests**: Capitalism, Economics, Education, Ecology and Environmentalism, Globalization, Human Rights, International Issues/Relations, Labor/Labor Studies, Politics, Social Change, Social Justice, Sustainable Development, Third World
**Motto**: "Radical democracy."

Founded in 1985, The Apex Press provides critical analyses of old and new approaches to significant economic, social and political issues in the U.S. and throughout the world. The press places a special focus on economic and social justice, human rights, and impact of technology on contemporary society. The Council on International and Public Affairs seeks to further the study and public understanding of problems and affairs of the peoples of the United States and other nations of the world. Bootstrap Press publishes books on social economics and community economic change, as well as small- and intermediate-scale or appropriate technology. Examples of titles include Sam Pizzigati's *Greed and Good: understanding and overcoming the inequality that limits our lives*, a book that show how wealth inequality in the U.S. undermines nearly every aspect of our lives, and Peter Kellman's *Divided We Fall: the story of the paper workers' union and the future of labor*, a picture of workers fighting against overwhelming odds for justice.

### ARBEITER RING PUBLISHING
201E-121 Osborne St.
Winnipeg, MB R3L 1Y4 Canada
(204) 942-7058 Fax: (208) 944-9198
Email: info@arbeiterring.com Web: www.arbeiterring.com

**Editor**: worker collective
**ISBN prefix**: 1-894037
**Average number of new titles published per year**: 3
**Number of titles in print**: 19
**Distributors**: AK Press Distribution (US); Fernwood Books (Canada)
**Publication interests**: Anarchism, Anti-capitalism, Cultural Studies, Economics, Film, Globalization, Indigenous Populations, Labor/Labor Studies, Social Change, Social Issues, Social Justice, Socialism/Marxism

**Motto**: "Left-wing politics with a rock-n-roll attitude."

Founded in 1996, Arbeiter Ring ("Workers Circle") borrows its name from the radical Jewish fraternal organization. A century ago, socialist and anarchist locals of the Arbeiter Ring were active on the political and cultural level in Winnipeg. ARP is a not-for-profit organization organized as a worker's collective. The collective believes in participatory economics as an alternative to contemporary capitalism. Examples of titles include: Doug Smith's *How To Tax a Billionaire: the story of the project loophole case and the campaign for tax justice*; David McNally's *Another World is Possible: globalization and anti-capitalism*; and Michael Albert's *Thought Dreams: radical theory for the 21st century*, a book that will help readers better understand progressive theories.

## ARSENAL PULP PRESS
341 Water St., Suite 200
Vancouver, British Columbia, V6B 1B8 Canada
(604) 687-4233  Fax: (604) 687-4283
Email: contact@arsenalpulp.com  Web: www.arsenalpulp.com

**Editor**: Brian Lam
**ISBN prefix** : 1-55152
**Average number of new titles published per year**: 15
**Number of titles in print**: 160
**Distributors**: Publisher direct via the website's order form or by phone, (888) 600-PULP (USA & Canada); Consortium (USA); Jaguar Book Group (Canada)
Publication interests: **Anthologies, Biography/Memoir, Cookery, Cultural Studies, Erotica, Feminism, Gay, Gender Studies, Lesbian, Literary, Multiculturalism, Music, Poetry, Popular Culture, Politics, Sociology, Women's Issues/Studies**
**Motto**: "Provocative and stimulating books that challenge the status quo."

Founded in 1971 and originally called Pulp Press Book Publishers, the press began as a collective of university students and associates disenchanted by what they perceived to be the academic literary pretentions of Canadian literature at the time. Pulp became Arsenal Pulp Press in 1982 with a publishing program that was about the disenfranchised more than anything, whether it's Native issues, race and class, or gay literature. In 1988, Arsenal launched "Little Red Books" series, tiny books, now at 22 titles, of quotations and anecdotes on provocative issues and personalities. The Unknown City series present alternative guidebooks designed for tourists and hometowners alike for seven major U.S. and Canadian cities. Examples of titles include: Sarah Kramer's *La Dolce Vegan: vegan livin' made easy*; Daniel Francis' *The Imaginary Indian: the image of the Indian in Canadian culture*, a revealing history of the "Indian" image mythologized by popular Canadian culture, now in its fifth printing; *Hot and Bothered: short short fiction on Lesbian Desire*, vol. 4; *Quickies: short short fiction on gay male desire*, vol. 3; Joe Keithley's *I, Shithead: a life in punk*; and Robert Hunter's *The Greenpeace to Amchitka: an environmental odyssey*, a memoir of the initial voyage of John Cormack's fishing vessel dubbed The Greenpeace, winner of the 2nd Annual George Ryga Award for Social Awareness in B.C. literature (2005).

## ARTE PUBLICO PRESS
University of Houston
452 Cullen Performance Hall
Houston, TX 77204-2004
(713) 743-2998  Fax: (713) 743-2848
Email: artrec@mail.uh.edu  Web: www.artepublicopress.com

**Editor**: Gabriela Baeza Ventura, Executive Editor; Nicolas Kanellos, Director
**Affiliated press names**: Pinata Books
**Associated with**: The University of Houston
**ISBN prefix**: 1-55885
**Average number of new titles published per year**: 30
**Number of titles in print**: 280
**Distributors**: Publisher direct by mail, fax, or phone (800) 633-ARTE
**Publishing interests**: Adolescents, Bilingual, Biography/Memoir, Children/Juvenile, Civil Liberties, Cultural Studies, Hispanic/Latino, Latin American Studies, Literary, Minorities, Poetry, Reference, Social Justice, Social Issues, Women's Issues/Studies
**Motto**: "Recovering the past, creating the future."

Founded in 1979, Arte Publico Press is committed to reforming the national culture to more accurately include values and reflect Hispanic historical and contemporary contributions. It is the oldest and largest publisher of U.S. Hispanic literature. In 1992, the press launched the Recovering the U.S. Hispanic Literary Heritage project, the first nationally coordinated attempt to recover, index, and publish lost Latino writings that date from the colonial period to 1960. In 1994, Pinata Books was founded to produce literature for children and young adults to accurately portray U.S. Hispanic culture. Arte Publico publishes books of fiction, poetry, drama, literary criticism, and art by the leading figures in Mexican-American, Puerto Rican, Cuban, and U.S. Hispanic Literature, especially Hispanic women's literature. Many titles are in Spanish. The Hispanic Civil Rights Series seek to document the many contributions to public policy, education and community affairs by Hispanic civil rights organization and their leaders. Examples of titles include: Alicia Alacron's *The Border Patrol Ate My Dust*, first-hand testimonies of immigrants navigating the U.S. border; *Isabel Allende: recuerdos para un cuento/Isabel Allende: memories for a story*, an informative bilingual biography for children; and Luisa Capitillo's *Nation of Women: an early feminist speaks out/Mi opinion sobre las libertades, derechos y deberes de la mujer*, a bilingual edition of the first feminist text published by a Puerto Rican activist. Nicolas Kanellos' *Hispanic Periodicals in the United States, Origins to 1960: a brief history and comprehensive bibliography*, is a useful a reference book that examines the press in exile, the immigrant press, and the nativist press.

## ASIA AMERICAN WRITERS' WORKSHOP
16 W. 32nd St., Suite 10A
New York, NY 10001
(212) 494-0061  Fax: (212) 494-0062
Email: desk@aaww.org  Web: www.aaww.org

**Editor**: editor changes with each title
**Associated with**: Distributes Asian American titles from other presses
**ISBN prefix**: 1-889876
**Average number of new titles published per year**: 1
**Number of titles in print**: 9
**Other materials produced**: *The Asian Pacific American Journal* and *Ten*, a magazine about the writing and writers of Asian American literature
**Distributors**: publisher direct via the website
**Publication interests**: Anthologies, Asian American, Literary, Minorities, Poetry
**Motto**: "Asian American literature and awareness across the nation."

Founded in 1991, Asia American Writer's Workshop is a nonprofit community-based literary arts organization dedicated to the creation, development, publication, and dissemination of Asian American literature. The organization presents annually the Asian American Literary Award to honor Asian American writers of excellence. The press started in 1996 and is noted for anthologies of underrepresented Asian American experiences, for example, *Take Out: queer writing from Asian Pacific America*, edited by Quang Bao and Hanya Yanagihara, and *Echoes Upon Echoes: new Korean American writings*, edited by Elaine H. Kim and Laura Hyun Yi Kang.

## ATRIUM SOCIETY
P.O. Box 816
Middlebury, CT 05753
(800) 848-6021 Fax: (802) 462-2792
Email: mapp8@aol.com Web: www.atrium.org

**Editor**: Dr. Terrence Webster-Doyle, Director
**ISBN prefix**: 0-942941, 0-834804
**Average number of new titles published per year**: 2
**Number of titles in print**: 12
**Other materials produced**: *Martial Arts for Peace Journal*, Martial Arts for Peace curriculum program, Education for Peace curriculum program, videos
**Distributors**: Random House, (800) 773-3000
**Publication interests**: Adolescents, Children/Juvenile, Conflict Resolution, Martial Arts, Peace, Prejudice
**Motto**: "Resources for understanding conflict–individually and globally."

Founded in 1984, the Atrium Society mission is to educate about the source, nature and structure of conflict, to recognize how we have sustained it through conditioned thinking and action. The society and publications emphasize understanding and ending conflict before it starts. The Education for Peace project produces a series of children's books for ages 8 to 16, to help young people understand conflict in their lives and the world around them, and to create humane, nonviolent ways to deal with it. This includes dealing with a bully in the schoolyard and internationally in what we call war. When children don't have the opportunity to learn how to resolve conflict peacefully, they grow up believing that violence will solve the problems of human relationships. The Martial Arts for Peace project is a conflict education and character development program for young people and adults, ages 17 and up, that teaches how to cope with bullying and gain the social skills for ethical relationships. Examples of titles include *Why Is Everyone Always Picking on Us: understanding the roots of prejudice*, for young people 8 to 14 to find ways to free themselves of prejudice, and *Tug of War: peace through understanding conflict*, a book that encourages the study of conflict resolution as an integral part of a young person's education. The book won the Silver Benjamin Franklin Award for Excellence in Independent Publishing.

## AUNT LUTE BOOKS

P.O. Box 410687
San Francisco, CA 94141
(415) 826-1300 fax: (415) 826-8300
Email: books@auntlute.com Web: www.auntlute.com

**Editor:** Joan Pinkvoss, co-founder, Senior Editor and Executive Director
**Associated with:** Aunt Lute Foundation, a nonprofit corporation founded to publish and distribute books that reflect the complex truth of women's lives and the possibilities for personal and social change
**ISBN prefix:** 1-879960
**Average number of new titles per year:** 2
Number of titles in print: **34**
**Distributors:** publisher direct via the website or by phone (800) 949-5883; Consortium and Small Press Distribution
**Publication interests:** African American, Biography/Memoir, Cultural Studies, Feminist, Globalization, Lesbian, Literary, Minorities, Multiculturalism, Poetry, Political, Social Change, Third World, Women's Issues/Studies
**Motto:** "A multicultural women's press."

Founded in 1982, Aunt Lute Books seeks to cultivate and build new bodies of thought and understanding about and between women. The press publishes works of literature by women who have been traditionally under-represented in mainstream and small press publishing, and has a long history of publishing works by diverse women writers. Examples of titles include: the groundbreaking Chicana text, *Boderlands/Fontera* by Gloria Anzaluda; *Shell Shaker* by Choctaw author LeAnne Howe, winner of the 2002 Before Columbus American Book Award; *The Aunt Lute Anthology of U.S. Women Writers, Volume One: 17th - 19th Centuries*; *Positive/Negative: women of color and HIV/AIDS*, edited by Imani Harrington and Chyrell D. Bellamy, a collection of plays that look at both individual and community issues; and Leela Fernandez' *Transforming Feminist Practice: non-violence, social justice and the possibilities of a spiritualized feminism*, a critique of feminist practice both in social justice organizations and in the academy.

## AUTONOMEDIA

P.O. Box 568, Williamsburgh Station

Brooklyn, NY 11211-0568
(718) 963-2603 Fax: same
Email: info@autonomedia.org  Web: www.autonomedia.org

**Editor**: Jim Fleming
**Associated with**: Autonomedia Distribution distributes their own books and selected titles from many other like-minded small presses
**ISBN prefix**: 1-57027, 0-936756
**Average number of new titles published per year**: 6
**Number of titles in print**: 100
**Other materials produced**: *Semiotext(e)*, a literary journal that introduced postmodern French intellectual theory to U.S. readers with a focus on radical political and cultural theories, and the annual *Autonomedia Calendar of Jubilee Saints: Radical Heroes for the New Millennium* and the *Sheroes and Womyn Warriors Calendar*
**Distributors**: AK Press Distribution, SBC Distributors, Small Press Distribution, Marginal (Canada)
**Publication interests**: Activism, Alternative Culture, Anarchism, The Arts, Cultural Studies, History, Literary, Media Studies, Politics

Founded in 1984, Autonomedia publishes titles on radical media, politics and the arts. Examples of titles include: *Anarchitexts*, edited by Joanne Richardson, a global mix of voices from the new "underground:" artists, media producers, activists, and people who create an alternative society through their everyday practice; *Orgies of the Hemp Easter: cuisine, slang, literature, and ritual of cannabis culture*, edited by Hakim Bey and Abel Zug; and Michael Muhammad Knight's *The Taqwacores*, a day-to-day life in a Muslim punk house in Buffalo, NY.

## BEACON PRESS
25 Beacon St.
Boston, MA 02108-2892
(617) 742-2110  Fax: (617) 723-3097
Web: www.beacon.org

**Associated with**: Unitarian Universalist Association
**ISBN prefix**: 0-8070
**Average number of new titles published per year**: 50
**Number of titles in print**: 400
**Distributors**: Houghton Mifflin Co. (800) 225-3362, Fitzhenry & Whiteside, Ltd. (Canada)

**Publication interests**: African-American, Anti-racism, Art/The Arts, Children/Juvenile, Education, Ecology/Environmentalism, Feminist, Gay, Gender Studies, Globalization, History, Lesbian, Literary, Politics, Religion, Social Change, Social Justice, Spirituality, Women's Issues/Studies
**Motto**: "Spirit Art Justice Knowledge"

Founded in 1854 as the press of the American Unitarian Association, the name was changed to Beacon Press in 1902. Beacon books seek to change the way readers think about fundamental issues. They promote such values as freedom of speech and thought, the importance of racial and ethnic diversity, religious pluralism, an anti-racist, anti-oppression agenda, respect for our environment, and the importance of the arts in a civil society. Beacon is a leading publisher of books on education policy, school reform and teaching. Publications have sometimes advanced controversial political positions, notably Paul Blanshard's *American Freedom and Catholic Power* (1949) and *Right to Read* (1955), and at other times have offered ground-breaking classics such as Herbert Marcuse's *One-Dimensional Man*. There have been an extensive number of books on literary history and criticism by authors including Lionel Trilling and Katherine Mansfield, as well as "cause-oriented" books, such as *The Pentagon Papers* (1971/72), edited by Sen. Mike Gavel. Beacon's all-time bestseller is Philip Slater's *The Pursuit of Loneliness* (1970). Beacon's New Democracy Forum is a paperback series that explores creative and inclusive solutions to our most urgent national challenges. Bluestreak is a paperback series of innovative literary writing by women of all colors and includes works by Gayl Jones and Sonia Sanchez. The Black Women Writers Series publishes rediscovered literature of historical significance. The Beacon Best is an annual anthology of creative writing. Finally, Concord Library produces classic and contemporary works that reflect on the search for balance between human culture and the rest of nature. Examples of titles include *Many Children Left Behind: how the No Child Left Behind Act is damaging our children and our schools*, edited by Deborah Meier and George Wood, and Rashid Khalidi's *Resurrecting Empire: Western footprints and America's perilous path in the Middle East.*

**BELLA BOOKS**
P.O. Box 10543
Tallahassee, FL 32302
(800) 729-4992
Email: Linda@bellabooks.com   Web: www.bellabooks.com

**Editor**: Linda Hill, Publisher, multiple editors

**Affiliated press names**: distributes Rising Tide Press books
**ISBN prefix**: 0-967775
**Average number of titles published per year**: 27
**Number of titles in print**: 230
**Other material produced**: audio CDs
**Distributors**: publisher direct via website's shopping cart feature; Bella Distribution (800) 533-1973; CDS (800) 343-4499
**Publication interests**: Erotica, Fantasy, Lesbian, Literary, Mystery, Romance, Science Fiction, Sexuality, Suspense
**Motto**: "The next generation of lesbian fiction."

Founded in 2000, Bella Books goal is to become the publishing company of choice for lesbian fiction. The press specializes in fiction by and about lesbians in the genres of romance, mystery/thriller, science fiction, fantasy and erotica. Bella Books took over publishing many of Naiad Press's most popular authors. Through a special arrangement, Bella Books is making available for purchase 30 titles from Rising Tide Press. Karin Kallmaker's *Maybe Next Time*, received a Lammy Award from the Lambda Literary Awards for Best Romance. Also, Bella Books received the 2005 LGBT Independent Press Award at the Lambda Literary Awards ceremony.

### BETWEEN THE LINES
720 Bathurst St., Suite 404
Toronto, Ontario M5S 2R4 Canada
(416) 535-9914  Fax: (416) 535-1484
Email: btlbooks@web.ca  Web: www.btlbooks.com

**Editor**: Paul Eprile, Editorial Coordinator
**ISBN prefix**: 0-921284, 1-896357, 0-919946
**Average number of new titles published per year**: 10
**Number of books in print**: 140
**Distributors**: SBC Distributors (USA); University of Toronto Press and Fernwood (Canada);
**Publication interests**: Activism, Animal Rights, Capitalism, Cultural Studies, Economics, Education, Ecology/Environmentalism, Globalization, Health, History, International Issues/Relations, Labor/Labor Studies, Media Studies, Political, Poor/Poverty, Social Issues, Social Justice, Third World
**Motto**: "Books to feed your head."

Founded in 1977, Between the Lines strives to embrace critical perspectives on culture, economics, and society. The press has been referred to as left-wing, feminist, queer positive and anti-racist, all terms that the editors agree with. A number of the books are developed in conjunction with social movements, and are written by some of Canada's leading political and cultural thinkers. Readers look to BTL for challenging ideas, concepts and analysis not readily found in mainstream publications, for example, Mike Hudema's *An Action a Day Keeps Global Capitalism Away*, a book introducing fifty-two actions and examples of where they could be used.

The No-Nonsense Guide series has eighteen titles such as Maggie Black's *The No-Nonsense Guide to Water*, a defense of the explosive issue of water rights in communities worldwide, and Nikki van der Gaag's *The No-Nonsense Guide to Women's Rights*, an explanation of why women's rights are still an issue.

## BILINGUAL REVIEW/PRESS
P.O. Box 872702
Tempe, AZ 85287-2702
(480) 965-3867  Fax: (480) 965-8309
Email: brp@asu.edu  Web: www.asu.edu/brp

**Editor**: Gary D. Keller, General Editor
**Affiliated press names**: also called Bilingual Press; the Clasicos Chicanos/ Chicano Classics imprint keeps alive classics of Chicana and Chicano fiction
**Associated with**: University of Arizona's Hispanic Research Center
**ISBN prefix**: 0-927534, 1-931010
**Average number of new titles published per year**: 9
**Number of titles in print**: 150+
**Other materials produced**: *The Bilingual Review*, a scholarly review; *Griffithiana: Journal of Film History*; commemorative posters
**Distributors**: publisher direct via the website's order form; Small Press Distribution, Ingram Book Company
**Publication interests**: Anthologies, Art/The Arts, Bilingual, Biography, Hispanic/Latino, Latin American Studies, Literary, Poetry, Reprints, Short Stories, Social Justice
**Motto**: "Publishes the works of Hispanic writers."

Founded in 1974, Bilingual Review/Press publishes works of weight and significance by U.S. Hispanics, and is committed to publishing high-quality writing by both established and emerging writers. While most are written in English, some are bilingual in Spanish and others in Spanish only. Examples of titles include: Larry LaFountain's *Unas pintadas de azul/Blue Fingernails*, poems of the pains and pleasures of diasporic, cosmopolitan gay and lesbian Puerto Rican identities; *Fantasmas: supernatural stories by Mexican American writers*, edited by Rob Johnson, a book that combines fantasy, folktales and pulp fiction, the first collection of such stories; and, Gary Keller, et al, *Contemporary Chicana and Chicano Art: artists, works culture, and education*, artistic production and biographies of nearly 200 individual artists.

## BLACK & RED
P.O. Box 02374
Detroit, MI 48202
Email: bandred@yahoo.com

**Editor**: D. M. Borts
**ISBN prefix**: 0-934868
**Number of titles in print**: 22
**Distributor**: Publisher direct (request publications list); AK Press and Distribution (USA); Marginal (Canada)
**Publication interests**: History, Labor/Labor Studies, Political, Reprints, Socialism/Marxism, Translations

Founded in 1968, Black & Red publishes political leftist pieces mostly focused on labor issues, political resistance, and class struggle. Many are classic reprints and translations. The press is a publishing project carried out by volunteers. Examples of titles include: Situationist International's *On the Poverty of Student Life*, a new translation of the 1966 French edition; David Watson's *Beyond Bookchin: preface for a future social ecology* (1996); Guy G. Debord's *Society of the Spectacle*, the first English translation of the 1967 French edition; Noam Chomsky's *Objectivity and Liberal Scholarship*, reprint of the 1969 essay; and six works by Fredy Perlman, including *Against His-story, Against Leviathan* (1983). Prices for the books are exceptionally low and cover little more than the printing expenses, and individual copies will be sent free of charge to anyone who cannot afford to pay for them.

## BLACK CLASSIC PRESS
P.O. Box 13414
Baltimore, MD 21203
(410) 358-0980 Fax: (410) 358-0987
Email: bcp@charm.net Web: www.blackclassic.com

**Editor**: W. Paul Coates, Director
**Affiliated press names**: DuForcelf (imprint)
**ISBN prefix**: 1-57478, 0-933121
**Average number of new titles published per year**: 2
**Number of titles in print**: 39
**Other materials produced**: pamphlet series of classic reprints
**Distributors**: Publisher direct via website's order form or by phone, (800) 476-8870; Publishers Group West, Red Sea Press
**Publication interests**: Africa/African Studies, African American, African Diaspora, History, Literary, Poetry, Politics, Reprints
**Motto**: "Publishing important books by and about people of African descent."

Founded in 1978, Black Classic Press is devoted to publishing obscure and significant works by and about people of African descent. A goal is to extend the memory of important books that have helped in meaningful ways to shape the black diasporic experience and black understanding of the world. The press's catalog represents titles that are essential to any well-rounded understanding of the black experience, and includes titles that are both reprints and original works. The press specializes in reprinting works that are rare or out of print. Examples of titles include: William A. Owens' *Black Mutiny: the revolt on the schooner Amistad*, originally published 1953; *The Death of White Sociology*, edited by Dr. Joyce A. Ladner and originally published in 1973, a powerful call for the acceptance and appreciation of the uniqueness of black history and society in undertaking studies of black people and their communities; and Dorothy Porter's *Early Negro Writing, 1760-1837*, originally published 1971. Original works include *Beyond the Frontier: African American poetry for the 21st Century*, edited by E. Ethelbert Miller, an anthology of emerging writers and noted poets, and Walter Mosley's *What Next: a memoir toward world peace*, a book that dares to propose that African-Americans can have a voice and play a leading role in creating world peace.

## BLACK ROSE BOOKS

C. P. 1258 Succ. Place du Parc
Montreal, Quebec , H2W 2R3 Canada
(450) 621-1681  Fax: (651) 221-0124
Email: blakrose@web.net  Web: www.web.net/blackrosebooks

2250 Military Rd.
Tonawanda, NY 14225

**Editor**: Robert Dollins
**ISBN prefix**: 0-919618, 0-919619, 1-895431, 1-55164, 0-920057, 0-921689

**Average number of new titles published per year**: 15
**Number of titles in print**: 489
**Distributors**: University of Toronto Press (Canada), (800) 565-9523, AK Press and Consortium (USA), (800) 283-3572; individual orders (USA) (800) 565-9523, ask for operator BRB
**Publication interests**: Anarchism, Cultural Studies, Economics, Ecology/Environmentalism, Gender Studies, Globalization, History, International Issues/Relations, Media Studies, Minorities, Peace/Non-violence, Philosophy, Politics, Reprints, Social Justice, Sociology, Urban Issues/Studies, Women's Issues/Studies
**Motto**: "Independent publishing for independent minds."

Founded in 1970, Black Rose Books publishes books that deal with important concerns such as gender equality, ecology, cities and neighborhoods, and questions of peace, freedom and social justice. The name comes from a Middle Ages legend. During peasant uprisings, those who found freedom would also find the black rose in nature, and conversely those who found the black rose in nature would find freedom. Besides many first-time authors, the press also has well-established writers on its list, such as Noam Chomsky, Murray Bookchin, and George Woodcock. The press reprints forgotten classics, for example, the complete works of Peter Kropotkin. Examples of titles include: *Anarchism: a documentary history of Libertarian ideas, Volume 1: From Anarchy to Anarchism (300 CE to 1939)*, edited by Robert Graham; Mildred J. Loomis' *Decentralism: where it came from—where is it going?*, a grounding for today's activists in understanding of decentralism as not merely a rebellion against authoritarianism, but also faith in the possibility of a new kind of society; and James Winter's *Lies the Media Tells Us*, examples from major newspapers and television programs of the use, misuse, and abuse of information.

## BLACK SWAN PRESS/SURREALIST EDITIONS

P.O. Box 6424
Evanston, IL 60204
(773) 465-7774
Web address: www.surrealistmovement-usa.org/pages/black.html

**Editor**: Franklin and Penelope Rosemont
**Associated with**: Surrealist Movement in the United States, including the Chicago Surrealist Group
**ISBN prefix**: 0-941194
**Average number of new titles published per year**: 3

**Number of titles in print**: 22
**Distributor**: Small Press Distribution
**Publication interests**: Anarchism, Literary, Poetry, Political, Surrealism
**Motto**: "Poetry must be made by all."

Founded in 1968, Black Swan Press/Surrealist Editions is the publisher of a group of revolutionary artists, poets and writers who have a passionate risk-taking adventure involving nothing less than the emancipation of language. Surrealism as an organized movement originated in Paris in the last months of World War I. Andre Breton, the movement's principal theorist, published the first *Surrealist Manifesto* in 1924. Surrealism remains an international movement. The history of the U.S. movement can be read about in the press's *The Forecast is Hot: tracks and other collective declarations of the Surrealist Movement in the United States, 1966-1976*. Penelope Rosement's *Surrealist Experiences: 1001 dawns, 221 midnights* includes nearly two dozen texts originally published in surrealist journals plus eleven more that appear for the first time.

**BOOK PUBLISHING COMPANY**
P.O. Box 99
Summertown, TN 38483
(888) 260-8458
Email: info@bookpubco.com  Web: www.bookpubco.com

**Associated with**: The Farm, the largest vegetarian community in the U.S.
**ISBN prefix**: 0-913990, 1-57067
**Average number of new titles published per year**: 15
**Number of titles in print**: 212
**Distributors**: Amazon
**Publication interests**: American Indian, Children/Juvenile, Cookery, Ecology/Environmentalism, Health, Natural/Nature, Philosophy, Social Change, Sustainable Living, Vegetarianism
**Motto**: "Books to educate, inspire and empower."

Founded in 1974, the Book Publishing Company is an employee-owned, small press that promotes books that provide information on how to create a sustainable and healthful way of life. Cookbooks for vegetarians and health conscious individuals are the press's specialty. Best-selling classics include: *Spiritual Midwifery*, a classic book on home birth; *A Cooperative Method of Natural Birth Control*, a safe, non-invasive and effective method of birth control based on the recording and interpretation of signs and signals from a women's own body;

and *The New Becoming Vegetarian: the complete guide to adopting a healthy vegetarian diet.* The press also publishes books on Native American history and culture, for example, *Basic Call to Consciousness*, 3rd ed., from the editors at *Akwesasne Notes*, an impassioned plea of Native peoples for a profound change in the policies of developed nations, and a call to stop the destruction of the natural world and its peoples, and Vic Glover's *Keeping Heart on the Pine ridge: family ties, warrior culture, commodity foods, rez dogs, and the Sacred*, an anthology of original essays about the Pine Ridge Indian Reservation.

## CADDO GAP PRESS, INC.
3145 Geary Blvd., PMB #275
San Francisco, CA 94118-3316
(415) 666-3012  Fax: (415) 666-3552
Email: caddogap@aol.com  Web: www.caddogap.com

**Editor**: Alan H. Jones
**Associated with**: National Association for Multicultural Education Planning
**ISBN prefix**: 0-9625945, 1-880192
**Average number of new titles per year**: 2-3
**Number of titles in print**: 45
**Other materials produced**: *Multicultural Education*, a quarterly magazine, and twelve education periodicals for professional associations in education
**Distributors**: publisher direct by phone, fax or email
**Publication interests**: education, multiculturalism
**Motto**: "Your key source for educational publications."

Founded in 1989, Caddo Gap Press specializes in the fields of social foundations of education, teacher education, multicultural education, and educational curriculum and instruction. The books take on the challenge of embracing major categories of diversity and cultural understandings, and offer perspectives into how we can rise above our differences while maintaining our own cultural heritage. Examples of titles include Gregory J. Fritzberg's *In the Shadow of "Excellence": recovering a vision of educational opportunity for all*, and Cornel Thomas et al. *We Can Have Better Urban Schools*. Other titles are more along the lines of practical guides, for example, Barbara McEwan's *Practicing Judicious Discipline: an educator's guide to a democratic classroom*, and *We Know Who We Are: a history of the blind in challenging educational and socially constructed policies*, a study in policy archaeology.

## CALACA PRESS
P.O. Box 2309
National City, CA 91951
(619) 434-9036  Fax: (same)
Email: calacapress@cox.net  Web: www.calacapress.com

**Editor**: Consuelo Manriquez de Beltran and Brent E. Beltran
**ISBN prefix**: 0-971703, 0-9660773
**Average number of new titles published per year**: 2
**Number of titles in print**: 13
**Other materials produced**: spoken-word CDs (Raza Spoken Here CD
series) and *La Calaca Review: Un Bilingual Journal of Pensamiento & Palabra*
**Distribution**: Publisher direct by mail (with payment)
**Publication interests**: Bilingual, Hispanic/Latino, Poetry, Human Rights,
Literary, Minorities, Poetry, Social Justice
**Motto**: "Independent spirit, community activism and cultural self-
determination."

Founded in 1997, Calaca Press is an independent Chicano family-owned press
created to fill the gap in the lack of publishing opportunities for independent
Chicano writers. The publishers are committed to supporting new, emerging
and established writers representing the diversity of the contemporary Chicano and Latino experience. The publishers view the press's works as "a welcome resistance to the corporate cultural erasure of the so-called Latin Explosion." With a commitment to social justice and human rights, Calaca Press
strives to bring about change through the literary arts. Examples of titles include *For the Hard Ones: a lesbian phenomenology/Para las Duras: una fenomenologia
lesbiana* by queer activist and librarian, tatiana de la tierra, and *as our barrio
turns...who the yoke b on?* by Chicano poet alurista.

## CALYX BOOKS
P.O. Box B
Corvalis, OR 97339-0539
(541) 753-9384  Fax: (541) 753-0515
Email: calyx@proaxis.com  Web: www.proaxis.com/~calyx
**Editor**: M. Donnelly, Director
**ISBN prefix**: 0-934971
**Average number of new titles published per year**: 1-2
**Number of titles in print**: 37
**Other materials produced**: *CALYX Journal*

**Distributors**: Publisher direct via the website or by phone, (888) 336-2665; Consortium, Small Press Distribution
**Publication interests**: Anthologies, Art/The Arts, Feminist, Lesbian, Literary, Minorities, Poetry, Social Justice, Women's Issues/Studies
**Motto**: "An independent publisher of literature and art by women."

Founded in 1976 by four writers and artists to publish *CALYX Journal*, the publishing expanded in 1986 with the introduction of CALYX Books. CAYLX Books exists to nurture women's creativity by publishing fine literary and artistic work by women. Editorial decisions are made on the basis of quality not on the ability to sell. The press provides a forum for diversity and underrepresented writers and viewpoints. CALYX publishes both emerging and developed writers and is dedicated to keeping books in print. Examples of titles include: *Going Home to a Landscape: writings by Filipinas*, edited by Margarita Donnelly, Beverly McFarland and Micki Reaman; Chitra Banerjee Divadaruni's *Black Candle: poems about women from India, Pakistan and Bangladesh*; Mary I. Cuffe's *The Woman of Too Many Days: poems*, poetry by homeless women; and Ann Nietzke's *Natalie on the Street*, an explicit picture of homelessness in the United States.

## THE CANADIAN CENTRE FOR POLICY ALTERNATIVES
75 Albert St., Suite 410
Ottawa, ON K1P 5E7 Canada
(613) 563-1341  Fax: (613) 233-1458
Email: ccpa@policyalternatives.ca  Web: www.policyalternatives.ca

**Editor**: Bruce Cambell, Executive Director
**ISBN prefix**: 0-88627
**Average number of new titles published per year**: 5
**Number of titles in print**: 25
**Other materials produced**: *The Monitor*, a monthly magazine and *Our Schools, Our Selves*, a quarterly journal on education. Also, research reports and policy briefs, most of which are free online.
**Distributor**: Publisher direct via the website, or by phone or fax
**Publication interests**: Economics, Education, Energy, Globalization, Health, Labor/Labor Studies, Politics, Social Justice
**Motto**: "People need to know that there are workable alternatives."

Founded in 1980, The Canadian Centre for Policy Alternatives (CCPA) is a liberal think tank that offers an alternative to the message that we have no

choice about the policies that affect our lives, and promotes research on issues
of social and economic justice. The CCPA also conducts research projects,
such as the Alternative Federal Budget that has shown that government budgets can be created in a way that is both fiscally and socially responsible. There
are additional offices in British Columbia, Manitoba, Nova Scotia, and Saskatchewan. Policy areas covered include, for example, free trade, financial
markets, public sector, natural resources, public finance, and corporate rule.
Examples of titles include: Alexander M. Ervin's et al, *Beyond Factory Farming:*
*corporate hog barns and the threat to public health, the environment, and rural communities*;
Marita Moll's *The False Promises of Standardized Testing*; *Lessons from NAFTA: the*
*high cost of "free trade,"* by the Hemispheric Social Alliance, and Andrew Jackson's and Matthew Sanger's *When World's Collide: implications of international trade*
*and investment agreements for non-profit social services.*

## CANADIAN COMMITTEE ON LABOUR HISTORY
Faculty of Arts Publications, FM 2005
Memorial University of Newfoundland
St. John's, Newfoundland A1C 5S7 Canada
(709) 737-2144  Fax: (709) 737-4342
Email: cchl@mun.ca  Web: www.mun.ca/cclh

**Editor**: revolving committee
**ISBN prefix**: 0-9629060, 1-894000
**Average number of new titles published per year**: 1
**Number of titles in print**: 27
**Other material produced**: *Labour/Le Travail: Journal of Canadian Labour*
*Studies*; videotapes
**Distributor**: Publisher direct via the website's order form
**Publication interests**: Communism, History, Labor/Labor Studies, Poli-
tics, Socialism
**Motto**: "Promoting all aspects of working class and labour history."

Founded in 1985, the Canadian Committee on Labour History (CCLH) encourages study of working-class communities, culture, ethnicity, family life,
gender, sexuality, migration, ideology, politics and organization. CCLH sponsors the annual Eugene A. Forsey Prize in Canadian Labour and Working-
Class History. In 1919, at the height of post-war labour revolt, the Royal Canadian Mounted Police took responsibility of national security. The CCLH
published in 8 volumes the *R.C.M.P. Security Bulletins*, edited by Gregory S.
Kealey and Reg Whitaker, covering 1919-45 on the Canadian state security

system, including topics of ideology and subversive activity. Examples of other titles include: *Labouring the Canadian Millennium*, edited by Bryan D. Palmer, writings on work and workers, history and historiography; Cy Gonick's *A Very Red Life: the story of Bill Walsh*; and Roger Stonebanks' *Fighting for Dignity: the Ginger Goodwin story*, about labor leader and socialist Ginger Goodwin, who was killed by the police while he tried to evade conscription during World War I.

## CAROLINA WREN PRESS
120 Morris St.
Durham, NC 27701
(919) 560-2738  Fax: (919) 560-2759
Email: carolina@carolinawrenpress.org
Web: www.carolinawrenpress.org

**Editor**: The press is a completely volunteer operation
**Affiliated press names**: Lollipop Power Books, an imprint of children's literature
**ISBN prefix**: 0-932112 (Carolina Wren), 0-914996 (Lollipop Power)
**Average number of new titles published per year**: 2
**Number of titles in print**: 39
**Distributors**: Publisher direct online via the website's order form
**Publication interests**: African-American, Bilingual, Children/Juvenile, Feminist, Gay, Hispanic/Latino, Lesbian, Literary, Minorities, Multiculturalism, Parenting, Poetry, Women's Issues/Studies
**Motto**: "New authors, new audiences"

Founded in 1976, Carolina Wren Press is a nonprofit organization whose mission is to seek out work committed to multicultural ideals, and publish quality writing, especially by writers historically neglected by mainstream publishing. Founded in 1984, Lollipop Power specializes in multicultural, nonsexist, and non-traditional children's books. Many titles are bilingual in Spanish and English. The editors recruit authors of promise, including new authors, authors of color, women authors, and gay and lesbian authors. Annually conducts the Sonja H. Stone Fiction Competition for underrepresented writers. Best-selling Carolina Wren titles include William Henry Lewis' *In the Arms of Our Elders*, winner of the 1995 Sonja H. Stone Fiction Competition, and Elaine Goolsby's *Letters: Lost and Found*. Best-selling Lollipop Power Books include Dava Walker's *Puzzles: a young girl copes with sickle cell disease* and Ellen Bass' *I Like You to Make Jokes With Me, but I Don't Want You to Touch Me* (bilingual in Spanish).

## CHARLES H. KERR PUBLISHING COMPANY
1740 W. Greenfield Ave., Suite 7
Chicago, IL 60626
(773) 465-7774
Email: chicagosurrealism@earthlink.net  Web: www.charleshkerr.org

**Editor**: Franklin and Penelope Rosemont
**ISBN prefix**: 0-88286
**Average number of new titles published per year**: 5
**Number of titles in print**: 64
**Distributor**: Publisher direct (773) 465-7366
**Publication interests**: African-American, Anarchism, Biography, Economics, History, Labor/Labor Studies, Poetry, Political, Reprints, Social Change, Socialism/Marxism, Translations, Unions/Unionizing
**Motto**: "Subversive literature for the whole family since 1886."

Founded in 1886, the Charles H. Kerr Publishing Company continues to meet a real need for radical, socialist, and labor history. The press has been referred to as "that Wobbly publisher in Chicago," but takes its charge more seriously producing "books for an endangered planet." In the early 20th century, the Kerr Company became the world's leading English-language radical publisher. It is now organized as a worker-owned cooperative, not-for-profit educational association. The press keeps in print classic works by and about the labor union movement and other revolutionary works, for example, Clarence Darrow's *Crime and Criminals*, a masterpiece of social criticism and the struggle for freedom, and the *Autobiography of Mother Jones*. Between 1906-9, the press issued Ernest Untermann's translation of the three volumes of Marx's *Das Capital*, the first such full-text English translation. The publications are not only a living link with the most vital radical traditions of the past, but also an organic part of today's struggles for peace and justice in an ecologically balanced world. The press has reprinted the works of Eugene Debs, Mary Marcy, Jack London, Carl Sandburg, and hundreds of other outstanding figures as well as published unpublished writings by T-Bone Slim, Claude McKay, and Slim Brundage. Kerr's "Poets in Revolt" Series includes volumes of poems by IWW organizer Covington Hall, anarchist Voltairine de Cleyre, and present-day Wobbly Carlos Cortez. Original monographs include Franklin Rosemont's *Joe Hill: the IWW and the making of a revolutionary working class counterculture* and Carolyn Ashbaugh's *Lucy Parsons: American revolutionary*.

## CHELSEA GREEN PUBLISHING COMPANY

P.O. Box 428, 85 N. Main St., Suite 120
White River Junction, VT 05001
(802) 295-6300 Fax: (802) 295-6444
Email: mbaldwin@chelseagreen.com Web: www.chelseagreen.com

**Editor**: Margo Baldwin, President and Publisher
**Associated with**: distributor of books from other small, like-minded publishers
**ISBN prefix**: 1-890132
**Average number of new titles published per year**: 20
**Number of titles in print**: 105
**Other materials produced**: audiobooks, CDs, CVDs (distributed)
**Distributor**: Publisher direct via the website's order form or by phone, (800) 639-4099
**Publication interests**: Architecture, Conservation, Ecology/Environmentalism, Economics, Health, Natural/Nature, Politics, Reference, Social Issues, Sustainable Development
**Motto**: "The politics and practice of sustainable living."

Founded in 1984, Chelsea Green Publishing Company's re-oriented its mission in 2003 from publishing books on sustainable living to include the politics and practice of sustainable living. "Our purpose is to stop the destruction of the natural world by challenging the beliefs and practices that are enabling this destruction and by providing inspirational and practical alternatives that promote sustainable living." The editors are dedicated to restorative economics—built around an integrated concern for intellectual capital, social capital, natural capital, and financial capital. Best-selling titles include *The Straw Bale House*, *The New Organic Grower*, and *Four Season Harvest*. Other titles include John Taylor's *A Shelter Sketchbook*, earth-friendly building techniques from ancient times to the present, and Jean Giono's *The Man Who Planted Trees*, a timeless story of Elzeard Bouffier, who spent his life planting one hundred acorns a day to transform the landscape. Examples of titles include Michael Ratner's and Ellen Ray's *Guantanamo: what the world should know*, an expose of America's secret interrogation camp and how it effects us, and Derrick Jensen's and George Draffan's *Welcome to the Machine: science, surveillance, and the culture of control*, about how surveillance and control technologies infiltrate every aspect of modern life.

## CHICORY BLUE PRESS, INC.
795 East Street North
Goshen, CT 06756
(860) 491-2271  Fax: (860) 491-8619
Email: sondraz@optonline.net  Web: www.chicorybluepress.com

**Editor**: Sondra Zeidenstein
**ISBN prefix**: 1-887344, 0-9619111
**Average number of new titles published per year**: 1-2
**Number of titles in print**: 21
**Distributor**: Publisher direct via the website's order form, or by phone or fax; Small Press Distribution
**Publication interests**: Aged/Aging, Anthologies, Biography/Memoir, Feminist, Literary, Minorities, Poetry
**Motto**: "Strong voices of women over sixty."

Founded in 1987, Chicory Blue Press is a small, feminist literary press that focuses on the writing of women over sixty. The press publishes paperbacks and chapbooks from the perspective of older women so they can imagine themselves to be part of a varied, vital community, and not as an anonymous, marginalized, stereotyped "senior." From the point of view of age and gender, older women are the most underrepresented among published writers, and older women writers from minority culture are even scarcer. The books represent accounts of coming to truth at this vital stage in life. A title example is *The Crimson Edge: older women writing*, vol. 2, edited by Sondra Zeidenstein, a book of anthologies of fiction, memoir and poetry.

## CHILDREN'S BOOK PRESS
2211 Mission St.
San Francisco, CA 94110-1811
(415) 821-3080  Fax: (415) 821-3081
Email: info@childrensbookpress.org  Web: www.childrensbookpress.org

**Editor**: Ruth Tobar, Executive Director
**ISBN prefix**: 0-89239
**Average number of new titles published per year**: 6
**Number of titles in print**: 60
**Distributors**: Publishers Group West, Publishers Group Canada
**Publication interests**: African American, American Indian, Anthologies Asian American, Bilingual, Children/Juvenile, Ethnic, Folktales, His-

panic/Latino, Minorities, Multiculturalism, Poetry, Race/Race Relations, Social Change
**Motto**: "Multicultural literature for children."

Founded in 1975, Children's Books Press has a mission to help broaden the base of children's literature by publishing multicultural and bilingual stories that reflect the diversity and experiences of minority and new immigrant communities in the United States. The press's goal is to promote a society where people know about many different cultures and everyone's culture is valued. The editors view their efforts as part of a larger movement to create a children's literature of inclusion, giving all children a sense of their culture, history, and importance. The authors and artists have a strong commitment to and connection with their communities, and many are activists committed to affecting social change. The publication's focus is on picture books for elementary school-aged children about contemporary life in the Latino/Chicano, African American, Asian American, Native American, multi-racial and other minority and new immigrant communities. The books present positive role models for at-risk youth. The press, one of the few nonprofit publishers of children's books, is involved in the community through sponsorship of public events. Example of titles include *I See the Rhythm,* painting by Michele Wood and text by Toyomi Igus, a chronicle of the history, mood, and movement of 500 years of African American music, and Monica Gunning's *A Shelter in Our Car,* a book about a girl who lives in a car with her mother while they both go to school and plan for a real home. Juan Felipe Herrera's *Featherless (Desplumado),* illustrated by Ernesto Cuevas, Jr., won the 2004 IPPY Award in the Multicultural Fiction in the Juvenile/Young Adult category.

## CHUSMA HOUSE PUBLICATIONS
P.O. Box 467
San Jose, CA 95103
(408) 947-0958  Fax: (408) 279-6381
Email: chusmahouse@earthlink.net  Web: www.chusmahouse.com

**Editor**: Charley Trujillo, founder
**ISBN prefix**: 1-891823
**Average number of new titles published per year**: 1
**Number of titles in print**: 17
**Distributor**: Publisher direct via the website's order form, or by fax
**Other materials produced**: CDs, DVDs, videos

APBNA

**Publication interests**: Hispanic/Latino, Literary, Minorities, Poetry, Social Justice
**Motto**: "Bringing quality literature to the *gente*" (people).

Founded in 1990, Chusma House Publications' philosophy is on of self-determination—Chicanos do not have to look to mainstream institutions to publish their intellectual and artistic work. Chusma is an archaic Spanish word that meant galley slaves; the editors chose it to mean "the common people." The editors are committed to the publication of high quality writing by both established and emerging Chicano and Chicana writers. Examples of titles include Patrisia Gonzales' *The Mud People: testimonies, chronicles and remembrances*, a series of essays that chronicle and witness the history of eight Mexican social movements from the 1930s to 1993, and Charley Trujillo's and *Soldados: Chicanos in Viet Nam*, 19 narratives of Chicano veterans in the Vietnam War.

## CINCO PUNTOS PRESS
701 Texas
El Paso, TX 79901
(915) 566-9072  Fax: (915) 566-5335
Email: info@cincopuntos.com  Web: www.cincopuntos.com

**Editor**: Bobby Byrd and Lee Byrd
**ISBN prefix**: 0-938317
**Average number of new titles published per year**: 7
**Number of titles in print:** 85
**Other materials produced**: CDs, audiocassettes and videos of some of the books for children
**Distributor**: publisher direct via the website or by phone, (800) 566-9072; Consortium
**Publication interests**: Adolescents, Bilingual, Children/Juvenile, Cultural Studies, Education, Folktales, Hispanics/Latinos, Immigration, Latin American Studies, Literary, Minorities, Poetry, Politics, Translations

Founded in 1985, Cinco Puntos Press focuses on the literature of the American Southwest, particularly on the U.S./Mexico border, and Mexico. Cinco Puntos publishes mostly books for children and adolescents, many bilingual, but also translations of Mexican fiction, and some notable Latino writers, among them Benjamin Alire Saenz, Lius Alberto Urrea, Dagoberto Gilb and Ricardo Sanchez.  There are teacher's guides for a number of the children's titles. The best selling title is the children's book by Joe Hayes, *La Llorona: the weeping woman*, one of the best known folkstories of Hispanic America. Joe Hayes won the 2004 IPPY Award for Story Teller of the Year. The press received a lot of publicity for the publication *The Story of Colors/La Historia de los Colores* by Subcommandante Marcos, a delightful myth about how the gods created color. It might have entered the canon of children's literature had it not been written by the leader of the insurgent rebels in Chiapas, Mexico (the Zapatistas), an act that cost the press a NEA grant. An example of a book for adults is Gary Cartwright's *Dirty Dealing: an American parable*, about drug smuggling on the Mexican border and the 1979 assassination of Federal Judge John Wood leading to one of the largest FBI investigations in history up to that time. Joe Hayes, author of *Ghost Fever (Mal de Fantasma)* and *La Llorona (The Weeping Woman)*, won the 2005 Independent Publisher's Ten Outstanding Books of the Year in the Story Teller of the Year category.

## CITY LIGHTS BOOKS
261 Columbus Ave.
San Francisco, CA 94133
(415) 362-8193  Fax: (415) 362-4921
Email: staff@citylights.com  Web: www.citylights.com

**Editor**: Elaine Katzenberger
**Associated with**: City Lights Bookstore
**ISBN prefix**: 0-87286
**Average number of new titles published per year**: 15
**Number of titles in print**: About 200
**Distributor**: Small Press Distribution or Consortium (USA); Marginal (Canada)
**Publication interests**: Alternative Culture, Biography/Memoir, Feminist, Gay, Lesbian, Literary, Poetry, Politics, Translations
**Motto**: "A literary meeting place."

Founded in 1953 by Peter D. Martin and Lawrence Ferlinghetti, City Lights Books focuses on cutting-edge fiction, poetry, memoirs, literary translations, and books on vital social and political issues. City Lights is known and respected for its commitment to innovative and progressive ideas, and its resistance to forces of conservatism and censorship. The publications continue the Beat legacy of anti-authoritarian politics and insurgent thinking. Prominent authors include Bertolt Brecht, Charles Bukowski, William S. Burroughs, Ward Churchill, Karen Finley, Allen Ginsberg, Michael Parenti, and Ellen

Ullman. Examples of titles include: Jack Kerovac's *Book of Dreams* with an Introduction by Robert Creeley, and an unabridged edition of Kerovac's dream accounts; *San Francisco Beat: talking with the poets*, edited by David Meltzer. Ward Churchill's *Kill the Indian, Save the Man: the genocidal impact of American Indian residential schools*; *Revolutionary Romanticism: a drunken boat anthology*, edited by Max Blechman, a book that draws on almost two centuries of intertwined traditions of cultural and political subversion,;and Juan Goytisolo's *Landscapes of War*, translated from the Spanish by Peter Bush, examines the tensions that exist between the West and Islamic societies. Luis Cernuda's *Written in Water* was the winner of the 2005 Lambda Literary Award for Gay Men's Poetry.

## CLARITY PRESS, INC.
3277 Roswell Road NE, Suite 469
Atlanta, GA 30305
(877) 613-1495  Fax: (404) 231-3899 or (877) 613-7868
Email: clarity@islandnet.com  Web: www.bookmasters.com/clarity/

**Editor**: Diana G. Collier
**ISBN prefix**: 0-932863
**Average number of new titles published per year**: 3-4
**Number of titles in print**: 28
**Distributor**: Publisher direct via the website (uses PayPal) or by phone, (800) 729-6423; SCB Distributors (800) 729-6423 (USA); Fernwood Books (Canada)
**Publication interests**: Development Studies, Economics, Globalization, Human Rights, Indigenous Peoples, International Issues/Relations, Minorities, Politics, Poverty, Social Justice, Sustainable Development, Third World
**Motto**: "Creating a human rights culture."

Founded in 1984, Clarity Press is dedicated to assisting in the creation of a human rights culture—a "lived awareness" of human rights principles. The press publishes books on the human dimension of current issues, with particular focus on human rights and social justice. The works shed new light on pressing human rights issues and promote new directions in keeping with international human rights norms. Examples of titles include: Oliver Schmidt's *The Intelligence Files: today's secrets, tomorrow's scandals*, a book that unveils the mechanisms of governments and secret services and offers a shocking insight into frequently illicit and routine immoral undertakings whose harm to individuals, groups and countries is seldom recognized or understood by the public at large, and Rick Anderson's *Home Front: the government's war on soldiers*, an examination of the health-related issues facing American military personnel and veterans.

## CLEIS PRESS
P.O. Box 14697
San Francisco, CA 94114
(415) 575-4700  Fax: (415) 575-4705
Email: dlevinson@cleispress.com  Web: www.cleispress.com

**Editor**: Frederique Delacoste and Felice Newman
**Affiliated press names**: Midnight Editions, imprint, www.midnighteditions.com
**ISBN prefix**: 1-57344
**Average number of new titles published per year**: 20
**Number of titles in print**: 150
**Distributor**: publisher direct (800) 780-2279; Publishers Group West and Publishers Group West Canada
**Publication interests**: Art/The Arts, Biography/Memoir, Comics/Comix, Erotica, Gay, Gender Studies, Hispanic/Latino, Human Rights, Lesbian, Literary, Poetry, Sexuality, Women's Studies
**Motto**: "Hot titles."

Founded in 1980, Cleis Press focuses on publishing lesbian, gay, bisexual and gender studies, sex guides and erotica, and is the largest independent queer publishing company in the U.S. Cleis has published the works of notables such as Gore Vidal, Joan Nestle, Annie Sprinkle, and Susie Bright. The books and authors have won numerous Lambda Literary Awards and the Society for Human Sexuality named the press's sex guides the Best Sex Education Series. Examples of titles include: *The Queer Encyclopedia of Music, Dance and Musical Theater*, edited by Claude J. Summers; Cleis's "best" titles: *Best Gay Erotica Stories* (the 2005 edition won the 2005 Lambda Literary Award for Best Gay Erotica), *Best Lesbian Erotica Stories, Best Women's Erotica*, and seven other titles; *Stories Wicked: Sexy Tales of Legendary Lovers*, edited by Mitzi Szereto, chronicles fantasy encounters with Sigmund Freud, Joan Collins, Warren Beatty and others; Frederique Delacoste's and Priscilla Alexander's *Sex Work: writings by women in the sex industry*, 2nd ed.; and *Conversaciones: relatos por padres y madres de Hijas lesbianas y Hijos gay* (Talking with parents of lesbian, gay, bisexual and transgendered Latinos), the first collection of Spanish-language coming out stories by and for Latino men and women. Midnight Editions' mission is to enlarge our understanding of human rights by publishing works from regions where repression and censorship endanger creative expression, for example, Melanie Friend's *No Place Like Home: echoes from Kosovo*, photographs and interviews that present a profoundly complex document of recent Balkan history.

## COFFEE HOUSE PRESS
27 N. 4th St., #400
Minneapolis, MN 55401
(612) 338-0125 Fax: (612) 338-4004
Email: form available on website Web: www.coffeehousepress.org

**Byline**: "Where good books are brewing."
**Editor**: Allan Kornblum
**ISBN prefix**: 0-918273, 1-56689
**Average number of new titles published per year**: 14
**Number of titles in print**: 216
**Distributor**: Small Press Distribution, Consortium
**Publication interests**: Literary, Poetry, Short Stories
**Motto**: "Where good books are brewing."

Founded in 1984, Coffee House Press has become an award-winning, non-profit literary publisher. The books presents writing of people who have been underrepresented in published literature. The books are generally from emerging and mid-career authors. The press took its name from the long tradition of coffee houses as places for the free exchange of ideas, where each individual had equal time for expression, regardless of station or background. Examples of titles include: William Melvin Kelley's *dem*, a 1967 reprint classic of the Black Arts Movement and a surrealistic satire of the convoluted and symbiotic relationship between whites and blacks; Bonnie J. Morris' *Girl Reel*, a survey of women and lesbians in television and film, 1970s-90s; Selah Saterstrom's *The Pink Institution*, about four generations of women in a tragic Mississippi family that never fully recovered from the Civil War; and *The Moon in Its Flight* by Gilbert Sorrentino, a two-time PEN/Faulkner Award finalist; and *Paul Metcalf: Collected Works*, vols. I, II, and III, from a leading author associated with the Black Mountain writers.

## COMMON COURAGE PRESS
P.O. Box 702, 1 Red Barn Road
Monroe, ME 04951
(207) 525-0900 Fax: (207) 525-3068

Email: form available on website under "Contact" Web:
www.commoncouragepress.com

**Editor**: Greg Bates
**ISBN prefix**: 1-56751
**Average number of new titles published per year**: 20
**Number of titles in print**: 160
**Distributor**: publisher direct via the website or by phone (800) 497-3207
(buy direct and save 35% on each title); Consortium
**Publication interests**: Activism, Ecology/Environmentalism, Economics,
Feminist, Gender Studies, Globalization, Health, Indigenous Populations,
International Issues/Relation, Labor Studies, Media Studies, Politics,
Race/Race Relations, Social Justice
**Motto**: "Books for informed descent."

Founded in 1990, Common Courage Press publishes books for social justice
relating to corporate power, race, ecology, welfare, media politics, U.S. policy
from Central America to the Middle East, and many other areas. The press
seeks to provide an analysis of problems from a range of perspectives, and to
aid activists and others in developing strategies for action. Notable authors
include Noam Chomsky, Howard Zinn, Jean Bernard Aristide, Jennifer Har-
bury, Philip Berrigan and Jude Bari. Examples of titles include: Larry Ever-
est's *Oil, Power and Empire: Iraq and the U.S. global agenda*, an expose on how the
U.S. war on Iraq is part of a plan for U.S. global domination; Michael K.
Smith's and Matt Wuerker's *The Madness of King George: the ingenious insanity of our
most misunderestimated President*; and Douglas F. Dowd's *The Broken Promises of
America*, vols. 1 and 2, a reference work with 160 entries from arrogance to
zoos.

## COPPER CANYON PRESS
P.O. Box 271
Port Townsend, WA 98368
(877) 501-1393  Fax: (360) 385-4985
Email: poetry@coppercanyonpress.org
Web: www.coppercanyonpress.org

**Editor**: Joseph Bednarik
**Affiliated press names**: Kage-an Books, imprint
**Associated with**: Centrum, a nonprofit arts agency, Fort Worden State
Park, Port Townsend

**ISBN prefix**: 0-914742, 1-55659
**Average number of new titles published per year**: 16
**Number of titles in print**: 187
**Other materials produced**: CDs
**Distributor**: publisher direct (877) 501-1393; Small Press Distribution, Consortium
**Publication interests**: Anthologies, Bilingual, Poetry, Reprints, Translations
**Motto**: the pressmark symbol--the Chinese character for poetry made up of two parts: word and temple

Founded in 1972, Copper Canyon Press is often considered the premier publisher in the U.S. devoted exclusively to poetry. The press's mission is to build the awareness and appreciation of, and audience for, a wide range of emerging and established American poets as well as poetry in translation from many of the world's cultures, classical and contemporary. The press publishes poetry exclusively selecting from a wide range of styles from many different world cultures. The Kage-an Books imprint focuses on translations. The press is committed to the belief that poetry is essential to the human spirit and a necessary element in a thriving culture. Authors include Thomas McGrath, Lucille Clifton, Carolyn Kizer, W.S. Merwin, Su Tung-p'o, Hayden Carruth, Denise Levertove, Octavio Paz, Czeslaw Milosz, and many others. The all-time bestselling book is, Pablo Neruda's *The Book of Questions* (updated, bilingual edition, 2001), composed of 316 unanswerable questions where poems integrate the wonder of a child with the experiences of an adult. Other titles include: *On Poetry and Craft: selected prose*, by Theodore Roethke, one of the most famous and outspoken poets this country has ever known; *Only Breed, Only Light*, by poet and disability activist, Stephen Kuusisto; and *Complete Poems of Kenneth Rexroth*, presenting poems of nature and protest with biting social and political commentary.

## CREATION BOOKS
P.O. Box 1137
New York, NY 10156
[phone and fax numbers not available]
Email: the.rabbit@creationbooks.com  Web: www.creationbooks.com

**Editor**: James Williamson
**Associated with**: Creation Bookstore, Los Angeles, California
**ISBN prefix**: 1-84068

**Average number of new titles published per year**: 20
**Number of titles in print**: 93
**Distributor**: Consortium (USA); Marginal (Canada)
**Publication interests**: Art/The Arts, Erotica, Film, Music, Sexuality, Surrealism

Founded in 1989, Creation Books uses books as components in "an attempt to assemble a unique monument to the terrible sadness of the world from the human perspective." The books and editorial philosophy pivot around the revolutionary writings and art of visionary iconoclasts, such as de Sade, Apollinaire, Wilde, Lovecraft and Dali. Publications feature those who have expressed their singular, creative impulse through rock and pop music, underground and cult cinema, body modification and fetishism, and their own bizarre and bloody deeds. Besides the publication interests, additional headings could include occult, apocalypse, manga, fetishisms, cults, and other topics that descend to the dark side of life. Examples of titles inlcude: Robert Short's *The Age of Gold: surrealist cinema*, Doyle Green's *Lips Hips Tits Power: the films of Russ Meyer*, Francis King's *Megatherion: the magical world of Aleister Crowley*, an account of Crowley's occult philosophy and technique; Alan Parker's *Vicious: too fast to live*, story of Sid Vicious from his childhood to his final fix, and Suehiro Marus's *Ultra-Gash Inferno*, a unique style of manga fusing sex and violence.

## CULTURAL SURVIVAL, INC.
215 Prospect
Cambridge, MA 02139
(617) 441-5400  Fax: (617) 441-5417
Email: csinc@cs.org  Web: www.cs.org

**Editor**: Ellen Lutz, Executive Director
**ISBN prefix**: 0-939521
**Average number of new titles published per year**: 4
**Number of titles in print**: 44
**Other materials produced**: *Cultural Survival Quarterly*, *Cultural Survival Voices*, a semi-annual newspapers, *Weekly Indigenous News*, Action Update (online), and Indigenous Action Network, an online network that matches Indigenous peoples or groups that request service with those who have the skills to meet their needs.
**Distributor**: Ingram

**Publication interests**: Aboriginal Studies, Cultural Studies, Development Studies, Ecology/Environmentalism, Economics, Globalization, Human Rights, Indigenous Peoples, International Issues/Relations, Politics, Social Justice, Sustainable Development, Third World, Women's Issues/Studies
**Motto**: "Promoting the rights, voices, and visions of indigenous peoples."

Founded in 1972, Cultural Survival, Inc. explores the interconnected issues that affect indigenous and ethnic communities, including environmental destruction, land rights, sustainable development, and cultural preservation. Cultural Survival was founded by Harvard University professor of Anthropology David Maybury-Lewis, who also directs PONSACS, the Program on Nonviolent Sanctions and Cultural Survival at Harvard's Weatherhead Center for International Affairs. The impulse for the founding of Cultural Survival came from the process of "development" being undertaken in the Amazonian regions of South America during the 1960s. The "opening up" of the Amazonian hinterland and the drastic effects this had on the indigenous peoples living there dramatized the urgent need to defend the human right of these "victims of progress." Cultural Survival also seeks to inform students and the public at large about indigenous issues and their significance for all of us through its education program. *Cultural Survival Quarterly*, the primary publication, analyzes of how indigenous peoples have successfully responded to serious crises, and proposes new strategies for responding directly to critical needs. Because each issue is thematic, the journals are also sold as monographs. Examples from volume 28 (2004) are *World Transformed: indigenous people's health in changing rainforests* and *Indigenous Women's Empowerment Begins with Communication*. Many articles are available free online.

**CURBSTONE PRESS**
321 Jackson St.
Willimantic, CT 06226-1738
(860) 423-5110  Fax: (860) 423-9242
Email: info@curbstone.org  Web: www.curbstone.org

**Editor**: Alexander Taylor and Judith Ayer Doyle
**ISBN prefix**: 1-880684, 0-915306
**Average number of new titles per year**: 10
**Number of titles in print**: 151
**Distributors**: publisher direct via website's order form, or by phone; Consortium, Small Press Distribution

**Publication interests**: Art/The Arts, Civil Liberties, Cultural Studies, Hispanic/Latino, History, Human Rights, Intercultural Understanding, Latin American Studies, Literary, Minorities, Poetry, Political, Poverty, Social Change, Social Justice, Third World, Translations, Women's Issues/Studies
**Motto**: "Literature that illuminates the issues of our time."

Founded in 1975, Curbstone Press is a nonprofit, literary arts organization that focuses on creative literature that examines social issues, encourages a deeper understanding between cultures, and reflects a commitment to promoting human rights. The press has two interdependent goals, first, publishing creative literature that promotes human rights and intercultural understanding, and second, bringing writers and programs deep into the community to promote literacy, knowledge about many cultures, and an appreciation of literature. It is this dual focus on publishing and educational programming that makes Curbstone unique among nonprofit presses. Curbstone has developed a strong list of books by African American, Latino, Central American, and Vietnamese writers, including the Voices from Vietnam Series and Poets from Vietnam Series. The press's Living Literature program brings writers into communities to promote literacy, knowledge about many cultures, respect for human rights, and appreciation of good literature, among people of all ages. Curbstone seeks out the highest aesthetic expression of the dedication to human rights in poetry, stories, novels, testimonials, and photography. Everything the press publishes mixes art and politics. In 2002, the press began awarding the Miguel Marmol Prize, named for the legendary Salvadorian labor union leader, enabling a Latina/o writer to publish a first novel written in English. Nearly three-quarters of the books are translations, and in 2001 Curbstone won a NEA Award for translation programs. Examples of titles include Doan Le's *The Cemetery of Chua Village*, the seventh volume in the "Voices from Vietnam" series, the book explores greed, marriage, divorce, aging, and human rights, and J.M.G. Le Clezio's *Wandering Star*, a translated title about the price of war and exile. Mary Helen Lagasse's *The Fifth Sun* won the 2004 IPPY Award in the Multicultural Fiction category.

## DALKEY ARCHIVE PRESS
ISU Campus 8905
Normal, IL 61790-8905
(309) 438-7555  Fax: (309) 438-7422
Email: contact@dalkeyarchive.com  Web: www.dalkeyarchive.com

**Byline**: "Preserving literature for future generations."

**Editor**: John O'Brien
**Associated with**: Center for Book Culture
www.centerforbookculture.org, Illinois State University
**ISBN prefix**: 0-916583, 1-56487
**Average number of new titles published per year**: 20
**Number of titles in print**: 250
**Other materials produced**: *Review of Contemporary Fiction* and *CONTEXT: A Forum for Literary Arts and Culture*
**Distributor**: publisher direct via website's printable order form
**Publication interests**: Literary, Poetry, Reprints, Translations

Founded in 1984, Dalkey Archive Press exists to challenge assumptions about the nature of literary art, its audience, and the means by which readers can and should be reached. The press started with the intention of restoring to print "just a few books," ones that really didn't have much of a chance of ever getting back into print through a commercial publishing house. Among the first books published were Gilbert Sorrentino's *Splendide-Hotel*, Nicholas Mosley's *Impossible Object*, and Douglas Woolf's *Wall to Wall*. The books represent world literature from the past one hundred years, and translations from twenty countries, especially from Europe including Russia. Translations represent about 35 percent of all the books. The editors look for books that "work against what is expected, that they in some way challenge received notions, whether those are literary, social or political." From the start the press has kept all of its fiction in print. Founded in 1980, the Center for Book Culture is a nonprofit organization serving readers and writers through the promotion and publication of books that define our heritage, challenge conventional ways of seeing the world, and demand the highest imaginative and intellectual response. Authors include many who are unknown except perhaps in narrow circles, to more recognizable authors such as Ismael Reed and luminaries such as Gertrude Stein. Examples of titles include William Eastlake's *The Bamboo Bed*, a book that treats with hilarity and outrage the grim absurdity of war, and Danilo Kis's *A Tomb for Boris Davidovich*, a stunning statement on political persecution.

## DOLLARS & SENSE
740 Cambridge St.
Cambridge, MA 02141
(617) 876-2434  Fax: (617) 876-0008
Email: dollars@dollarsandsense.org
Web: www.dollarsandsense.org

**Editor**: Amy Gluckman and Adrian Scharf
**ISBN prefix**: 1-878585
**Average number of new titles published per year**: 3
**Number of titles in print**: 11
**Other materials produced**: *Dollars & Sense*, a bimonthly magazine of economic issues and opinion
**Distributors**: Publisher direct via the website's shopping cart feature
**Publication       interests**:       Anthologies,       Capitalism,       Ecology/Environmentalism, Economics, Globalization, Government Regulation, Housing, International Issues/Relations, Politics, Social Justice, Unemployment, Urban Issues/Studies
**Motto**: "Left perspectives on current economic affairs."

Founded in 1974, Dollars & Sense publishes books that explain the workings of the U.S. and international economies. Originally sponsored by the Union for Radical Political Economics, the magazine was produced by a collective of URPE members to challenge the mainstream's account of how the U.S. economy works. The press is still a collective, but now with an editorial staff. The primary emphasis is on the journal, *Dollars & Sense*. The best articles from the journal are repackaged into a number of the edited books and anthologies meant for general and classroom use. Examples of titles include: Charles Sackrey's and Geoffrey Schneider's *Introduction to Political Economy*, 3rd edition, a book that covers the works of the three most influential economists of modern times—Marx, Veblen and Keynes—who are simply ignored in most economics courses; *Current Economic Issues: progressive perspectives from Dollars & Sense*, the 8th edition covers from the 1990's stock market crash to the Iraq war; *Real World Globalization*, the 8th edition, a guide to rapidly changing global trends in trade, investment, labor relations, and economic development; and *The Wealth Inequality Reader*, edited by Chuck Collins, et al, twenty-five essays that explore wealth inequality in the United States--causes, consequences, and strategies for change.

## DOWN THERE PRESS
938 Howard St., Suite 101
San Francisco, CA 94103
(800) 289-8423 or (415) 974-8990  Fax: (415) 974-8989
Email: customerservice@goodvibes.com
Web: www.goodvibes.com/dtp/dtp.html

**Editor**: worker-owned, woman-run cooperative
**Affiliated press names**: Yes Press, imprint
**Associated with**: Open Enterprises Cooperative, Inc. (corporate name) and Good Vibrations retail stores, San Francisco and Berkeley
**ISBN prefix**: 0-940208
**Average number of new titles published per year**: (no titles published 2004-)
**Number of titles in print**: 20
**Other material produced**: audiobooks (Passion Press) and videos and DVDs (Sexpositive Productions)
**Distributor**: publisher direct via website's shopping bag feature or by phone (800) 289-8423 or fax (415) 974-8989; SCB
**Publication interests**: Adolescents, Children/Juvenile, Erotica, Health, Sexuality
**Motto**: "Books with a sex positive philosophy."

Founded in 1975, Down There Press is the nation's only independent publisher devoted exclusively to the publication of sexual health books for children and adults. Joani Blank, sex therapist and educator, started the press in her pursuit to provide needed books on sexuality. The first book published was Blank's *The Playbook for Women about Sex* followed by *The Playbook for Men about Sex*. All the books provide realistic physiological information with non-judgmental techniques for strengthening sexual communication. The press also publishes erotica, both literary and photographic for women and men. Many works are for adults only and the website states that one must be 21 or over to enter. Examples of titles include: Martha Cornog's *The Big Book of Masturbation: from angst to zeal*, winner of the 2004 Benjamin Franklin Award for Best Reference Book; Joani Blank's *Still Doing It: women and men over 60 write about their sexuality*; *A Kid's First Book About Sex*, by Joani Blank with illustrations by Marcia Quackenbush, a book that teaches about sexual activity apart from reproduction for ages 5-9, Blank's *The Playbook About Sex for Kids* for ages 6-11, and Isadore Alman's *Sex Information, May I Help You?*, for ages 16-adult.

## EARTHSCAN PUBLICATIONS
8-12 Camden High St.
London NW1 0JH United Kingdom
+44 (0) 20 7387 8558  Fax: +44 (0) 20 7387 8998
Email: earthinfo@earthscan.co.uk  Web: www.earthscan.co.uk

**Editor**: Jonathan Sinclair Wilson

**Associated with**: Earthscan publishes information on behalf of 119 national and international institutions, from ActionAid to Wuppertal Institute, and produces books in association with a wide range of governmental and non-governmental organizations.
**ISBN prefix**: 1-85383, 1-84407
**Average number of new titles published per year**: 70
**Number of titles in print**: 300+
**Other materials produced**: 3 bimonthly journals: *Renewable Energy World, Cogeneration and On-site Power Production*, and *Waste Management World*
**Distributor**: Publisher direct via website's Bookshop feature, or by telephone +44(0) 1903 828 503 or email orders@earthscan.co.uk; Stylus Publishing (U.S.) www.styluspub.com , (800) 232-0233; Renouf Publishing Co. (Canada) www.renoufbooks.com, (613) 745-2665
**Publication interests**: Conservation, Cultural Studies, Development Studies, Ecology/Environmentalism, Economics, Globalization, Natural/Nature, Politics, Social Change, Social Issues, Sustainable Development, Third World
**Motto**: "Delivering sustainability."

Founded in 1988, Earthscan Publications joined in 2003 with another publisher in environmental science, technology, and sustainable development, James & James (Scientific Publications, Ltd). The combined publishers are now known as Earthscan. Through their publications and other media, the editors seek to increase understanding of environmental issues and their implications at all levels, to influence opinion and policy toward sustainable forms of development, and to promote the various businesses, industries, and organizations that provide the infrastructure to make this happen. *State of the World*, a bestseller published annually in 28 languages, has each edition draw on the expertise of World Watch Institute writers and researchers. Examples of titles include Vijay V. Vaitheeswaran's *Power to the People: how the coming energy revolution will transform an industry, change our lives and maybe even save the planet*, and Tim Lang's and Michael Heasman's *Food Wars: the battle for mouths, minds and markets*, a focus on the global politics of food and health.

## FANTAGRAPHICS BOOKS
7563 Lake City Way, N.E.
Seattle, WA 98115
(206) 524-1967 Fax: (206) 524-2104
Email: fbicomix@fantagraphics.com
Web: www.fantagraphics.com

**Editor**: Gary Groth
**Affiliated press names**: Eros Comix
**ISBN prefix**: 0-930193, 1-56097
**Average number of new titles published per year**: 35
**Number of titles in print**: 400+
**Other materials produced**: Comics and *The Comics Journal*, a monthly trade magazine
**Distributor**: Publisher direct via website's bookstore or by phone, (800) 657-1100; W.W. Norton
**Publication interests**: Alternative Culture, Anthologies, Art, Cartoons/Cartoonists, Comics/Comix, Erotica, Fantasy, Popular Culture, Reprints, Sexuality
**Motto**: "Publisher of the world's greatest cartoonists."
Founded in 1976, Fantagraphics Books is the world's leading publisher of cutting-edge work by today's most popular alternative comic artists, as well as collections of underground comix artists and classic comic strips. Some material is x-rated. The press publishes works that define the attitudes and aesthetics of contemporary popular culture. The publications include reprints of classic works from the golden age of comic strips—Popeye, Pogo, Prince Valiant, etc., fifty works of Jules Feiffer, and the sixties and seventies work from underground cartoonists, such as Vaughn Bode and R. Crumb, acknowledged as the "Father" of underground comics. Examples of titles include Ho Che Anderson's *King: a comics biography of Martin Luther King, Jr.* and Wilfred Santiago's *In My Darkest Hour*, about a 28-year-old Latin American transient who confronts pervasive feelings of inadequacy, anger, guilt, and escalating alienation.

## THE FEMINIST PRESS AT THE CITY UNIVERSITY OF NEW YORK
365 Fifth Ave., Suite 5406.
New York, NY 10016
(212) 817-7920  Fax: (212) 817-1593
Email: jroncker@gc.cuny.edu
Web: www.feministpress.org

**Editor**: Livia Tenzer
**ISBN prefix**: 1-55861, 0-912670, 0-935312
**Average number of new titles published per year**: 10
**Number of titles in print**: 200+

**Other materials produced**: *Women's Studies Quarterly* and *Women and Sports: WSQ*

**Distributor**: Publisher direct via website's order form, or by phone (212) 817-7925 or fax (212) 817-1593; Consortium

**Publication interests**: Adolescents, Biography/Memoir, Children/Juvenile, Cultural Studies, Feminist, International Issues/Relations, Literary, Politics, Reprints, Third World, Women's Issues/Studies

**Motto**: "A force in literary publishing and social transformation."

Founded in 1970, The Feminist Press is a nonprofit literary and educational publisher dedicated to publishing work by and about women. The press is called the flagship of the women's movement in the U.S. and is the oldest women's press in the nation. It was among the first to give voice to African American women writers. Projects include Women Changing the World, an international biography series of individuals who have made extraordinary contributions to the global community despite tremendous adversity and discrimination. Books for young readers include The GIRLS FIRST! Series of biographies, folktales and fables, novels, and picture books. The International Women's Writing Project publishes literary works by distinguished women writers from Africa, Asia, Europe and Latin America. The Women Writing Africa is a major project of cultural reclamation that includes Suzette Haden Elgin's *Native Tongue*, a reprint of the 1984 classic trilogy (Vol. 2, *The Judas Rose* and vol. 3, *Earthsong*) that earned wide critical praise and cult status not only among science fiction fans, but also among followers of women's literature and feminist theory and language buffs of all persuasions. Examples of other titles include Riverbend's *Baghdad Burning: a girl blog from Iraq*, a young Iraqi woman gives a human face to war and occupation, and *Developing Power: how women transformed international development*, edited by Arvonne S. Fraser and Irene Tinker.

## FERAL HOUSE

P.O. Box 39910
Los Angeles, CA 90039
(323) 666-3311
Email: info@feralhouse.com  Web: www.feralhouse.com

**Editor**: Adam Parfrey
**ISBN prefix**: 0-922915
**Average number of new titles published per year**: 8
**Number of titles in print**: 50
**Other materials produced**: distributes films and audio discs

**Distributor**: Consortium (beginning spring 2006); Marginal (Canada)
**Publication interests**: Alternative Culture, Art/The Arts, Biography/Memoir, Comics/Comix, Conspiracy, Cultural Studies, Erotica, Film, Music, Political, Popular Culture, Sexuality, True Crime
**Byline**: "The publisher that refuses to be domesticated."

Founded in 1988, Feral House publishes books on the fringes of society's mainstream: research on unconscious reality, mind control, biographies of the eccentric and sometimes insane, satanism, and accounts of ultra-violence. Examples of titles include: Jim Redden's *Snitch Culture: how citizens are turned into the eyes and ears of the state*; Mel Gordon's *Voluptuous Panic: the erotic world of Weimar Berlin*; Jim Hogshire's *Pills-a-go-go: a fiendish investigation into pill marketing, art, history and consumption*; John Carter's *Sex and Rockets: the occult world of Jack Parsons*; H. Michael Sweeney's *The Professional Paranoid: how to fight back when investigated, stalked, harassed, or targeted by any agency, organization, or individual*; and *Apocalypse Culture II*, edited by Adam Parfrey, the sequel to the flagship book of Feral House. *Suicide Girls*, edited by Missy Suicide, a book of pin up rock and goth girls, was winner of the 2005 IPPY Award in Erotica.

## FERNWOOD PUBLISHING

8422 St. Margaret's Bay Rd., Suite 2A, Box 5
Black Point, Nova Scotia B0J 1B0 Canada
(902) 857-1388  Fax: (902) 857-1328
Email: info@fernwoodbooks.com  Web: www.fernwoodbooks.ca

**Editor**: Errol Sharpe, President
**Associated with**: Fernwood Books represents and distributes books from 19 publishers
**ISBN prefix**: 1-55266
**Average number of new titles published per year**: 18-20
**Number of titles in print**: 202
**Distributor**: Independent Publishers Group (USA); Broadview Press, (705) 743-8990, handles Canadian orders for Fernwood Books, customerservice@broadviewpress.com
**Publication interests**: Critical Theory, Cultural Studies, Ecology/Environmentalism, Gender Studies, Globalization, Health, History, Indigenous Populations, International Issues/Relations, Media Studies, Politics, Race/Racial Relations, Social Work, Women's Issues/Studies
**Motto**: "Publish critical works, break new ground, challenge existing norms."

Founded in 1991, Fernwood Publishing's objective is to publish critical works that address social issues with a focus in the social sciences and humanities. Fernwood's Global Issue Series, co-published with Zed Books, are short, accessible think pieces that address leading global issues of relevance today, for example, Walden Bello's *Deglobalization: ideas for a new world economy*. The annual *Socialist Register*, co-published with Merlin Press, has since 1964 brought together leading writers of the left to investigate aspects of a common theme. In the 2004 edition of *New Imperial Challenge*, editors Leo Panitch and Colin Leys explore how U.S. led imperialism has transformed global power relations. Other titles include Jim Harding's *After Iraq: war, imperialism and democracy* and Isaac Saney's *Cultural Inclusion: supporting children to value diversity and challenge racial prejudice*.

## FICTION COLLECTIVE TWO (FC2)
Department of English
Florida State University
Tallahassee, FL 32306-1580
(850) 644-2260  Fax: (850) 644-6808
Email: fc2@english.fsu.edu
Web: fc2.org

**Editor**: R.M. Berry, acting publisher
**Affiliated press names**: Black Ice Books, Fiction Collective (previous name)
**Associated with**: Florida State University (executive offices), Illinois State University (book production)
**ISBN prefix**: 0-914590, 0-932511, 1-57366, 0-918411 (Black Ice Books)
**Average number of new titles published per year**: 6-10
**Number of titles in print**: 170+
**Distributor**: Publisher direct via the website's order form; Northwestern University Press, Small Press Distribution
**Publication interests**: Avant-garde, Literary, Poetry
**Motto**: "Fiction that redefines the rules."

Founded in 1974, Fiction Collective Two is committed to unsettling the bounds of literature and broaden the audience for America's more adventurous writing. The press is a not-for-profit publisher with an editorial board consisting of between five and twelve FC2 authors. The press is committed to preserving cultural resources that might otherwise be silenced or lost and prides itself in keeping its backlist in print. New writers are aggressively sought out. Mainstream publishers consider the writing as too challenging, innovative or heterodox for the commercial milieu. Black Ice Books, founded in 1993, is a merging of avant-garde with the popular. FC2 books have been nominated for or won a number of awards including the American Book Award, Western States Book Award, PEN West Award, and the BEA Firecracker Award. Award-winning authors include Clarence Major, Gerald Vizenor and Rob Hardin.

**FIREBRAND BOOKS**
2232 S. Main St., #272
Ann Arbor, MI 48103
(248) 738-8202  Fax: (248) 738-7786
Email: firebrand@firebrandbooks.com  Web: www.firebrandbooks.com

**Editor**: Karen Oosterhous
**ISBN prefix**: 1-56341, 0-932379
**Average number of new titles published per year**: 12
**Number of titles in print**: 106
**Distributor**: Publisher direct (800) 343-4499; CDS
**Publication interests**: African American, Asian American, Biography/Memoirs, Erotica, Feminist, Gender Issues, Lesbian, Literary, Sexuality, Women's Issues/Studies

Founded in 1985, Firebrand Books is a feminist and lesbian publishing house committed to producing quality work in a wide variety of genres by ethnically and racially diverse authors.

The publications have garnered twelve Lambda Literary Awards and four American Library Association Gay/Lesbian/Bisexual Book Awards. The publications include nine books of cartoons by Alison Bechdel as part of the popular *Dykes to Watch Out For* series. Examples of titles include Judith Frank's *Crybaby Butch*, a book that investigates the meaning of butch identity as it reinvents itself from one generation to the next, also winner of the 2005 Lambda Literary Award's Trustee's Award for Debut Lesbian Fiction; *Politics of the Heart: a lesbian parenting anthology*, edited by Sandra Pollack and Jeanne Vaughn; and *Venus of Chalk* by Susan Stinson, "the most criminally underrated dyke novelist in the world," according to *Diva Magazine*, February 2004.

## FLORICANTO PRESS

650 Castro St., Suite 120-331
Mountain View, CA 94041-2055
(415) 552-1879 Fax: (702) 995-1410
Email: cs@floricantopress.com Web: www.floricantopress.com

**Editor**: Roberto Cabello-Argandona
**Associated with**: Inter American Development Corp.
**ISBN prefix**: 0-915745
**Average number of new titles published per year**: 2
**Number of titles in print**: 30
**Other materials produced**: *LECTOR: The Hispanic Book Review Journal* and *La Red/The Net: The Hispanic Journal of Education, Commentary and Reviews*; digital products
**Distributor**: Publisher direct via website's bookcart feature, or by phone, fax, email, or regular mail; Inter American Development is the exclusive distributor (same address, phone, fax, email as the press)
**Publication interests**: Bilingual, Biography/Memoir, Children/Juvenile, Ethnic, Feminist, Hispanic/Latino, History, Latin American Studies, Minorities, Psychology, Reference, Women's Issues/Studies
**Motto**: "Dedicated to promote Latino discourse, thought and culture."

Founded in 1982, Floricanto Press is a vehicle for materials on Mexican and Hispanic cultures, Cinco de Mayo, and Hispanic heritage. The materials fall into the broad categories of biography, social sciences, and humanistic discourse. The La Mujer Latina Series is a series of feminist creative, social and historiographical writings by and about Latino women. *Bilindex*, a collection of subject headings, is the Spanish equivalent of the Library of Congress Subject Headings list. Other reference works include Spanish language dictionaries, Spanish-English bilingual dictionaries, and books on English as a second language. The La Mujer Latina Series is a collection of feminist, social and historiographical writings by and about Latino women. Books on Cinco de Mayo include Roberto Cabello-Argandona's *Cinco de Mayo: a symbol of Mexican resistance*. Other titles focus on Chicano Studies, including Burton Moore's *Love and Riot in Los Angeles: the life of Oscar Zeta Acosta*, the man who awakened the Chicano movement in Los Angeles and served as a catalyst for change and hope for the community, and Raoul Lowery Contreras' *The Illegal Alien: a dagger into the heart of America?*, an analysis of illegal immigration and its growing impact on the American economy and way of life.

## FOOD FIRST BOOKS
398 60th St.
Oakland, CA 94608
(510) 654-4400  Fax: (510) 654-4551
Email: foodfirst@foodfirst.org  Web: www.foodfirst.org

**Editor**: Peter Rosset, Co-Director; Clancy Drake, Managing Editor
**Associated with**: Institute for Food and Development Policy, a member-supported "peoples" think tank and an education-for-action center. Food First Information and Action Network (FIAN) is the action and campaigning partner of the Institute.
**ISBN prefix**: 0-935028
**Average number of new titles published per year**: 2
**Number of titles in print**: 20
**Other materials produced**: videos, development reports, policy briefs, educational material, fact sheets, and Food Rights Watch, the email newsletter
**Distributor**: Publisher direct via the website's shopping cart feature
**Publication interests**: Ecology/Environmentalism, Education, Globalization, Human Rights, Hunger, Indigenous Populations, International Issues/Relations, Minorities, Politics, Poverty, Social Change, Social Issues, Social Justice, Sustainable Development
**Motto**: "For the right to be free from hunger."

Founded in 1975 by Frances Moore Lappe and Joseph Collins following the success of the book, *Diet for a Small Planet*, Food First Books commit to establishing food as a fundamental human right. The materials highlight root causes and value-based solutions to hunger and poverty around the world. With half of its income coming from individual contributions, Food First maintains its independence, objectivity and commitment to the struggles of common people all over the world. Examples titles include: *Alternative to the Peace Corps* (biennial); *Shafted: free trade and America's working poor*, edited by Christine Ahn, a book giving voice to working people and how trade agreements have effected them; Angus Linsay Wright's and Wendy Wolford's *To Inherit the Earth: the landless movement and the struggle for a new Brazil*, about Brazil's Landless Workers' Movement; and Kenny Bruno's and Joshua Karliner's *Earthsummit Biz: the corporate takeover of sustainable development*.

## FREEDOM PRESS
Angel Alley, 84b Whitechapel High Street
London E1 7QX, United Kingdom
Telephone: 01-247-7249
Email: distro@freedompress.org.uk
Web: vega.soi.city.ac.uk/~louise/freehome.html

**Editor**: unpaid volunteers
**Associated with**: Freedom Bookshop, a London anarchist bookstore
**ISBN prefix**: 0-900384
**Average number of new titles published per year**: varies from about 1 to 4
**Number of titles in print**: 76
**Other material produced**: *Freedom*, an anarchist newspaper, *Raven*, an anarchist quarterly journal, and pamphlets
**Distributor**: Publisher direct via the website; AK Press Distribution (USA)
**Publication interests**: Anarchism, Comics/Comix, Cultural Studies, Economics, Politics, Reprints, Socialism/Marxism
**Motto**: "Opposed to bosses and governments of every kind."

Founded in 1886, Freedom Press emerged from the British socialist movement, and is now the world's oldest anarchist publisher publishing a range of books covering all aspects of anarchist theory and practice. Although the editors concentrated on the periodical, they also produced other publications—first pamphlets, then booklets, and books, mostly works by foreign writers, for example, Peter Kropotkin, Emma Goldman, and Mikhail Bakunin. The press publishes books of Wildcat strips, anarchist comics starring a wild cat commenting on topical issues, for example, Donald Rooum's *Wildcat Anarchists against Bombs*. Examples of titles include, Ronald Creagh's and Sharif Gemie's *The Shadow Under the Lamp: essays on September 11*, an analysis of 9/11 and its origins, and Tony Allen's *A Summer in the Park: A Journal of Speakers' Corner*, an account of the "take-no-prisoners gladiatorial confrontation" that is Speakers' Corner.

## FREEDOM VOICES PUBLICATIONS
P.O. Box 423115
San Francisco, CA 94142
(415) 558-8759
Email: info@freedomvoices.org Web: www.freedomvoices.org

**Editor**: Ben Clarke
**Other affiliated press names**: TallMountain Circle Books; acquired New Earth Publications
**Associated with**: Tenderloin Reflection and Education Center, San Francisco, a center committed to providing essential human services to underserved people and organizing public readings of writing workshops
**ISBN prefix**: 0-9625153
**Average number of new titles published per year**: 4
**Number of titles in print**: 26
**Other material produced**: Participates in research projects for popular education and produces education materials, in-progress collaborative texts, chapbooks, and periodicals used in grassroots education programs; posters
**Distributor**: Publisher direct via the website's order form; Small Press Distribution
**Publication interests**: Alaskan Native, Education, Minorities, Poetry, Poor/Poverty, Social Issues, Social Justice

Founded in 1991, Freedom Voices publishes works that speak to or from communities on the margins. Editorial decisions are made by a collective of writers, activists, and street scholars. Both Freedom Voices and TallMountain Circle Books have published works by Mary TallMountain, a Native Alaskan and elder who wrote about life along the Yukon River and street life in inner city San Francisco. She was also active in the Native American Literature renaissance. Examples of titles include: *September 11 and the U.S. War: beyond the curtain of smoke*, edited by Roger Burbach and Ben Clarke, a collection of essays outlining U.S. policies that contributed to the tragedy of 9/11 (published with City Lights); George Wynn's *Back to the Streets*, short stories and poems first published in the street newspapers of Boston, San Francisco, Montreal and Seattle; and Margot Pepper's *Through the Wall: a year in Havana*, a memoir about life and love in Cuba.

## GABRIEL DUMONT INSTITUTE
2 - 604 22nd St. West
Saskatoon, Saskatchewan S7M 5W1 Canada
(306) 657-5711  Fax: (306) 244-0250
Email: info@gdins.org  Web: www.gdins.org

**Editor**: editing is done in-house
**Associated with**: University of Saskatchewan and the University of Regina
**ISBN prefix**: 0-920915

**Average number of new titles published per year**: 4
**Number of titles in print**: 80
**Other material produced**: *Journal of Indigenous Studies*; audio and visual resources; posters
**Distributor**: publisher direct via the website's bookcart feature
**Publication interests**: Children/Juvenile, Education, History, Indigenous Populations, Reference

Founded in 1985, Gabriel Dumont Institute of Native Studies and Applied Research is the educational arm of the Metis Nation of Saskatchewan. The Institute promotes the renewal and the development of Métis culture through research, materials development, collections and the distribution of those materials and the development and delivery of Métis-specific educational programs and services. Gabriel Dumont was a famous Metis general and buffalo hunter. The press publishes and promotes the works of emerging Metis writers and artists. Reference works include *Metis Legacy*, an annotated bibliography on Metis history, a photo collection of Metis culture, and a large collection of other material, and *Resources for Metis Researchers*. The Metis Historical Booklet Series contains six works. A title example is Murray Dobbin's *One-and-a-Half Men*, the story of Jim Brady and Malcom Norris, Métis patriots by Murray Dobbin, a dedicated democratic socialist originally from Saskatchewan, and now a journalist, writer and teacher who has written on northern issues and Aboriginal Canada's movement for social justice.

## GARAMOND PRESS

P.O. Box 1243                          3576 California Rd.,
Peterborough, Ontario                  P.O. Box 1015
K9J 7H5                                Orchard Park, NY 14127-1015
Canada
(705) 743-8990  Fax: (705) 743-8385
Email: customerservice@broadviewpress.com
Web: www.garamond.ca or www.broadviewpress.com

**Editor**: Michael Harrison, Publisher and President
**Affiliated press names**: parent company Broadview Press, an independent, academic publisher
**ISBN prefix**: 1-55193, 0-920059
**Average number of new titles published per year**: 5
**Number of titles in print**: 78
**Distributor**: publisher direct via website's order form, or by phone or fax

**Publication interests**: Development Studies, Ecology/Environmentalism, Economics, Gender Studies, Globalization, Labor/Labor Studies, Politics, Race/Racial Studies, Social Change, Social Justice, Third World
**Motto**: "Canada's first independent academic publisher."

Founded in 1981, Garamond Press's mandate is to provide an alternative to multinational textbook publishers and university presses, publishing critical works in such areas as political economy, labor studies, popular culture and gender studies. The press was founded by Women's Press, Between the Lines publishing, and Fernwood Books. Examples of titles include: *The World Guide: an alternative reference to the countries of our planet*, 1979- (annual); Henry A. Giroux's *The Terror of Neoliberalism: authoritarianism and the eclipse of democracy*, argues that neoliberalism's cultural dimensions erode the public participation that is the very foundation of democratic life; *Caring For/Caring About: women, home care and unpaid caregiving*, edited by Karen R. Grant, et al.; and Gary Teeple's *The Riddle of Human Rights*, makes the case that "human rights" by definition is far from a settled matter, their legal status is quite varied, their uses and defense widely inconsistent between jurisdictions, and respect for them is blatantly limited.

## GAY SUNSHINE PRESS/LEYLAND PUBLICATIONS
P.O. Box 410690
San Francisco, CA 94141
(415) 626-1935  Fax: (415) 626-1802
Web: www.gaysunshine.com and www.leylandpublications.com
(Must be 18 or older to enter the website)

**Editor**: Winston Leyland
**ISBN prefix**: 0-940567, 0-917342, 0-943595 (Leyland)
**Number of titles in print**: 37 (Gay Sunshine) and 51 (Leyland)
**Other materials produced**: comics
**Distributor**: Publisher direct via the website's printable order form; Koen
**Publication interests**: Comics, Cultural Studies, Erotica, Gay, Literary, Political, Sexuality, Translations

Founded in 1975, Gay Sunshine Press produces books about gay male history, sex, politics, and culture. Founded in 1984, Leyland Publications focuses on popular gay culture and sexuality, for example, books on film. The editor, Winston Leyland, is considered a pioneer in gay publishing. The books include works by such famous writers as Gore Vidal, Tennessee Williams, Jean Genet, Allen Ginsberg, as well as works by young American writers and gay literature in translation from Japan, China, Latin America and Russia. One particular focus is on Buddhism and homosexuality, for example, *Queer Dharma: voices of gay Buddhists*, vols. 1 and 2, edited by Winston Leyland. Another focus is on minority and ethnic gay groups, for example, *Black Men White Men: Afro American gay life and culture*; *Out of the Closet into Our Hearts: celebrating our gay/lesbian family members*, edited by Laura Siegel & Nancy Lamkin Olson, a collection of true personal accounts written by the families (parents, siblings, grandparents, children and extended family) of gay men, lesbians, bisexuals and transgendered people.

## GRAYWOLF PRESS

2402 University Ave., Suite 203
St. Paul, MN 55114
(651) 641-0077  Fax: (651) 641-0036
Email: wolves@graywolfpress.org  Web: www.graywolfpress.org

**Editor**: Fiona McCrae, Publisher and Director
**ISBN prefix**: 1-55597, 0-915308
**Average number of new titles published per year**: 16
**Number of titles in print**: 163
**Distributor**: Publisher direct via the website's shopping cart feature; Farrar, Straus & Giroux
**Publication interests**: Anthologies, Biography/Memoir, Cultural Studies, Gay, Lesbian, Literary, Literary Criticism, Poetry, Short Stories, Translations
**Motto**: "A rare breed of publisher."

Founded in 1974, Graywolf Press's mission is to produce excellence, intelligence, and creativity in contemporary literature. It is considered one of the nation's leading nonprofit literary publishers. Graywolf wishes to aid in the cultivation of "a wide and contemplative habit of mind," as Bertrand Russell once said. The press publishes two translations annually with the support of the Lannan Foundation and co-sponsors with the Literary Arts Institute of the College of St. Benedict the annual S. Mariella Gable Prize, a $15,000 advance award for a previously unpublished literary novel that will by published by Graywolf. Examples of titles include: *By Herself: women reclaim poetry*, edited by Molly McQuade, where contemporary women poets reconsider their art form on their own terms; *The Private I*, edited by Molly Peacock, essays on our contradictory feelings about protecting and violating privacy; and Barrie Borich's

*My Lesbian Husband*, winner of the GLBT Book Award of the American Library Association, questions whether the names we give our relationships changes their meaning.

## GREEN CANDY PRESS

601 Van Ness Ave., E3-918
San Francisco, CA 94102
(415) 824-6636
Email: editorial@greencandypress.com
Web: www.greencandypress.com

**Editor**: Andrew McBeth
**ISBN prefix**: 1-931160
**Average number of new titles published per year**: 6-10
**Number of titles in print**: 30
**Distributor**: Publishers Group West
**Publication interests**: Comics/Comix, Erotica, Gay, Lesbian, Marijuana, Sexuality
**Motto**: "A whole new flavor."
Founded in 2000, Green Candy Press actively scours the cultural fringe for new writers, illustrators, photographers and other deviants who produce materials in areas such as drugs, S&M, and gay and lesbian culture. Examples of titles include: Greg Green's *The Cannabis Grow Bible: the definitive guide to growing marijuana for recreational and medicinal use*; Shapiro's *The Book of Sick: a mixed bag of gay and lesbian sweeties*, a look at the stereotypes of gay and lesbian culture; and Michael Troy's *Homo Hero's Big Book of Fun and Adventures*, an interactive book of gay and male erotica and fun activities.

## GREEN DRAGON PRESS

2267 Lake Shore Blvd., Suite 1009
Toronto, Ontario M8V 3X2 Canada
(800) 305-2057 (416) 251-6366  Fax: (416) 251-6365
Email: equity.greendragonpress@sympatico.ca
Web: www3.sympatico.ca/equity.greendragonpress

**ISBN prefix**: 1-896781, 0-9691955, 0-9696977
**Average number of new titles published per year**:
**Number of titles in print**: 18
**Other materials produced**: videos, posters, curriculum materials
**Distributor**: publisher direct via the website's printable order form

**Publication interests**: Discrimination, Gender Studies, History, Reference, Social Issues, Women's Issues/Studies

Green Dragon Press focuses on women's history, equity issues, and harassment prevention. The materials are for teachers, librarians and everyone who wants to know more about women's stories and harassment prevention. The materials also includes curriculum materials, for example, Carla Rice's and Venessa Russell's *Embodying Equity: body image as an equity issue*, a manual for educator and service providers that addresses the intersection of body image, identity, oppression and equality. Examples of titles include: P. A. Stanton's, Rose Fine-Meyer's and Stephanie Kim Gibson's *Unfolding Power: documents in 20th century Canadian women's history*; Karleen Pendleton Jimenez's *Are You a Boy or a Girl?*, a story of a child thinking through who she is; and Sharon Merritt's *HERstory: women from Canada's past*, 3 vols.

## THE GREENFIELD REVIEW PRESS

2 Middle Grove Road
Greenfield Center, NY 12833
(518) 583-1440  Fax: (518) 583-9741
Web: www.greenfieldreview.org

**Editor**: Joseph Bruchac III
**ISBN prefix**: 0-912678, 0-87886
Average number of new titles published per year: **no recent activity**
**Number of titles in print**: 42
**Distributor**: Publisher direct via the website's bookcart feature; Small Press Distribution
**Publication interests**: Alaskan Native, American Indian, Anthologies, Asian American, Ethnic, Folklore, Hispanic/Latino, Indigenous Populations, Literary, Minorities, Multiculturalism, Poetry, Prison/Prisoners

Founded in 1969, The Greenfield Review Press's mission is to make available works by writers the editors feel are some of the finest contemporary poets and storytellers. The press's first book was a collection of inmate poems smuggled out of Soledad Prison. Since then, the press has become home for a great diversity of voices making it one of the most multicultural presses publishing today. The range of diverse voices within the press's publications can be found in the series titles and book titles. Series titles include, for example, the Frank Waters Memorial Series, first books of prose by American Indian writers, and the Prison Poets Series. The press also produces the Ithaca House poetry series and the Bowman Books folktales. Example of titles include: *Breaking Silence: an anthology of contemporary Asian American Poetry*, edited by Joseph Bruchac; *Reclaiming the Vision: past, present and future Native voices of the Eighth Generation*, edited by Lee Francis and James Bruchac; and Ron Welburn's *Coming Through the Smoke and Dreaming*, poems written to the deep and lasting ties of culture and blood forged over the last five centuries between African Americans and Native Americans.

## HANGING LOOSE PRESS
231 Wyckoff St.
Brooklyn, NY 11217
(212) 206-8465  Fax: (212) 243-7499
Email: print225@aol.com  Web: www.hangingloosepress.com
**Editor**: Robert Hershon, Dick Lourie, and Mark Pawlak
**ISBN prefix**: 1-882413, 0-914610, 1-931236
**Average number of new titles published per year**: 8
**Number of titles in print**: 130
**Other materials produced**: *Hanging Loose* magazine, one of the country's oldest continuously published independent journals of poetry and fiction
**Distributor**: Publisher direct via the website's printable order form; Koen (selected titles); Small Press Distribution (all titles)
**Publication interests**: Anthologies, Literary, Poetry, Translations
**Motto**: "Good literature stays good."

Founded in 1966, Hanging Loose Press emphasizes works by new writers while keeping every title published in print. In turning 40 years old, the press is one of the oldest independent presses in the country. Ideally, writers have been discovered in the magazine and then presented in book form. The process has led the press to do first books by such writers as Kimiko Hahn, Sherman Alexie, Indran Amirthanayagam, Dennis Nuskse, Carol Cox and Cathy Cockrell. The editors take great pride in never having had to publish special issues for women or gays or people of color because those writers have always been represented in the press's publications. In 1968, the magazine introduced a regular section devoted to writing by talented high school students that was then published in anthologies: *Bullseye: stories and poems by outstanding high school writers* and *Smart Like Me: high school age writing from the sixties to now*. Other titles include: five books by Sherman Alexie, (with some 90,000 copies in print) including *The Business of Fancy Dancing: the screenplay*; Arnold Mesches' *The FBI Files*, turns 26 years of his FBI surveillance files into art consisting of a book of collages, 50's era images, and hand-written script all surrounded by colorful borders; and *Present Tense: poets in the new world*, edited by Mark Pawlak, an anthology of contemporary political poetry by American poets.

## HARRINGTON PARK PRESS
10 Alice St.
Binghamton, NY 13904-1580
(607) 722-5857  Fax: (607) 722-1424
Email: getinfo@haworthpressinc.com
Web: www.haworthpressinc.com/imprints/details.asp?ID=HPP

**Editor**: John P. De Cecco, San Francisco
**Affiliated press names**: Haworth Press, parent company; Alice Street Editions and Southern Tier Editions, imprints
**ISBN prefix**: 1-56023, 0-918393, 0-7890
**Average number of new titles published per year**: 38
**Other materials produced**: 13 lesbigay journals
**Distributor**: Haworth Press (800) 429-6784 (USA) and (607) 722-6362 (Canada)
**Publication interests**: Biography/Memoir, Ethnic/Ethnic Studies, Feminist, Gay, Gender Studies, Lesbian, Literary, Men's Issues/Studies, Sexuality, Social Justice, Women's Issues/Studies

Founded in 1985, Harrington Park Press focuses on gay, lesbian, bisexual, transgender, and other gender studies. The press originally published only nonfiction, but now has branched out to publish gay and lesbian fiction. The Alice Street Editions imprint provides a voice for lesbian novels, essays, erotica, science fiction, memoirs, and popular nonfiction, and the Southern Tier Editions imprint publishes the best in gay men's fiction. Titles include studies about homosexuality in other parts of the world, for example, Alison J. Laurie's *Lesbian Studies in Aotearoa/New Zealand*, about health applications, for example, Christopher J. Alexander's *Gay and Lesbian Mental Health: a source book for practitioners*, and reference titles, for example, *Speaking for Our Lives: historic speeches and rhetoric for gay and lesbian rights (1892-2000)*, edited by Robert B. Marks Ridinger. There have also been a number of award winning titles, for example, *Queer Crips: disabled men and their stories*, edited by Bob Guter and John Killacky, winner of the Lambda Literary Award in the LGBT Nonfiction Anthology category, and Robert Taylor's *Whose Eye is on the Sparrow?*, a gay romance and winner of the 2005 IPPY Award in the Gay/Lesbian category.

## HAYMARKET BOOKS
P.O. Box 180165
Chicago, IL 60625
(773) 583-7884
Email: info@haymarketbooks.org  Web: www.haymarketbooks.org

**Associated with**: Center for Economic Research and Social Change
**ISBN prefix**: 1-931859
**Number of titles in print**: 27
**Other material produced**: audio tapes
**Distributor**: publisher direct via website's shopping cart feature, or by phone or mail; Consortium. Haymarket is also a distributor for many other progressive titles (more than 500).
**Publication interests**: Anarchism, Economics, Globalization, History, International Issues/Relations, Labor/Labor Studies, Latin American Studies, Media Studies, Middle East Studies, Politics, Race/Race Relations, Reprints, Social Justice, Socialism/Marxism, Women's Issues/Studies
**Motto**: "Solidarity of labor."

Haymarket Books is a nonprofit, progressive book distributor and publisher that believes activists need to take ideas, history and politics into the many struggles for social justice today. The editors take inspiration and courage from the namesake, the Haymarket Martyrs, who gave their lives fighting for a better world. Books cannot change the world simply by being read, but rather their lessons and ideas must be put into practice. By learning the lessons of past victories as well as defeats can arm a new generation of fighters for a better world. Examples of titles include: Sharon Smith's *Women and Socialism: essays on women's liberation*; Alexander Rabinowitch's *The Bolsheviks Come to Power: the Revolution of 1917 in Petrograd*; and Leon Trotsky's *Literature and Revolution*, a reprint of the 1925 classic.

## HOLY COW! PRESS
P.O. Box 3170, Mount Royal Station
Duluth, MN 55803
(218) 724-1653  Fax: same number
Email: holycow@cpinternet.com  Web: www.holycowpress.org

**Editor**: Jim Perlman
**ISBN prefix**: 0-930100
**Average number of new titles published per year**: 6

**Number of titles in print**: 73
**Distributor**: Publisher direct using the website's printable order form or Book Cart feature with payment through PayPal; Consortium and Small Press Distribution
**Publication interests**: American Indian, Anthologies, Biography/Memoir, Literary, Poetry, Short Stories, Translations

Founded in 1978, Holy Cow! Press is devoted to searching out and publishing regional poetry, fiction, biographies, anthologies, and critical essays. Though generally not considered an alternative press, Holy Cow! has been considered one of the best small independent presses in the nation. The press is one of a handful of presses that devote attention to original works by Native American writers, including Duane Niatum, Anne M. Dunn and Joseph Bruchac. Examples of titles include Else Lasker-Schuler's *Star in My Forehead*, translated by Janine Canan, poems of the author's innocence from the brutality of the Nazi age and the tested resilience of her Jewish background, and James R. Bailey's *Spirit of the Ojibwa: images of Lac Courte Oreilles elders*.

## HUMAN RIGHTS FIRST
333 Seventh Ave., 13th fl.
New York, NY 10001-5004
(212) 845-5200 (212) 845-5299
Email: communications@humanrightsfirst.org
Web: www.humanrightsfirst.org

**Editor**: Mike Posner, Executive Director
**ISBN prefix**: 0-934143
**Average number of new titles published per year**: 1-2
**Number of titles in print**: 31
**Other material produced**: working and briefing papers, and RightsWire, a free email newletter, *U.S. Law and Security Digest*, a weekly report, *Asylum Protection News*, *Defender Alert Network*
**Distributor**: publisher direct through website payable by check or credit card
**Publication interests**: Civil Liberties, Human Rights, International Issues/Relations, Law/Legal Studies, Refugees, Social Justice

Founded in 1978 as the Lawyers Committee for Human Rights, Human Rights First works in the United States and abroad to create a secure and humane world by advancing justice, human dignity and respect for the rule of law. The organization supports human rights activists who fight for basic freedoms and peaceful change at the local level; protect refugees in flight from persecution and repression; help build a strong international system of justice and accountability; and make sure human rights laws and principles are enforced in the United States and abroad. Examples of titles include: *Antisemitism in Europe: challenging official indifference*; *Holding the Line: a critique of the Department of State's Annual Country Reports (for 2002) on human rights practices*; and three reports on the erosion of civil liberties in the U.S. since 9/11 – *Accessing the New Normal: liberty and security for the post-September 11 United States; A Year of Loss: reexamining civil liberties since September 11;* and *Imbalance of Powers: how changes to U.S. law and security since 9/11 erode human rights and civil liberties.*

## HUMAN RIGHTS WATCH
350 Fifth Ave., 34th fl.
New York, NY 10118-3299
(212) 290-4700  Fax: (212) 736-1300
Email: hrwnyc@hrw.org  Web: www.hrw.org

**Editor**: Sobeira Genao, Publications Manager
**ISBN prefix**: 1-56432
**Average number of new titles published per year**: 75
**Number of titles in print**: 500
**Other materials produced**: short country reports, *Human Rights Watch Quarterly Newsletter*
**Distributor**: Publisher direct via the website's shopping feature. Also, many reports can be downloaded in PDF format free of charge from the website under "Publications."
**Publication interests**: Africa/African Studies, Asia/Asian Studies, Developing Countries, Economics, Ethnic, Globalization, Human Rights, Hunger, International Issues/Relations, Latin American Studies, Law/Legal Studies, Middle East Studies, Political, Prison/Prisoners, Refugees, Social Justice, Third World, Women's Studies/Issues
**Motto**: "Defending human rights worldwide."

Founded in 1978, Human Rights Watch publications report on investigations of human rights abuses in more than seventy countries around the world. Each report is an attempt to get at the truth. The publications address the human rights practices of governments of all political stripes, of all geopolitical alignments, and of all ethnic and religious persuasions. Human Rights Watch is an independent, non-governmental organization, supported by contributions from private individuals and foundations worldwide. It accepts no government funds. The organization defends freedom of thought and expression, due process and equal protection of the law, and a vigorous civil society. Also, the organization documents and denounces murders, disappearances, torture, arbitrary imprisonment, discrimination, and other abuses of internationally recognized human rights. The goal is to hold governments accountable if the rights of people have been transgressed. Since the 1980s, the organization has gradually added special programs devoted to the rights of women, children, workers, common prisoners, refugees, migrants, academics, gays and lesbians, and people living with HIV/AIDS. Many of the publications are in booklet form amounting to less than 100 pages. Besides the prominent annual, *Human Rights Watch World Report*, examples of titles include: *Blood, Sweat, and Fear: workers' rights in the U.S. meat and poultry plants*; *Divorced from Justice: women's unequal access to divorce in Egypt*; and *Hated to Death: homophobia, violence, and Jamacia's HIV/AIDS epidemic*.

## ITDG PUBLISHING
Bourton Hall
Bourton-on-Dunsmore
Rugby, Warwickshire CV23 9QZ United Kingdom
+44(0)1926 63401 Fax: +44(0)1926 63402
Email: itpubs@itpubs.org.uk Web: www.itdg.org

**Editor**: Helen Marsden
**Associated with**: The Schumacher Centre for Technology and Development
**ISBN prefix**: 1-853395
**Average number of new titles published per year**: 25
**Number of titles in print**: 300+ (including distribution from other presses)
**Other materials produced**: the journal *Small Enterprise Development* and *Waterlines*, a journal of low-cost water sanitation
**Distributors**: publisher direct, www.development.bookshop.com; Stylus Publishing, LLC (USA) (800) 232-0223, www.styluspub.com
**Publication interests**: Conservation, Development Studies, Energy, Ecology/Environmentalism, Globalization, Health, Indigenous Populations, International Issues/Relations, Politics, Poverty, Social Change, Sustainable Development, Third World, Women's Issues/Studies
**Motto**: "Helping people to use technology in the fight against poverty."

Founded in 1966 as the Intermediate Technology Group, ITDG Publishing builds the skills and capabilities of people in developing countries through the dissemination of information in all forms, including book and journal publishing, and online book sales (www.developmentbookshop.co.uk). ITDG was founded by the radical economist, E.F. Schumacher, to prove that his philosophy "small is beautiful" could bring real and sustainable improvement to people's lives. ITDG Publishing is the publishing arm of the Intermediate Technology Development Group, an organization that specializes in helping people to use technology for practical answers to poverty in developing countries. The organization publishes on all aspect of development and appropriate technology. Best sellers include Jon Hellin's and Sophie Higman's *Feeding the Market: South American farmers, trade and globalization*, a debate about the pros and cons of globalization and the changes in policies and markets that are needed, and *Microfinance: evolution, achievement and challenges*, edited by Malcolm Harper, analyzes major development in microfinance in the last 12 year. Examples of other titles include *Removing Unfreedoms: citizens as agents of change in urban development*, and *Bridging Research and Policy in Development*, edited by Julius Court, Ingie Hovland and John Young, a practical approach to getting the lessons of development research converted into changes in government and aid agency policy.

### INFORM, INC.
120 Wall St., 14th fl.
New York, NY 10005-4001
(212) 361-2400  Fax: (212) 361-2412
Email: inform@informinc.org  Web: www.informinc.org

**Editor**: Joanna Underwood, President
**ISBN prefix**: 0-918780
**Average number of new titles published per year**: 2
**Number of titles in print**: 40
**Other materials produced**: *Inform Reports* (quarterly newsletter), fact sheets and summaries (available free online)
**Distributor**: publisher direct via website's PayPal purchase feature or by phone, (212) 361-2400, ext. 240
Publication interests: Development Studies, Ecology/Environmentalism, Economics, Education, Health, International Issues/Studies, Politics, Sustainable Development, Transportation
**Motto**: "Strategies for a better environment."

Founded in 1974, Inform, Inc. is an independent, nonprofit research organization that conducts research aimed at practical solutions to complex environmental and health-related problems throughout the world. Inform helps governments, business community groups, educational institutions, and environmental leaders reduce pollution and waste, promote sustainable product designs, and convert to cleaner-fueled transportation. The publications examine the effects of business practices on the environment and human health and identify practical ways of living and doing business that ensure environmentally sustainable growth. Inform, Inc. believes that meaningful progress depends on a public that is well informed about environmental problems, on dialogue rather than confrontation, and on collaboration among business, government and communities to achieve lasting solutions. Primary areas of focus include sustainable transportation, waste prevention, and toxic chemicals and human health. Examples of publications include: Alicia Culver's et al., *Cleaning for Health: products and practices for a safer indoor environment*; Bette K. Fishbein's *Waste in the Wireless World: the challenge of cell phones*, an examination of the waste issues posed by cell phones and other wireless electronic devices; and James S. Cannon's *The Transportation Boom in Asia: crisis and opportunity for the United States*, details how soaring oil use and expanding transportation in China and India have put these countries on a collision course with the U.S. A number of publications are available free online for downloading in PDF format.

## INSTITUTE FOR LOCAL SELF-RELIANCE
927 15th St., NW, 4th fl.
Washington, DC 20005
(202) 898-1610  Fax: (202) 898-1612
Email: info@ilsr.org  Web. www.ilsr.org

**Editor**: Neil Seldman, President; Mark Wilger, Publications Manager
ISBN prefix: **0-917582**
**Associated with**: Self-Reliance, Inc., a consulting affiliate of ILSR that delivers technical expertise and professional services to cities, industry and community development groups
**Average number of new titles published per year**: 2
**Number of titles in print**: 17
**Other materials produced**: *The Carbohydrate Economy*, a quarterly newsletter; *The New Rules*, a quarterly journal; five different free e-bulletins; fact sheets; reports; home arsenic testing kit

**Distributor**: publisher direct via website's shopping cart feature or by phone (612) 379-3815
**Publication interests**: Conservation, Development Studies, Ecology/Environmentalism, Economics, Education, Energy, Politics, Social Change, Sustainable Development, Urban Issues/Studies
**Motto**: "Ecologically and locally controlled economies."

Founded in 1974, the Institute for Local Self-Reliance (ILSR) is a nonprofit research and educational institution that provides technical assistance and information on environmentally sound economic development strategies. ILSR was the first to apply the concept of local self-reliance to urban areas with a vision of ecological and locally controlled economies. ILSR's urban townhome became a working model of the institute's ideas, with rooftop hydroponic gardens, solar collectors, and a commercial basement sprout operation, and composting toilet. Program areas include the New Rules Project: designing rules as if community matters; Carbohydrate Economy Clearinghouse: growing the next economy; Waste to Wealth: reuse, recycling and scrap-based manufacturing along with building deconstruction; Sustainable Minnesota: moving Minnesota toward a sustainable energy future; and HealthyBuilding.net: building with people and the environment in mind. Sample titles include Stacy Mitchell's *The Home Town Advantage: how to defend your main street against chain stories and why it matters*, and Brenda Platt's *Resources Up in Flames: the economic pitfalls of waste incineration versus a zero waste approach in the global South*, twenty reason why waste incinerators could spell financial disaster for host communities.

## INTERLINK PUBLISHING
46 Crosby St.
Northampton, MA 01060-1804
(800) 238-LINK  Fax: (413) 582-7057
Email: info@interlinkbooks.com  Web: www.interlinkbooks.com

**Editor**: Phyllis Bennis
**Affiliated press names**: Interlink Books and two imprints: Olive Branch Books and Crocodile Books (children's books); the Interlink Publishing Group represents nine other publishers
**ISBN prefix**: 1-56656; 0-940793
**Average number of new titles published per year**: 90
**Number of titles in print**: 800

**Distributor**: publisher direct via website's shopping basket feature, or by phone or fax
**Publication interests**: Art/The Arts, Children/Juvenile, Cookery, Health, History, Literary, Multicultural, Music, Political, Religion, Translations, Vegetarianism, Women's Issues/Studies
**Motto**: "Changing the way people think about the world."

Founded in 1987, Interlink Publishing is an independent publishing house specializing in world travel, world literature, world history and politics, world music, health and cooking (including vegetarian cooking), art, and children's books. Many of the books are on Celtic culture and travel. Olive Branch Press publishes socially and politically relevant nonfiction, concentrating on topics and areas of the world often ignored by the Western media. Crocodile Books publishes high-quality illustrated children's books from around the world for children ages 3 to 8, for example, Julia Johnson's *A Gift of the Sands*, a tale of life in the Arabian Gulf, and Leo Tolstoy's *How Much Land Does a Man Need?*, where a man is promised as much land as he can walk around in one day. The International Folk Tales Series, for adults and young adults, present folk tales from Burma, Sudan, Bengal, Siberia, Scotland, Fuji, and other locations. The Illustrated History series explores our recent past in order to prepare for this century. Two recent translated titles in this series are Antonella Salomoni's *Lenin and the Russian Revolution*, and Yves Chevrier's *Mao and the Chinese Revolution*. The Emerging Voices New International Fiction series is designed to bring to North American readers unheard voice of writers, especially women, from throughout the world who have wide acclaim at home but are unknown here. Other recent titles include David Ray Griffin's *The 9/11 Commission Report: omissions and distortions: a critique of the Dean-Zelikow Report*, and *Shattering the Stereotypes: Muslim women speak out*, edited by Fawzia Atzal-Khan.

## INTERNATIONAL LABOUR OFFICE

1828 L St., NW, Suite 600              4, route des Morillons
Washington, DC 20036                   CH-1211 Geneva 22
                                       Switzerland
(202) 653-7652  Fax: (202) 653-7687
Email: washington@ilo.org or ilo@ilo.org
Web: us.ilo.org or www.ilo.org

**Editor**: Juan Somavia, Director-General
**ISBN prefix**: 92-2, 92-9014
**Associated with**: United Nations

**Average number of new titles published per year**: 20
**Number of titles in print**: 390
**Other materials produced**: *World of* Work, the magazine of the ILO, *International Labour Review*, a quarterly journal, CD-ROMs, videos
**Distributor**: ILO Publications Center (USA), (301) 638-3152; Renouf Publishing Co. (USA & Canada), 888-551-7470, www.renoufbooks.com
**Publication interests**: Development Studies, Economics, Gender Studies, Globalization, Human Rights, International Issues/Relations, Labor/Labor Studies, Political, Social Change, Social Issues, Social Justice, Sustainable Development, Third World, Unions/Unionizing, Women's Issues/Studies
**Motto**: "Promoting decent work for all."

Founded in 1919, the International Labour Office (ILO), is a specialized agency in the United Nations working as the authoritative source for global data on labor. The ILO seeks to promote social justice and internationally recognized human and labor rights. The organization sets minimum standards of basic labor rights, provides technical assistance in vocational training and rehabilitation, and promotes the development of independent employers' and workers' organizations. The International Institute for Labour Studies, established 1960, is an autonomous unit within the ILO to further public involvement in social issues of concern to the organization through a variety of publications. The publications fall into the categories in child labor, labor issues, labor statistics, employment, social protection, gender issues and women at work, occupational safety and health, and management and training. The series, Studies on the Social Dimension of Globalization, publishes titles such as, Raymond Torres' *Towards a Socially Sustainable World Economy: an analysis of the social pillars of globalization*. Examples of titles include: the annual *Yearbook of Labour Statistics*; *Philosophical and Spiritual Perspectives on Decent Work, Jobs and Income in a Globalizing World*; *Preventing and Responding to Violence at Work*; and Ronald Dore's *New Forms and Meanings of Work in an Increasingly Globalized World*.

## INTERNATIONAL PUBLISHERS COMPANY
235 W. 23rd St., 5th fl.
New York, NY 10011-2302
(212) 366-9816  Fax: (212) 366-9820
Email: service@intpubnyc.com  Web: www.intpubnyc.com

**Editor**: Betty Smith
**Affiliated press names**: New World Paperbacks, an imprint of reprint titles

**ISBN prefix**: 0-7178
**Average number of new titles published per year**: 4-5
**Number of titles in print**: 200+
**Distributor**: publisher direct via the website's order form, or by telephone, fax, mail, email
**Publishing interests**: Economics, History, International Issues/Relations, Labor/Labor Studies, Philosophy, Politics, Reprints, Socialism/Marxism, Unions/Unionizing
**Motto**: "Books to help you understand and change the world."

Founded in 1924, International Publishers Company publishes books by Marx, Engels, Lenin and other Marxist scholars and activists. The press has published copies of all the books by Marx and Engels. A large, ongoing project is the publication of *the Collected Works of Karl Marx and Friedrich Engels*, vols. 1-50 with additional volumes forthcoming. Numerous titles are reprints of classic Marxist texts from authors such as Philip Bonosky, W.E.B. DuBois, and Antonio Gramsci. The publications have a strong focus on the labor movement, and includes Philip S. Foner's multi-volume, *History of the Labor Movement in the United States*. Examples of other titles include: *People versus Profits: the columns of Victor Perlo, 1961-1999*, edited by Ellen Perlo, Stanley Perlo and Arthur Perlo; Willis H. Truitt's *Marxist Ethics: needs and rights, morality and the arts, and ethics in our "new world"*; and Virginia Brodine's *Red Roots, Green Shoots*, a collection of the late author's articles about environmental issues with special attention to uniting the labor and environmental concerns into a united struggle.

## INTERNATIONAL RELATIONS CENTER
P.O. Box 2178
Silver City, NM 88062-2178
(505) 388-0208  Fax: (505) 388-0619
Email: irc@irc-online.org  Web: www.irc-online.org

**Editor**: Deb Preusch, Executive Director
**Affiliated press names**: previously Resource Center Press and Interhemispheric Resource Center Press
**ISBN prefix**: 0-911213
**Average number of new titles published per year**: 1-2
**Number of titles in print**: 21
**Other materials produced**: occasional papers; *IRC Insider*, a bi-monthly newsletter; In Focus, briefs on foreign policy produced with the Institute for

Policy Studies; Progressive Response, an e-zine; *borderlines*, a monthly bulletin
of U.S.-Mexico border issues; and Borderline Updates, an e-zine
**Distributor**: publisher direct via website's shopping cart feature payable
through PayPal or printable order form. Titles on foreign policy and global-
ization topics from other publishers are also available.
**Publication interests**: Ecology/Environmentalism, Economics, Foreign
Policy, Globalization, International Issues/Relations, Labor/Labor Studies,
Peace, Political, Social Change, Social Justice, Sustainable Development
**Motto**: "People-centered policy alternatives."

Founded in 1979 as the Interhemispheric Resource Center Press, the International Relations Center works to make the U.S. a more responsible member of
the global community by promoting progressive strategic dialogues that lead
to new citizen-based agendas. The IRC works through four primary projects:
Americas Program presents policy options, Global Affairs Program works to
make the U.S. a more responsible global leader and partner, Global Good
Neighbor promotes dialogue and action aimed at forging a new vision for
foreign policy, and Right Web heightens public awareness of the outrageous
policies advocated by the right and their network of power. The organization
has not published any new books for the past two years, but does not rule out
future publications. A number of current titles on U.S. foreign policy and
globalization topics from other alternative presses are available from the website's bookstore, as well as older IRC books from the U.S.-Mexico Series and
books on Central America. The website has a number of articles free for
downloading.

## ISHMAEL REED PUBLISHING COMPANY
P.O. Box 3288
Berkeley, CA 94703
(510) 428-0116
Email: ireedpub@yahoo.com

**Editor**: Ishmael Reed
**ISBN prefix**: 0-918408
**Average number of new titles published per year**: 1
**Number of titles in print**: 20
**Other materials produced**: Konch magazine online,
www.ishmaelreedpub.com;Vines, a quarterly webzine
**Distributor**: Small Press Distribution; Xlibris

**Publication interests**: Africa/African Studies, Literary, Minorities, Poetry, Political, Third World

Founded in 1973, Ismael Reed Publishing works to create forums for aspiring writers from diverse ethnicities, locations and eras. The publishing company has given voice to engaging and powerful, though largely ignored, writers of various cultures, for example, it boast the first book published by a Chinese-American, Shawn Wong's *Homebase*, and the first book of poetry by an Inuit, Sister Goodwin's *There's a Lagoon in My Backyard*. The editor, Ishmael Reed, is a prominent writer who has written many novels and books of poetry, all published by other publishing firms. A good collection of his works can be found in his *The Reed Reader* (Basic Books, 2000). Examples of books include: *25 New Nigerian Poets*, edited by Toyin Adewale-Gabriel, new and politically relevant writers from a country in turmoil; Imamu Amini Baraka's *Un Poco Low Coups*; and Kathryn Waddell Takara's and Carla Blank's *New and Collected Poems*.

## ISLAND PRESS
1718 Connecticut Ave., NW
Washington, DC 20009-1148
(202) 232-7933  Fax: (202) 234-1328
Email: info@islandpress.org  Web: www.islandpress.org

**Editor**: Todd Baldwin, Editor-in-Chief
**Affiliated press names**: Shearwater Books
**Associated with**: distributes books for the Foundation for Deep Ecology, IUCN–The World Conservation Union, Natural Lands Trust, Natural Resources Defense Council, and The Nature Conservancy
**ISBN prefix**: 1-55963
**Average number of new titles published per year**: 40
**Number to titles in print**: 400+
**Other materials produced**: Eco-Compass, an email update and alert; Island Currents, an online newsletter
**Distributor**: publisher direct via the website's shopping cart feature or by phone (800) 621-2736; Broadview Press, (705) 743-8990 or customerservice@broadviewpress.com (Canada)
**Publication interests**: Conservation, Development Studies, Ecology/Environmentalism, Economics, Energy, Globalization, Health, Law/Legal Studies, Natural/Nature, Policy Studies, Political, Social Change, Sustainable Development
**Motto**: "The environmental publisher."

Founded in 1984, Island Press's mission is to stimulate, shape, and communicate the ideas that are essential for solving environmental problems. The press is the only nonprofit organization in the United State whose principal purpose is the publication of books on environmental issues and natural resource management. It was established to meet the need for peer-reviewed, solutions-oriented information that addressed the multidisciplinary nature of environmental problems. Technical information from a variety of disciplines is translated into accessible and informative books for citizen activists, educators, students, and professionals involved in the study or management of environmental programs. Besides the above publication interests, topics addressed include biodiversity, land use and planning, ecosystems, forest management, agriculture, marine science, and climate change. Founded in 1992, Shearwater Books produces material that explores through literary nonfiction and autobiography, the relationships of nature, science and human culture. Examples of titles include: *The Eco Guide to Careers That Make a Difference*; Fred Pearce's *Keepers of the Spring: reclaiming our water in an age of globalization*; and Dan L. Perlman's and Feffrey C. Midler's *Practical Ecology for Planners, Developers and Citizens*, a book on land use planning, conservation biology, and biodiversity and wildlife. Chip Ward's *Hope's Horizon: three visions for healing the American land* won the 2004 IPPY Award in the Environment/Ecology/Nature category.

## JUST US BOOKS
356 Glenwood Ave.
East Orange, NJ 07017
(973) 672-7701  Fax: (973) 677-7570
Email: justusbooks@mindspring.com  Web: www.justusbooks.com

**Editor**: Wade Hudson and Cheryl Willis Hudson
**Affiliated press names**: Afro-Bets Kids and Santofa Books (classics for young people)
**ISBN prefix**: 0-940975
**Average number of new titles published per year**: 5
**Number of titles in print**: 64
**Other materials produced**: posters, tee shirts
**Distributor**: publisher direct via website's shopping basket feature
**Publication interests**: Africa/African Studies, African American, Biography/Memoir, Children/Juvenile, Education, History
**Motto**: "Good books make a difference."

Founded in 1988, Just Us Books focuses on black history, culture, and experiences for children 2 to 12 years of age. The editors believe the key problem in children's literature is not getting kids to read, but coming up with characters children can relate to. The publishers look for certain key factors in the evaluation of Afrocentric themes: positive images that leave lasting impressions; accurate factual information that is enjoyable to read; cultural authenticity; a clear and positive perspective for people of color in the 21$^{st}$ century; self-affirming material; strong three-dimensional characters; and a vehicle that opens the windows of knowledge, information and self-discovery. Examples of titles include: *AFRO-BETS ABC Book*; Veronica Freeman Ellis' *First Book about Africa*; *Book of Black Heroes from A to Z* (vol. 1), *Great Women in the Struggle* (vol. 2), and *Scientists, Healers and Inventors* (vol. 3); *Black History Handbook*, a ready reference guide filled with activities for incorporating African American history with classroom related studies; and Mari Evans' *Dear Corinne: Tell somebody! Love, Annie*, a powerful story about the devastating effects of child sexual abuse.

## KAYA

224 Riverside Dr., #1B
New York, NY 10025
(212) 229-1445
Email: kaya@kaya.com  Web: www.kaya.com

**Editor**: Juliana Koo, Managing Editor
**ISBN prefix**: 1-885030
**Average number of new titles published per year**: 1
**Number of titles in print**: 14
**Distributor**: Amazon; DAP/Distributed Art Publishers (800) 338-BOOK; Small Press Distribution (800) 869-7553
**Publication interests**: Art/The Arts, Asia/Asian Studies, Asian American, Literary, Minorities, Poetry, Third World
**Motto**: "A literary voice for the vastness of the Pacific Rim."

Founded in 1994 by Soo Kyung Kim, Kaya is a nonprofit publisher dedicated to new and innovative literature and the recovery of important and often overlooked works from Asian, Pacific Islander, and API Asian diasporic authors. Works include fiction, poetry, critical essays, art, and culture. Books include a best seller in New Zealand, Sia Figiel's *Where We Once Belonged*, the first work by a Samoan woman published in the U. S. Examples of titles include Denise Uyehara's *Maps of City and Body: shedding light on the performances of Densie Uyehara*, the first in a series of books on Asian diasporic performance artists, and Ishle Yi Parks' *The Temperature of the Water*, the first collection of poetry by the Poet Laureate of Queens, New York. Koon Woon's *The Truth in Rented Rooms*, poetry of immigrant life, homelessness, and the Beats, was the winner of the PEN Oakland's Josephine Miles Award.

## KEGEDONCE PRESS
Cape Croker Reserve, RR #5
Chippewas of Nawash First Nation
Wialton, Ontario N0H 2T0 Canada
(519) 371-1434   Fax: (519) 371-5011
Email: info@kegedonce.com   Web: www.kegedonce.com

**Editor**: Kateri Akiwenzie-Damm, publisher, managing editor and an Anish-naabe writer
**ISBN prefix**: 0-9731396
**Average number of new titles published per year**: 1
**Number of titles in print**: 9
**Distributor**: publisher direct via website's order form; LitDist Co. (800) 591-6250 (Canada and USA)
**Publication interests**: Aboriginal Studies, Anthologies, Indigenous Populations, Literary, Poetry
**Motto**: "w 'daub awae... speaking true"

Founded in 1993, Kegedonce Press is a Native owned and operated company committed to the development, promotion and publication of the work of indigenous writers nationally and internationally, particularly in New Zealand and Australia. The editors believe that sharing markets for First Peoples, Native American, Maori, Aboriginal, and Indigenous writers generally will assist in developing an international readership interested in the writings of wider range of Indigenous writing. The publishers foster the creative cultural expression of Indigenous Peoples through the publication of beautifully crafted books which involve Indigenous Peoples in all levels of production and by supporting activities which promote Indigenous literary development and the development of Indigenous publishing.  Examples of titles include: Basil H. Johnston's *Honour Earth Mother*; Kateri Akiwenzie-Damm's *Without Reservation: Indigenous erotica*; and *Skins: contemporary Indigenous writing*, compiled by Kateri Akiwenzie-Damm and Josie Douglas.

## KELSEY STREET PRESS
50 Northgate
Berkeley, CA 94708
(510) 845-2260 Fax: (510) 548-9185
Email: info@kelseyst.com Web: www.kelseyst.com

**Editor**: Patricia Dienstfrey and Rena Rosenwasser
**ISBN prefix**: 0-932716
**Average number of new titles published per year**: 4
**Number of titles in print**: 44
**Distributor**: Small Press Distribution—SPD order form available on the website
**Publication interests**: Art/The Arts, Literary, Poetry, Women's Issues/Studies
**Motto**: "Poetry by women."

Founded in 1974, Kelsey Street Press publishes innovative writing by emerging writers, women of color, and lesbians. The press was started by a group of writers who felt compelled to address the historical marginalization of women writers by mainstream publishers. The first books were handset and printed on a letterpress in the basement of a house on Kelsey Street in Berkeley. The books represent a unique series of collaborations between poets and visual artists. Examples of titles include: Mei-Mei Berssenbrugge's *Nest*, winner of the Asian American 7th Annual Prize for Literature; Cecilia Vicuna's *Instan*, a long poem by a Chilean poet, performance artist, and sculptor; and Carol Mira Kove's *Occupied*, protest poetry about Afghanistan and the Iraq War.

## KUMARIAN PRESS
1294 Blue Hills Ave.
Bloomfield, CT 06002
(860) 243-2098 Fax: (860) 243-2867
Email: kpbooks@kpbooks.com Web: www.kpbooks.com

**Editor**: Krishna Sondhi, President and Publisher, Jim Lance, Editor and Associate Publisher
**Affiliated press names**: Frog Books
**Associated with**: distributes books for Oxfam GB; publishes in association with other organizations
**ISBN prefix**: 1-56549, 1-887208, 0-931816

**Average number of new titles published per year**: 18
**Number of titles in print**: 200+
**Distributor**: publisher direct by phone, (800) 289-2664, mail, fax, or email
**Publication interests**: Conflict Resolution, Development Studies, Ecology/Environmentalism, Economics, Gender Studies, Globalization, Health, Human Rights, International Issues/Relations, Peace, Politics, Social Change, Social Justice, Third World, Women's Issues/Studies
**Motto**: "A world in which distinctions such as 'Third World' will no longer exist."

Founded in 1977, Kumarian Press responds to the expressed need for books on international development and management that are geared to the needs of developing countries. The press's name is coined from a combination of the publisher's middle name, Kumari, and the first name,Ian, of the vice president, Ian Mayo-Smith. Besides the above publication interests, the press publishes books on civil society and NGOs, humanitarianism, microfinance, and governance. The press is a pioneer in publishing books emphasizing the people centered approach to development. Example of titles include: *World Disasters Report* (annual), edited by Jonathan Walter, a look at how humanitarian agencies and governments can best help disaster-affected communities to recover, become stronger, and more disaster resilient; *Global Civil Society, volume 2: dimensions of the nonprofit sector*, edited by Lester M. Salamon, an ambitious attempt to measure the size of charity; Ronaldo Munck's *Globalization and Social Exclusion: a transformationalist perspective*, a road map of globalization that places inequality at the forefront; and Severyn T. Bruyn's *A Civil Republic: beyond capitalism and nationalism*, illuminates the boundary between civil society and social economy.

## LANTERN BOOKS

1 Union Square West, Suite 201
New York, NY 10003
(212) 414-2275   Fax: (212) 414-2412
Email: editorial@lanternbooks.com   Web: www.lanternbooks.com

**Editor**: Martin Rowe, Publisher
**Associated with**: Lantern Books is a division of Booklight, Inc., a website promotion and publishing company, and U.S. distributor for Findhorn Press, Stealth Technologies, and Samhita Publications.
**ISBN prefix**: 1-590560
**Average number of new titles published per year**: 25

**Number of titles in print**: 80
**Other materials produced**: audiobooks
**Distributor**: publisher direct via website's order form, or by phone, (800) 856-8664, or mail to P.O. Box 960, Herndon, VA 20172-0960; Hushion House Publishing (Canada), www.hushion.com
**Publication interests**: Animal Rights, Ecology/Environmentalism, Health, Natural/Nature, Politics, Religion, Social Issues, Spirituality, Vegetarianism

Founded in 1999, Lantern Books publishes books for all wanting to live with greater spiritual depth and commitment to the preservation of the natural world. Publication interests fall into non-alternative categories of new age spirituality, religion, and psychology, and into alternative categories of animal advocacy, nature and the environment, social thought and vegetarianism. Examples of titles include: Norm Phelps' *The Dominion of Love: animal rights according to the Bible*; Steven Best's and Anthony J. Nocella, II's *Terrorists or Freedom Fighters? Reflections on the liberation of animals*; Craig Rosebraugh's *Burning Rage of a Dying Planet: speaking for The Earth Liberation Front*; and David A. Kidd's *The Story of a Grassroots Activist: a call for renewed civic action*.

## LATIN AMERICAN BUREAU
1 Amwell St.
London EC1R 1UL United Kingdom
+44(0)20 7278 2829   Fax: +44(0)20 7833 0715
Email: info@lab.org.uk   Web: www.lab.org.uk

**Editor**: Marcela Lopez Levy
**ISBN prefix**: 1-899365
**Average number of new titles published per year**: 6
**Number of new titles in print**: 96
**Distributor**: publisher direct via website's bookstore, or by phone 0845 458 9910, or email, lab@centralbooks.com; Monthly Review Press (USA), mreview@icg.org; Fernwood Books (Canada)
**Publication interests**: Development Studies, Economics, Education, Gender Studies, Globalization, Human Rights, Latin American Studies, Media Studies, Politics, Social Justice
**Motto**: "Research, publishing and education on Latin America and the Caribbean."

Founded in 1977, the Latin American Bureau is an independent research and publishing organization that works on issues of social justice and human rights in Latin America and the Caribbean. LAB is also engaged in a number of large projects designed to raise European awareness of Latin American and the Caribbean. The publications seek to broaden public understanding of the concerns of people in Latin America and the Caribbean, as well as highlight the cultural diversity of the region. The press co-publishes with a range of publishers in Latin America and the United States. Besides the above publication interests, publications fall in the areas of tourism and the environment, trade and development, and indigenous rights. LAB Short Books strattle feature-length journalism and full-length books documenting key struggles in the Latin American region. LAB's In Focus country guides provide the inside story on Latin America and the Caribbean politics, culture, history and society packed into 100 pages. Examples of titles include Elizabeth Jelin's *State Repression and the Struggles for Memory*, an exploration of how memory and politics intertwine and the forms in which memory, and forgetting, shape individual and collective identities, and *Confronting Globalisation: economic integration and popular resistance in Mexico*, edited by Timothy A. Wise, Hilda Salazar and Laura Carlsen, documents resistance to Washington's neo-liberalism.

## LATIN AMERICAN LITERARY REVIEW PRESS
P.O. Box 17660
Pittsburgh, PA 15235
(412) 824-7903   Fax: (412) 824-7909
Email: latin@angstrom.net   Web: www.lalrp.org

**Editor**: Yvette Miller
**ISBN prefix**: 0-935480, 1-891270
**Average number of new titles published per year**: 4
**Number of titles in print**: 83
**Other material produced**: *Latin American Literary Review*, a semi-annual, scholarly journal devoted to the literature of Latin America and Brazil
**Distributor**: publisher direct via website's order forms, one for emailing and one that can be printed and mailed or faxed; Bilingual Press Review, brp@asu.edu
**Publication interests**: Bilingual, Literary, Music, Poetry, Translations, Women's Issues/Studies

Founded in 1980, Latin American Literary Review Press was established with the principal objective to familiarize readers outside the field with Latin American literature. The emphasis has been on publishing translations of creative writing, literary criticism bilingual Spanish/English editions of poetry, and Spanish music. Example of titles include: Alejandro Hernandez Diaz' *The*

*Cuban Mile*, a study of the psychology of risk and desire; *Cruel Fictions, Cruel Realities*, edited and translated by Kathy S. Leonard, a first hand glimpse into the Latin American soul through the writings of prominent women authors, most appearing here for the first time in English translation; and Marjorie Agosin's *Melodious Women*, poems dedicated to the individuality and contributions to society of 45 women from Virginia Wolfe to Chilean folk singer Gala Torres.

## LASP GASP
777 Florida St.
San Francisco, CA 94110
(415) 824-6636  Fax: (415) 824-1836
Email:  email form available on website  Web: www.lastgasp.com

**Editor**: Ron Turner
**Affiliated press names**: Priaprism Press
**Associated with**: Last Gasp Distribution—sells more than 20,000 titles from 600+ publishers, including some 200 different comic books
**ISBN prefix**: 0-86719
**Average number of new titles published per year**: 17
**Number of titles in print**: 128
**Distributor**: publisher direct via website's shopping cart feature
**Publication interests**: Alternative Culture, Anarchism, Art/The Arts, Avant-garde, Comics/Comix, Erotica, Gay, Lesbian, Occultism, Punk, Sexuality, Surrealism
**Motto**: "Mind candy for the masses."

Founded in 1970, Last Gasp publishes and distributes a very eclectic assortment of comix, books and magazines which present a dizzying collection of independent, marginal and avant-garde titles. Subjects range from anarchy to fetish fashions, horticulture to occultism, beatnik literature to erotic manga, and avant-garde graphics to artistic terrorism. The press is one of the largest and oldest publishers and purveyors of underground comic books in the world, as well as being a distributor of sorts of weird and wonderful subversive literature, graphic novels, tatoo and art books. The press is especially known for publishing the autobiographical work of cartoonists like R. Crumb, Justin Green, and Rand Holmes, and has published the work of famous illustrators, artists and writers, including R. Crumb (Wierdo), Bill Griffith (Zippy the Pinhead), and Frank Kozik (Man's Ruin). Lasp Gasp distributes titles of noteworthy authors from the fifties and sixties, including Timothy Leary (10 titles),

Charles Bukowski (39 titles), and William S. Burroughs (14 titles). Examples of titles include: Keister's *Dead Kennedys: unauthorized biography*; Diane de Prima's *Dinners and Nightmares*, an early beat classic; and *Pop Surrealism: the rise of underground art*, edited by Kristen Anderson, a survey of the movement featuring 23 artists.

## LAWRENCE HILL BOOKS
814 N. Franklin St.
Chicago, IL 60610
(312) 337-0747  Fax: (312) 337-5110
Email: frontdesk@chicagoreviewpress.com
Web: www.chicagoreviewpress.com/CRP/

**Editor**: Linda Matthews, Publisher and Yuval Taylor, Senior Editor
**Affiliated press names**: imprint of Chicago Review Press which also owns Independent Publishers Group
**ISBN prefix**: 1-55652, 0-88208
**Average number of new titles published per year**: 5
**Number of titles in print**: 45
**Distributor**: Independent Publishers Group (800) 888-4741 or orders@ipgbook.com
**Publication interests**: Africa/African Studies, African American, Biography/Memoir, Civil Liberties, History, Minorities, Political, Race/Race Relations, Reprints, Slavery, Social Justice

Founded in 1973, Lawrence Hill Books provides a home for controversial works from a progressive political perspective, particularly books that reflect Black America and Africa. The press is especially strong in biography, including slave narratives and history. The publishers created the Library of Black America, publishing titles, for example, *Frederick Douglass: selected speeches and writings*. Examples of titles include Nikki Giovanni's *Ego-tripping and Other Poems for Young People*, a collection of poetry that captures the essence of the African-American experience for young people, and Damali Yao's *How to Rent a Negro*, a biting satire of racism in American life. Classic titles include *Assata: an autobiography*, the life story of African American revolutionary Shakar, and *Soledad Prison: the prison letters of George Jackson*.

## LEE & LOW BOOKS
95 Madison Ave., Suite 606
New York, NY 10016
(212) 779-4400  Fax: (212) 683-1894
Email: general@leeandlow.com  Web: www.leeandlow.com

**Editor**: Tom Low, Jason Low, Craig Low (Bebop Books)
**Affiliated press names**: Bebob Books, imprint, www.bebopbooks.com
**ISBN prefix**: 1-880000, 1-58430
**Average number of new titles published per year**: 13
**Number of books in print**: 85
**Distributor**: publisher direct (888) 320-3190, ext. 25, fax, email,
orders@leeandlow.com; on the web at booksense.com or amazon.com; Fitz-
henry & Whiteside (Canada) (800) 387-9776
**Publication interests**: Adolescents, African American, American Indian,
Asian American, Biography/Memoirs, Children/Juvenile, Civil Rights, His-
panic/Latino, Minorities, Multiculturalism
**Motto**: "Multicultural literature for children."

Founded in 1991 by Philip Lee and Thomas Low, Lee & Low Books has a
goal to meet the need for stories that children and adolescents of color can
identify with and that all children and adolescents can enjoy. The books are
about African, Asian, Latino, and Native Americans in contemporary and
historic settings. Bebob Books features multicultural stories for children who
are just learning to read. The editors make a special effort to work with artists
of color. The titles have won a number of major awards and honors, including
the Coretta Scott King Award, the Parents' Choice Award, and the Parenting
magazine Reading-Magic Award. Many of the titles have been translated into
Spanish. Examples of titles include: Dia Cha's *Dia's Story Cloth: the Hmong people's journey to freedom*, a book about a family's displacement as told through the
story cloth stitched by Dia's aunt and uncle; Jeannine Atkin's *Anni and the Tree
Huggers*, a story of a village girl in India who inspires the women around her to
save their beloved forest; and Leslie Jones Little's *Children of Long Ago*, a celebration of African American childhood in the early 1900s told through 17
poems.

## LOOMPANICS UNLIMITED
P.O. Box 1197
Port Townsend, WA 98368
(360) 385-5087  Fax: (360) 385-7785

Email: service@loompanics.com Web: www.loompanics.com

**Editor**: Michael Hoy, President
**ISBN prefix**: 0-915179, 1-55950
**Average number of new titles published per year**: 17
**Number of titles in print**: 85
**Distributor**: publisher direct by phone (800) 380-2230, fax, email, or regular mail
**Publication interests**: Alternative Culture, Anarchism, Civil Liberties, Erotica
**Motto**: "The lunatic fringe of the libertarian movement."

Founded in 1975, Loompanics Unlimited is publisher of some of the world's most controversial and unusual books, as well as a retailer for many books from many presses. The books are for anyone interested in the strange, the arcane, the odd-ball, or the diabolical, for example, how-to books for anarchists, survivalists, iconoclasts, investigators, and mercenaries. The books represent the undying spirit of human freedom and resistance to tyranny. All titles are sold for informational purposes only. Certain materials in Loompanics books and catalog could be in violation of various federal, state and local laws if actually carried out or constructed. Loompanics does not advocate the breaking of any law. Examples of titles include: Uncle Fester's *Secrets of Methamphetamine Manufacture*, 7th edition; M.D. Farber's *The Psychological Roots of Religious Belief: searching for angels and the parent-god*; and Bill Wilson's *Under the Table and into Your Pocket: the how and why of the underground economy*, describes ways of getting around the money-grubbing hand of the government.

## LOTUS PRESS, INC.
P.O. Box 21607
Detroit, MI 48221
(313) 861-1280 Fax: (313) 861-4740
Email: lotuspress@aol.com Web: www.lotuspress.org

**Editor**: Naomi Madgett, Poet Laureate of the City of Detroit
**Affiliated press names**: Penway Books
**ISBN prefix**: 0-916418
**Average number of new titles published per year**: 1-2
**Number of titles in print**: 62
**Distributor**: publisher direct via website's order form available for postal mailing

**Publishing interests**: African American, Poetry
**Motto**: "Flower of a new Nile."

Founded in 1972, Lotus Press, Inc. is a nonprofit publisher publishing poetry only, usually by African Americans. The press has been considered a forum for many black voices. The poems cover a great deal of variety in style and subject matter. The press "gets" many African American themes in a way that other publishers might not. Lotus has published some of the leading African American writers such as Toi Derricote and Gayl Jones. Examples of books include: Ruth Ellen Kocher's *Desdemona's Fire*, a book of ambitious poems expressing intense subjectivity, harsh inner-city reality, and classical and mythological allusion; James C. Kilgore's *African Violet: poem for a blackwoman*; and Lance Jeffers' *O Africa, Where I Baked My Bread*.

## MEP PUBLICATIONS
University of Minnesota, Physics Bldg.
116 Church St., SE
Minneapolis, MN 55455-0112
(612) 922-7993  Fax: (612) 922-0858
Email: marqu002@tc.umn.edu
Web: webusers.physics.umn.edu/~marquit

**Editor:** Doris G. Marquit, Managing Editor
**Affiliated press names:** imprint of the Marxist Educational Press
**ISBN prefix:** 0-930656
**Average number of new titles published per year:** 1
**Number of titles in print:** 31
**Other materials produced:** *Nature, Society, and Thought*, a quarterly interdisciplinary journal of Marxist studies (author/title index, 1987-2003 available online)
**Distributor:** publisher direct with payments through PayPal, check or money order
**Publication interests:** African American, Civil Liberties, Economics, Globalization, History, Human Rights, International Issues/Relations, Labor/Labor Studies, Philosophy, Politics, Poverty, Race/Race Relations, Socialism/Marxism

Founded in 1977, MEP Publications is the publication arm of the Marxist Educational Press, a nonprofit, educational organization that sponsors, stimulates and develops Marxist scholarship by providing forums for the exchange of ideas and experiences among those interested in the dialectical-materialist intellectual tradition. MEP receives no institutional subsidies. Examples of publications include: James S. Allen's *Organizing in the Depression South: a communist's memoir; Dialectics of the U.S. Constitution: selected writings of Mitchell Franklin*, edited by James M. Lawler, a discussion of how the development of natural law from an idealist to a materialist concept in the transition from feudalism to capitalism is reflected in the drafting of the Constitution and its interpretation today; and Priscilla Metscher's *James Connolly and the Reconquest of Ireland*, a reassessment of James Connolly who was prominent in Irish, British, and U.S. labor movement, a Marxist scholar, and a militant Irish patriot.

**MAISONNEUVE PRESS**
P.O. Box 2980
Washington, DC 20013-2980
(301) 277-7505  Fax: (301) 277-2467
**Email:** rm@maisonneuvepress.com
**Web:** www.maisonneuvepress.com

**Editor:** Robert Merrill
**Affiliated with:** Institute for Advanced Cultural Studies
**ISBN prefix:** 0-944624
**Average number of new titles published per year:** 6
**Number of titles in print:** 36
**Distributor:** publisher direct via website order form; AK Press and Distribution, and Marginal (Canada)
**Publication interests:** Cultural Studies, Development Studies, Ecology/Environmentalism, Economics, Globalization, History, International Issues/Studies, Poetry, Politics

Founded in 1988, Maisonneuve Press is a nonprofit organization that seeks to advance the revisions of knowledge and re-evaluation of values that will lead to a world in which the dignity of every human being matters the most. A goal is to bring the traditional university based scholar to the forefront of political activism and likewise bring the agenda of practical political activism to the university curriculum and research. The Institute for Advanced Cultural Studies is a nonprofit organization committed to progressive social change through cultural analysis and education. Postmodern Positions, a book series edited by Robert Merrill, about competing paradigms based on race, class, gender, ideological/religious identity, or geography, and the rise of the global marketplace. Examples of titles include: Stephen C. Pelletiere's *Iraq and the International*

*Oil System: why we went to war in the Gulf*, an assertion that the desire to control Persian Gulf's oil supply sent the United States to war against Iraq in both 1991 and 2003; Chris Maser's *The Perpetual Consequences of Fear and Violence: re-thinking the future*, argues that current conflicts in the war on terrorism are doing tremendous damage to the future generations; and *The War on Children*, edited by Lenora Foerstel, seeks to prove that the most significant damage during recent wars will be wrought on the children of the region.

## MANIC D PRESS
Box 410804
San Francisco, CA 94141
(415) 648-8288  Fax: same
**Email:** info@manicdpress.com
**Web:** www.manicdpress.com

**Editor:** Jennifer Joseph
**ISBN prefix:** 0-916397
**Average number of new titles published per year:** 8-10
**Number of titles in print:** 75
**Distributor:** publisher direct via website's bookcart feature; Publishers Group West (US and Canada), Small Press Distribution, Last Gasp
Publication interests: Alternative Culture, Anthologies, Comics/Comix, Erotica, Gay, Gender Studies, Lesbian, Poetry, Punk, Sexuality, Women's Issues/Studies
**Motto:** "Eat, sleep, read, coexist."

Founded in 1984, Manic D Press publishes a mix of fiction, poetry, art, and nonfiction writing that is by nature experimental or unusual and includes emerging and well-established writers and artists. The press has been referred to as the best quintessentially San Franciscan publisher. *Poetry Slam: the competitive art of performance poetry*, edited by Gary Mex Glazner, is a bestseller. Examples of titles include: *The Insomniac Reader: stories of the night*, edited by Kevin Sampsell, an anthology of short fiction exploring the dark side, literally and figuratively; *From the Inside Out: radical gender transformation, FTM and beyond*, edited by Morty Diamond, illuminates the experiences of those who identify as FTM (female to male); and Jon Longhi's *Wake Up and Smell the Beer*, a fictional chronicle of a year in the underground counter-cultural life of a San Francisco guy. The press is also known for books on alternative travel.

## MEHRING BOOKS

P.O. Box 1306
Sheffield S9 3UW United Kingdom
(0114) 244 0055  Fax: (0114) 244 0224
Email: sales@mehringbooks.co.uk  Web: www.mehringbooks.co.uk

**ISBN prefix**: 0-929087
**Affiliated press names**: formerly Labor Press Books
**Associated with**: publication and distribution arm of the Socialist Equality Party
**Average number of new titles published per year**: 2-3
**Number of titles in print**: 40
**Other materials produced**: pamphlets
**Distributor**: publisher direct via website's shopping cart feature, www.wsws.org/cgi-bin/store/commerce.cgi; USA sales: P.O. Box 48237, Oak Park, MI 48237, (248) 967-2924
**Publication interests**: Globalization, History, International Issues/Relations, Labor/Labor Studies, Philosophy, Politics, Socialism/Marxism, Translations
**Motto**: "The foremost publisher of socialist books."

Mehring Books is dedicated to producing high-quality editions of socialist books and pamphlets in the English language. The titles encompass contemporary political analysis, history, culture and the arts, and include works by Leon Trotsky and other leading representatives of classical Marxism. The press is named after Franz Mehring (1846-1919), a writer, literary critic, and historian of the Second International, the Marxist movement before World War I. The publishers believe that one of the greatest lies in the course of the 20th century was the false identification between Stalinism and socialism. Western historians and bourgeois ideologues used the crimes committed by the bureaucracy to discredit a socialist perspective. Mehring Books sets out to clarify the historical record. Many of the books are available in English for the first time. Examples of books include *Globalization and the International Working Class: a Marxist assessment*, a statement of the International Committee of the Fourth International, and Aleksandr Konstantinovich Voronsky's *Art as the Cognition of Life: selected writings, 1911-1936*, translated and edited by Frederick S. Choate, writings by one of the authentic representatives of classical Marxism in the field of literary criticism.

## MEIKLEJOHN CIVIL LIBERTIES INSTITUTE
Box 673
Berkeley, CA 94701-0673
(510) 848-0599 Fax: (510) 848-6008
Email: 2005@mcli.org Web: www.mcli.org

**Editor**: Ann Fagan Ginger, Executive Director
**Associated with**: Center for the Covenant, San Francisco State University, and the India Legal Center for Human Rights and Law, Bombay, India
**ISBN prefix**: 0-913876
**Average number of new titles published per year**: 1
**Number of titles in print**: 11
**Other materials produced**: Peace Law Packets, *Human Rights Now*, a quarterly newsletter, Issue Sheets
**Distributor**: publisher direct via website's shopping basket
**Publishing interests**: Civil Liberties, Human Rights, Law/Legal Studies, Peace, Reference, Social Change, Social Justice
**Motto**: "A unique center for human rights and peace law."

Founded in 1965, the Meiklejohn Civil Liberties Institute is a human rights and peace law center, an organizer for the right to education, an information clearinghouse on social change, an advocate of government accountability, a training center, and a repository of history. The institute was named for Alexander Meiklejohn, the great civil libertarian, and is part of the peace and justice community, empowering people to protect and expand their rights under law. The institute works documents and report violations of rights enumerated in the U.S. Constitution and international treaties, ensures enforcement of these laws in this country, and collects facts on human rights violations to include in reports to appropriate agencies (local, state, federal and United Nations), not to courts. It does not represent individuals whose rights have been violated. Examples of publications include: Ann Fagan Ginger's *How to Use "New" Civil Rights Laws after 9/11: what are the "new" laws, what cases have they won, how are they enforced; Human Rights and Peace Law Docket*, detailed descriptions of court cases, and *Human Rights Organizations and Periodicals Directory*, 11th edition (biennial). The institute was also responsible for the publication, *Challenging U.S. Human Rights Violations Since 9/11*, edited by Ann Fagan Ginger (Prometheus Books, 2005).

## MERCURY HOUSE
P.O. Box 192850
San Francisco, CA 94119-2850
(415) 626-7874  Fax:  (415) 626-7875
Email: mercury@mercuryhouse.org  Web: www.mercuryhouse.org

**Editor**: Kristen Janene-Nelson, Executive Director
**ISBN prefix**: 0-916515, 1-56279
**Average number of new titles published per year**: 4
**Number of titles in print**: 166
**Distributor**: publisher direct via website's printable order form or shopping cart feature; Consortium, Small Press Distribution
**Publication interests**: Cultural Studies, Ecology/Environmentalism, Literary, Natural/Nature, Poetry, Translations

Founded in 1985, Mercury House is guided by a dedication to literary values, to works of social significance, and to the free exchange of ideas. The press concentrates on literary fiction and it has long been respected for the literary quality of its fiction and nonfiction books. Its translations of fine works of literature offer an essential window to the world of another culture. The press is considered a prime example of a literary independent press in this country that adamantly keeps itself apart from the commercial publishing industry. A number of works by the press have won literary awards, for example, Ken Lamberton's *Wilderness and Razor Wire: a naturalist's observations from prison*, winner of the 2002 John Burroughs Medal for distinguished natural history writing, an eloquent study of the persistence of nature in a desert prison. Another example of a title is Leslie Baer-Brown's and Bob Rheim's *Earth Keepers: writers, artists and AIDS*, literary works by leading writes and artists affected by AIDS.

## MERLIN PRESS
P.O. Box 30705
London WC2E 8QD England
+44(0)20 7836 3020  Fax: +44(0)20 7497 0309
Email: info@merlinpress.co.uk  Web: www.merlinpress.co.uk

**Editor**: Anthony Zurbrugg
**Affiliated press names**: Green Print, imprint
**ISBN prefix**: 0-805036, 1-854250 (Green Print)
**Average number of new titles published per year**: 12
**Number of titles in print**: 122

**Distributor**: publisher direct via website's shopping cart feature; Independent Publishers Group (USA); Fernwood Books (Canada)
**Publication interests**: Critical Theory, Ecology/Environmentalsim, Globalization, History, International Issues/Relations, Labor/Labor Studies, Politics, Reprints, Socialism/Marxism

Founded in 1958, Merlin Press was originated by people on the left wanting to reconsider the past and the future in light of the failures of Stalinist communism. The press publishes in the broad area of left, labor history and social sciences, and has produced a number of reprints of Marx, Levi-Strauss, and Georg Lukacs. The Chartist Studies Series focuses on the campaign for democracy in Victoria Britain and overseas. Chartists asserted the rights of ordinary people and were viewed as either dangerous radicals or proto-democrats. An example in the series is Keith Flett's *Chartism After 1848: the working class and the politics of radical education*. The *Socialist Register*, 1964-, is an annual publication considered compulsory reading for people who refuse to be resigned to the idea that there can be no alternative to our unacceptable society. Examples of titles include: *The Globalization Decade: a critical reader*, edited by Leo Panitch and Colin Leys; Jim Harding's *After Iraq: war, imperialism and democracy*; Ursula Huw's *The Making of a Cybertariat: virtual work in a real world*, the effect of technological innovations on employees; and David Icke's *It Doesn't Have to be Like This: green politics explained*.

## MILKWEED EDITIONS
1011 Washington Ave., South, Suite 300
Minneapolis, MN 55415-1246
(800) 520-6455, (612) 332-3192 Fax: (612) 215-2550
Email: webmaster@milkweed.org Web: www.milkweed.org

**Editor**: H. Emerson Blake
ISBN prefix: **0-915943, 1-57131**
**Average number of new titles published per year**: 12
**Number of titles in print**: 200+
**Distributor**: publisher direct via U.S. mail; Publishers Group West, and Publishers Group West Canada. Publisher encourages purchases through local bookstores.
**Publication interests**: Children/Juvenile, Ecology/Environmentalism, Literary, Minorities, Natural/Nature, Poetry, Social Change
**Motto**: "Publishes with the intention of making a humane impact on society."

Founded in 1979, Milkweed Editions' mission is to propagate the unique and beautiful by producing literature that promotes both personal reflection and cultural change. The press is the nation's largest nonprofit, independent literary publisher. The press produces high-quality books that places emphasis on cultural diversity, environmental stewardship, exceptionally crafted poetry, and insightful literature for adults. The Milkweeds for Young Readers program is designed to bring the very best writing to children in the middle grades. In 1993, as an adjunct to the juvenile publishing program for children 8 to 13, Milkweed launched the Alliance for Reading in collaboration with other organizations dedicated to making reading vital in the lives of children. The World as Home, <www.worldashome.org>, is a nonfiction series about the natural world, for example, *Cross-Pollinations: the marriage of science and poetry* by Gary Paul Nabhan, about an interdisciplinary life that combines a passion for science and a love of literature leading to discoveries that would be other wise inaccessible. Literature for a Land Ethic is an anthology series that addresses the need to preserve our last wild places, for example, Hank Lentfer's and Carolyn Servid's *Arctic Refuge: a circle of testimony*, a grassroots effort to bring a variety of voices to the debate over oil exploration in the Arctic National Wildlife Refuge. The Credo Series conveys the essential beliefs of American nature writers, for example, John Nichols' *An American Child Supreme: the education of a liberation ecologist.* Another title example is Susan Power's *Roofwalker*, a portrayal of men and women negotiating an impossible path between Native American culture and transplanted urban life in Chicago.

## MONTHLY REVIEW PRESS
122 W. 27th St.
New York, NY 10001
(212) 691-2555  Fax: (212) 727-3676
Email: promo@monthlyreview.org
Web: www.monthlyreview.org/mrpress.htm

**Editor**: Andrew Nash, Editorial Director
**ISBN prefix**: 1-58367, 0-85345
**Average number of new titles published per year**: 10-12
**Number of titles in print**: 300
**Other materials produced**: *Monthly Review* magazine, and *The Socialist Register*, an annual political journal which probes the challenges and opportunities facing the left from a socialist perspective

**Distributor**: publisher direct via website's online book purchase feature, or by phone (800) 670-9499 or fax; New York University Press (800) 996-6987; Fernwood Books (Canada)
**Publication interests**: Development Studies, Ecology/Environmentalism, Economics, Globalization, History, International Issues/Relations, Labor/Labor Studies, Latin American Studies, Politics, Social Justice, Social Issues, Socialism/Marxism, Third World, Women's Issues/Studies

Founded in 1957, Monthly Review Press was launched in the depths of the McCarthy/J. Edgar Hoover era by the editors of the socialist magazine, *Monthly Review*. Over the years, the press has published major international political-economic and historical studies. Monthly Review is committed to left publishing, and consistently carries the standard of thoughtful and critical radicalism. The books combine the best of the old left with creative insights of new social movements. Examples of titles include: *Pox Americana: exposing the American empire*, edited by John Bellamy and Robert W. McChesney, examines the nature and prospects of the war and occupation in the Middle East; Joan Greenbaum's *Windows in the Workplace: technology, jobs, and the organization of office work*, 2nd edition, shows how new technologies benefit capitalist profit and control over the workforce rather through greater efficiency; and *The Rosa Luxenburg Reader*, edited by Peter Hudis and Kevin B. Anderson.

## MORNING GLORY PRESS
6595 San Haroldo Way
Buena Park, CA 90620
(888) 612-8254  Fax: (888) 327-4362
Email: info@morninggl orypress.com  Web: www.morninggl orypress.com

**Editor**: Jeanne Lindsay
**ISBN prefix**: 1-885356
**Average number of new titles published per year**: 3-5
**Number of titles in print**: 29
**Other materials produced**: *PPT Express*, a quarterly newsletter for teachers and others working with pregnant and parenting teens; workbooks, guides, videos, games, and Comprehensive Curriculum Notebooks, lesson plans, handouts, objective, quizzes, and learning activities.
**Distributor**: publisher direct via website's printable order form or by phone (888) 612-8254; Independent Publishers Group

**Publishing interests**: Adolescents, Adoption/Adopted Children, Children/Juvenile, Domestic Violence, Education, Health, Parenting, Sexuality, Women's Issues/Studies
**Motto**: "Resources for pregnant and parenting teens."

Founded in 1977, Morning Glory Press's mission is to provide the best possible books for and about pregnant and parenting teens, adopted children, and partner abuse. These resources help serve the 200,000 teens that father babies born to teenage mothers each year in the U.S. The books are nonjudgmental and written directly to teenagers, many based on interviews with teens who were pregnant, had recently given birth, or who had placed a baby for adoption. Examples of books include: *Do I Have a Daddy?*, a picture book for the child who doesn't know his/her father; *Did My First Mother Love Me?*, a picture book for an adopted child; *Teenage Couples: caring, commitment and change*, a book on building relationships that last; *Teenage Couples: coping with reality*, a book on dealing with money, in-laws, babies, and other details of daily life; *Teenage Couples: expectations and reality*, teen views on living together, roles, work, jealousy, and partner abuse; and *Breaking Free from Partner Abuse: voices of battered women caught in the cycle of domestic violence*, selected by the Public Library Association as a "Distinguished Work" for new adult readers. The True to Life Series from Hamilton High captures teens where they live, for example, Marilyn Reynolds' *Love Rules*, about a young woman's awareness of the tragic effects of injustice on people of varied backgrounds and persuasions. Some titles have free study or discussion guides available for use with groups and individuals.

## NATION BOOKS
33 Irving Pl., 8th floor
New York, NY 10003
(212) 209-5448  Fax: (212) 982-9000
E-mail form available on website  Web: www.nationbooks.org

**Editor**: Carl Bromley
**Associated with**: a co-publishing adventure of the Nation Institute, www.nationinstitute.org, and the Avalon Publishing Group
**Affiliated press names**: publishes some titles under the imprint Thunder's Mouth/Nation Books, both imprints of the Avalon Publishing Group.
**ISBN prefix**: 1-56025
**Average number of new titles published per year**: 30
**Number of titles in print**: 84
**Distributor**: Publishers Group West (800) 788-3123

**Publication interests**: Cultural Studies, Economics, Feminism, Gender Studies, Globalization, History, Human Rights, International Issues/Relations, Politics, Race/Race Relations Social Justice
**Motto**: "The independent publishing alternative."

Founded in 2001, Nation Books is dedicated to continuing the long tradition of progressive, independent critical thought in America. Nation Books is the book publishing arm of The Nation Institute, founded in 1966 and producer of Radio Nation, a syndicated weekly current affairs program. The Institute is an independently funded and administered public charity committed to the creation of a just society and an informed public, as well as the preservation of rights protected under the First Amendment. The Institute also conducts an internship program to train young journalists to, as John Dewey said, "provoke, to incite, and to contribute to the national dialogue." Examples of titles include: Melissa Boyle Mahle's *Denial and Deception: an insider's view of the CIA from Iran-Contra to 9/11*, details the political and operational culture of the CIA in the post-Cold War era and reveals how the CIA failed to anticipate 9/11; *The Jonathan Schell Reader: on the United States at war, the long crisis of the American republic, and the fate of the earth*, the best selections from four decades of work from the famed author; and John Nicholas' *Against the Beast*, a collection of writings, speeches, comments and cartoons of four centuries of American antiimperialist campaigners.

## NEW CLARION PRESS
5 Church Row
Gretton, Cheltenham GL54 5HG United Kingdom
44 1242 620623  Fax: same
Email: chrisbessant@newclarionpress.co.uk
Web: www.newclarionpress.co.uk

**Editor**: Chris Bessant
**ISBN prefix**: 1-873797
**Average number of new titles published per year**: 2-3
**Number of titles in print**: 17
**Distributor**: publisher direct via phone, fax or email, sales@newclarionpress.co.uk; USA & Canada: Paul & Company Publishers Consortium, c/o IPG, Chicago, IL, (800) 888-4741, orders@ipgbook.com
**Publication interests**: Civil Liberties, History, Politics, Prisons/Prisoners, Social Policy, Socialism/Marxism

Founded in 1990, New Clarion Press is an independent publisher of books on history, politics, and social policy written from a radical and reforming perspective. Examples of titles include: David Renton's *Classical Marxism: socialist theory and the Second International*; *Class Struggle and Resistance in Africa*, edited by Leo Zeilig , offers a contemporary Marxist analysis of the continent; David Stack's *The First Darwinian Left: socialism and Darwinism, 1859-1914*, provides a detailed account of how socialists wrestled with the paradoxical challenges that Darwinism posed for their politics; and Anne Kerr's and Tom Shakespeare's *Genetic Politics: from eugenics to genome*, argues that eugenics continues to shape genetics today.

## THE NEW PRESS
38 Green St., 4th floor
New York, NY 10013
(212) 629-8802  Fax: (212) 629-8617
Email: newpress@thenewpress.com  Web: www.thenewpress.com

**Editor**: Andre Schiffrin
**Associated with**: press offices are provided by the City University of New York
**ISBN prefix**: 1-56584
**Average number of new titles published per year**: 50
**Number of titles in print**: 200+
**Distributor**: publisher direct via website's shopping cart feature, or by phone, (800) 233-4830 or fax; W.W. Norton; University of Toronto (Canada), www.utpress.utornto.ca
**Publication interests**: African American, American Indian, Asian American, Cultural Studies, Economics, Education, Gay, Globalization, Hispanic/Latino, History, Human Rights, Immigration, International Issues/Relations, Law/Legal Studies, Lesbian, Labor/Labor Studies, Media Studies, Minorities, Politics, Race/Race Relations, Social Issues, Social Justice, Women's Issues/Studies
**Motto**: "An independent publisher in the public interest."
Founded in 1990, The New Press is a not-for-profit publishing house established as a major alternative to the large, commercial publishers that operates editorially in the public interest. The New Press aims to provide ideas and viewpoints under-represented in the mass media, serve as an activist press that seeks to identify areas in which new books and materials are most needed, broaden the audience for serious intellectual work, and address the problems of a society in transition, highlighting attempts at reform and innovation in a

wide range of fields. The New Press operates an ambitious Outreach program that works with arts and media organizations to generate public discussion and debate on the major issues confronting American society today. Most titles are non-fiction, though some fiction is also published. Commercially successful authors have chosen to publish with the press, including Marguerite Duras, John Leonard and Studs Terkel. Examples of titles include: John Nicholas' *Dick: the man who is President*, makes a case that Dick Cheney runs the country; Christopher D. Cook's *Diet for a Dead Planet: how the food industry is killing us*, explains why our entire food system is in crisis; Jon Wiener's *Historians in Trouble: plagiarism, fraud and politics in the ivory tower*, examines the various history scandals of the last few years, arguing that media spectacles end careers only when powerful groups outside the profession demand punishment; and Richard G. Wilkinson's *Impact of Inequality: how to make sick societies healthier*.

## NEW SOCIETY PUBLISHERS
1680 Peterson Road
P.O. Box 189
Gabriola Island, British Columbia V0R 1X0 Canada
(250) 247-9737  Fax: (250) 247-7471
Email: info@newsociety.com  Web: www.newsociety.com

**Editor**: Chris Plant and Judy Plant
**Associated with**: distributes titles from the Centre for Alternative Technology (Wales), and *Real Goods Solar Living Sourcebook. The Complete Guide to Renewable Energy Technologies & Sustainable Living*, edited by John Schaeffer, from Gaiam (Broomfield, CO).
**ISBN prefix**: 0-86571
**Average number of new titles published per year**: 30
**Number of titles in print**: 135
**Other material produced**: DVDs
**Distributor**: publisher direct via website's order form or shopping cart feature, or by phone (800) 567-6772, email orders@newsociety.com, or fax (800) 567-7311; Consortium (U.S.); in Canada, Kate Walker and Co. (book trade) and Fernwood (academic and college market)
**Publication interests**: Activism, Architecture, Ecology/Environmentalism, Education, Energy, Globalization, Natural/Nature, Peace, Politics, Social Change, Social Issues, Social Justice, Sustainable Development
**Motto**: "Books to build a new society."

Founded in 1982, New Society Publishers' mission is to publish books that contribute in fundamental ways to building an ecologically sustainable and just society, and to do so with the least impact upon the environment. New Society is an activist publisher focusing mostly on positive, solutions-oriented books. Subject areas range from conflict education to conscientious commerce and more. As an activist press, New Society publishes on acid-free paper that is 100 percent old growth forest free, processed chlorine free, and printed with vegetable-based low VOC inks. It is the first North American press to become carbon neutral by purchasing carbon offsets equal to the amount of carbon produced by the printing process (213 tons of emissions). The press won the 2003 Jim Douglas British Columbia Publisher of the Year Award. Noteworthy is William Rees' and Mathis Wackernagel's *Our Ecological Footprint*, a book that has been translated into many languages. Examples of titles include Betsy Leondar-Wright's *Class Matters: cross-class alliance for middle class activists*, a guide to building bridges across class lines and collaborating more effectively in mixed-class social change efforts, and William H. Kemp's *The Renewable Energy Handbook: a guide to rural energy independence, off-grid and sustainable living*, a guide to reducing energy usage in the home.

## NEW VICTORIA PUBLISHERS, INC.
P.O. Box 27
Norwich, VT 05055
(802) 649-5297  Fax: same
Email: newvic@aol.com  Web: www.newvictoria.com

**Editor**: Claudia McKay and Beth Dingman
**ISBN prefix**: 0-934678
**Average number of new titles published per year**: 2-3
**Number of titles in print**: 80
**Other material produced**: took over Charis Video, distributor of lesbian and feminist videos and DVDs.
**Distributor**: publisher direct via website's order form or by phone (800) 326-5297; trade orders through Bookworld (800) 593-9673
**Publication interests**: Humor, Lesbian, Literary, Mystery, Romance
**Motto**: "Lesbian feminist books."

Founded in 1976, New Victoria Publishers publishes books describing and reflecting lesbian/feminist culture. The press is a nonprofit, literary and cultural organization publishing mostly mystery, romance, humor, and other fiction. There are a few nonfiction titles, such as Laura Post's *Backstage Pass:*

*interviews with women in music* and LaVerne Gagehabib's *Circles of Power: shifting dynamics in a lesbian-centered community*, a portrait of the lives, principles and dreams of the women of the Southern Oregon women's land community. The book is an in-depth view of self-sufficient communities based on feminist ideals of sharing and cooperation. In fiction, Jean Marcy's (actually two authors, Jean and Marcy) won the Lambda Literary Award 2001 in the Best Lesbian Mystery category for *Mommie Deadest*, the third novel in the Meg Darcy Mystery series.

## THE NORDIC AFRICA INSTITUTE/NORDISKA AFRIKANSTI-TUTET

P.O. Box 1703
SE - 751 47 Uppsala, Sweden
+46-(0) 18 56 22 00  Fax: +46-(0) 18 56 22 90
Email: nai@nai.uu.se  Web: www.nai.uu.se/indexeng.html

**Editor**: Lennart Wohlgemuth, Director
**ISBN prefix**: 91-7106
**Average number of new titles published per year**: 20-30
**Number of titles in print**: 300
**Other materials produced**: News from the Nordic Africa Institute, online newsletter (free)
**Distributor**: publisher direct via website, or by email (orders@nai.uu.se), phone or fax; North American orders via Stylus Publishing, www.styluspub.com, (800) 232-0223
**Publication interests**: Africa, Development Studies, Economics, Globalization, Health, History, Human Rights, Hunger, International Issues/Relations, Politics, Social Change, Social Issues, Third World, Urban Issues, Women's Issues/Studies
Founded in 1962, The Nordic Africa Institute is a leading center for research, documentation and information on contemporary Africa in the Nordic countries. The Institute publishes high-quality manuscripts, primarily the results of the research carried out at the Institute, meant to facilitate policy decisions on current African issues. The target groups for the publications are aimed at an international readership, especially research and education communities, decision-makers and development administrators, representatives of the media, and non-governmental organizations. The publications are in English, French and Swedish. Examples of titles include: Gislea Geisler's *Women and the Remaking of Politics in Southern Africa*, analyses post-colonial outcomes and examines the strategies employed by women's movements to gain a foothold in politics;

*Globalization and the Southern African Economies*, edited by Mats Lundahl, provides insight into how Southern African nations' participation in global development has unfolded in the past and into the problems and challenges of the future; and Eva Poluha's *The Power of Continuity: Ethiopia through the eyes of its children*, a study where children are used as a window to an Ethiopian society where hierarchical relations persist, despite the numerous political and administrative transformations of the past century.

## OCEAN PRESS

P.O. Box 3279                         P.O. Box 1186
North Melbourne                     Old Chelsea Station
Victoria 3001 Australia            New York, NY 10113-1186
61-3-9362  Fax: 61-3-9329-5040    (212) 260-3690

Email: info@oceanbooks.com.au
Web: www.oceanbooks.com.au

**Editor**: Deborah Shnookal
**Associated    with**:    The    Che    Guevara    Archive, www.oceanbooks.com.au/clibrary/, a companion site hosted by Ocean Press containing a library of writings by and about Che, a collection of images, and the Che Guevara Studies Center, Havana, Cuba.
**ISBN prefix**: 1-876175, 1-920888
**Average number of new titles published per year**: 20
**Number of titles in print**: 60
**Other materials produced**: DVDs
**Distributor**: publisher direct via websites's shopping cart feature; Consortium (USA)
**Publication interests**: Bilingual, Biography/Memoir, Globalization, History, International Issues/Relations, Latin American Studies, Politics, Social Change, Social Justice
**Motto**: "In the world to change the world."

Founded in 1989, Ocean Press publishes radical books on Cuba, Latin America, world politics, and social change. Authors include Ernesto Che Guevara, Fidel Castro, Noan Chomsky, Joe Slovo, Salvador Allende, Nidia Diaz, and Jose Marti. The press has an expanding list of Spanish language books and due to the special focus on Latin America the primary market is North America. The Radical History series seeks to restore the memory of events, struggles, and people erased from conventional (and conservative) histories and media, for example, *Chile: the other September 11*, edited by Pilar Aguilera and Ricardo Fredes, an anthology of reflection on the 1973 coup. Other examples of titles include: Che Guevara's *Motorcycle Diaries*, the youthful scribblings of Che's travels with Alberto Granado; Ignacio Ramonet's *Wars of the 21st Century: new threats, new fears*, argues that civil society must reclaim its place as the key protagonist on the international political stage; and Victor Serge's *What Every Radical Should Know About State Repression: a guide for activists*.

## ONLYWOMEN PRESS
40d St. Lawrence Terrace
London W10 5ST, United Kingdom
020 8354 0796  Fax: 020 8960 2817
Email: onlywomenpress@aol.com  Web: www.onlywomenpress.com

**Editor**: Lilian Mohin
**ISBN prefix**: 906500
**Average number of new titles published per year**: 2
**Number of titles in print**: 48
**Distributor**: publisher direct via "buy now" feature (orders go through Bookplace Ltd); Alamo Square, alamosquare@earthlink.net, (USA)
**Publication interests**: Feminist, Lesbian, Mystery, Poetry, Romance, Short Stories
**Motto**: "We prioritize lesbian authors."

Founded in 1974, Onlywomen Press is a radical lesbian publisher of feminist fiction, theory and poetry. Onlywomen books are mostly fiction, including crime, mystery and poetry. Nonfiction books focus on literary criticism and feminist theory. Examples of nonfiction titles include Ann Menasche's *Leaving the Life: lesbians, ex-lesbians and the heterosexual imperative*, and Sylvia Martin's *Passionate Friends: Mary Fullerton, Mabel Singleton, and Miles Franklin*, a study of female friendships.

## OPEN HAND PUBLISHING
P.O. Box 20207
Greensboro, NC 27420
(336) 292-8585  Toll-free (866) 888-9229  Fax: (336) 292-8588
Email: info@openhand.com  Web: www.openhand.com

**Editor**: Sandra S. Koritz and Richard A. Koritz
**ISBN prefix**: 0-940880

**Average number of new titles published per year**: 3
**Number of titles in print**: 22
**Other materials produced**: curriculum guides
**Distributor**: publisher direct via website's order form or bookcart feature payable through PayPal
**Publishing interests**: African American, Biography/Memoir, Children/Juvenile, Ethnic/Ethnic Studies, History, Literary, Minorities, Multiculturalism, Poetry, Politics, Race/Racism, Social Change, Women's Studies
**Motto**: "Multicultural books for adults and children."

Founded in 1981, Open Hand Publishing publishes books that promote both positive social change and respect and understanding among people of diverse cultures and ethnic groups. The Contribution Series, for children in the 4th and 5th grades and new readers, contains titles such as Ruth Pelz's *Women of the Wild West* and *Black Heroes of the Wild West*. Books for children ages 8 to 12 include examples such as Gilbert "Bobbo" Ahigble's and Louise Meyer's *Master Weavers from Ghana*, an introduction to the craft of weaving in West Africa, a book that helps Africa come alive for students. Other titles include: Ninotchka Rosca's *Jose Maria Sison: at home in the world--portrait of a revolutionary*, the initial title for the Anti-Imperialist Series, a biography of a Filipino revolutionary leader in his struggle to achieve freedom from the "embrace" of the U.S. government; *Stone on Stone/Piedra sobre Piedra*, edited by Zoe Anlesey, poetry by women of diverse heritage; Chuck Stone's *Squizzy the Black Squirrel: a fabulous fable of friendship*, dialogues about acceptance and friendship for 5 to 9 year olds, and winner of the 2004 Skipping Stone Magazine's National Honor Award in the "Multicultural and International Books" category.

## ORBIS BOOKS

Walsh Building, Box 308
Maryknoll, NY 10545-0308
(914) 941-7636, ext. 2477 or 2477  Fax: (914) 941-7005
Email: orbisbooks@maryknoll.org  Web: www.orbisbooks.org

**Editor**: Robert Ellsberg
**Associated with**: Maryknoll, the U.S.-based Catholic mission movement.
**ISBN prefix**: 1-57075
**Average number of new titles published per year**: 50-60
**Number of titles in print**: 400+
**Other materials produced**: *Maryknoll Magazine*, *Revista Maryknoll*, Web-based Action Alerts, videos and DVDs, posters, and other

**Distributor**: publisher direct via website's shopping cart feature, or by phone (800) 258-5838 Dept. WEB, or fax (914) 941-7005
**Publishing interests**: Developing Countries, Globalization, Human Rights, Hunger, Peace, Politics, Poor/Poverty, Refugees, Religion, Social Issues, Social Justice, Spirituality, Third World
**Motto**: "Peace, justice and the integrity of creation."

Founded in 1970, Orbis Book is the publishing imprint of Maryknoll founded to bring the voices of Third World peoples to First World ears. Orbis received the 2005 book award from Pax Christi, the nation's leading peace group. The books provide a global perspective on matters of faith, and are meant to amplify the voices of the poor on earth and foster dialog among people of different faiths. Books address global problems such as human rights abuses, world debt, making AIDS medication accessible, and providing for the world's poor. Examples of titles include: Jay McDonald's *Ghandi's Hope: learning from world religions as a path to peace*, emphasizes not that truth is one while the paths are many, but that the truths are many and make the world richer; James R. Brockman's *Romero: a life*, 25th anniversary edition of the definitive biography of Oscar Romero, the prophetic archbishop of San Salvador, assassinated while celebrating mass; and Robert Ellsberg's *Dorothy Day: selected writings*, a collection of works by the co-founder of the Catholic Worker movement and her lifelong option for the poor and her devotion to active nonviolence. Orbis also distributes books for Plough Publishing, a project of the Bruderhof, a community of people who live their lives based on Jesus' teachings of nonviolence, love of neighbors and enemies, and sexual purity.

## THE ORION SOCIETY
187 Main St.
Great Barrington, MA 01230
(413) 528-4422  Fax: (413) 528-0676
Email: orion@orionsociety.org  Web: www.oriononline.org

**Editor**: Jennifer Sahn
**ISBN prefix**: 0-913098
**Average number of new titles published per year**: 2
**Number of titles in print**: 12
**Other materials produced**: *Orion* magazine
**Distributor**: publisher direct via website's order feature
**Publication interests**: Activism, Conservation, Ecology/Environmentalism, Education, Ethics Natural/Nature, Politics

**Motto**: "Become engaged, choose your world."

Founded in 1982, The Orion Society's mission is to inform, inspire, and engage individuals and grassroots organizations in becoming a significant cultural force for healing nature and community. The Society was the 2004 winner of the Independent Press Association's IPPY Award for General Excellence in publications. The publications combine the focus of environmentalism with other broad topics including ethics, democracy, spiritual and culture. The New Patriotism Series are comprised of timely essays on the values and leadership of our nation, and our responsibilities as just citizens in a "new world order." The Nature Literacy Series offers both philosophical background and practical examples of place-based education in action emphasizing an interdisciplinary study of an individual's home ground–the continuum of nature and culture that defines community. Examples of titles include: David Sobel's *Placed-based Education: connecting classrooms and community*; Wendell Berry's *In the Presence of Fear: three essays for a changed world*; and Terry Tempest Williams' *The Open Space of Democracy: a perspective on the ethics and politics of place, spiritual democracy, and the responsibilities of citizen engagement.*

## OXFAM
274 Banbury Road                         26 West Street
Oxford OX2 7DZ England                      Boston, MA 02111
+44(0) 1865 312610         (800) 776-9326 Fax: (617) 728-2594
Email: oxfam@oxfam.org.uk, info@oxfamamerica.org
Web: www.oxfam.org.uk, www.oxfamamerica.org

**Associated with**: Oxfam International is an international group of independent non-governmental organizations, established in 12 countries, providing emergency assistance to over 40 countries.
**ISBN prefix**: 0-855984, 1-870727 (Oxfam GB)
**Number of titles in print**: 300
**Other materials produced**: *Oxfam Exchange* magazine, briefing papers and notes, discussion papers
**Distributor**: Stylus Publishing www.styluspub.com (U.S.), Fernwood Books (Canada)
**Publication interests**: Conservation, Developing Countries, Ecology/Environmentalism, Economics, Globalization, Health, Human Rights, Hunger, International Issues/Relations, Peace, Politics, Poor/Poverty, Refugees, Social Justice, Third World, Women's Issues/Studies
**Motto**: "A just world without poverty."

Founded in 1980, Oxfam is a development, relief, and campaigning organization dedicated to finding lasting solutions to poverty and suffering around the world. "Oxfam" was the original postal abbreviation for the Oxford Committee for Famine Relief, which was started in England in World War II to provide relief to war victims in Europe. Oxfam believes that the lives of all human beings are of equal value, and in a world rich in resources, poverty is an injustice that must be overcome. The organization works to eliminate the root causes of social and economic inequalities by challenging the structural barriers that foster conflict and human suffering and limit people from gaining the skills, resources and power to become self-sufficient. Most publications are in the form of briefing papers or research reports available free for downloading. Examples of books include: *Partnerships for Girls' Education*, a case study of what partnerships are most likely to increase opportunities for girls and women; *The Coffee Crisis Continues: situation assessment and policy recommendations for reducing poverty in the coffee sector*; and *Congressional Testimony: the implementation of DR-CAFTA*, presents the rules set forth in the DR-CAFTA legislation on agriculture, intellectual property, and investment that add up to a bad deal for farmers, workers and consumers in Central America and the Dominican Republic. Each of the two websites have different publication offerings.

## PACT PUBLICATIONS
1200 18th St. NW, Suite 350
Washington, DC 20036
(202) 466-5666  Fax: (202) 466-5669
Email: books@pacthq.org  Web: www.pactpublications.org

**Editor**: Sarah Newhall, President
**ISBN prefix**: 1-888753
**Affiliated press names**: Impact Alliance Press, an imprint, publishes books written by members of Impact Alliance, www.impactalliance.org
**Associated with**: distributes books from other organizations, such as Earthscan, Oxfam, Strategies for Hope, Save the Children, and Kummarian
**Average number of new titles published per year**: 8
**Number of titles in print**: 800+ including distributed titles from other publishers
**Distributor**: publisher direct via website's shopping cart feature, or through worldwide distributors listed in the website.
**Publication interests**: Activism, Development Studies, Education, Human Rights, Peace, Poverty, Social Change, Social Justice

**Motto**: "Sources for the international development community."

Founded in 1985, Pact Publications is an integrated publishing house that facilitates the development, design, production and distribution of progressive tools and materials for the international development community. Pact (Private Agencies Collaborating Together), www.pactworld.org, is a networked global organization that builds the capacity of local leaders and organizations to meet pressing social needs in dozens of countries around the world. The work is firmly rooted in the belief that local communities must be the driving force in ending poverty and injustice. The PAL Program (Publications at Low-cost) is a fund for southern agencies without the financial resources to purchase the materials. The Pact initiative grow out of grassroots participation and enterprise that help communities combat HIV/AIDS, protect the environment, operate village banks, resolve conflicts, enhance food security, empower women, and strengthen human rights and democratic participation. Examples of titles include Cynthia Sampson et al., *Positive Approaches to Peacebuilding: a resource for innovators*, and *Capitalizing on Knowledge: strategies for empowering communities through information and knowledge exchange.*

## PANGAEA
226 Wheeler St. South
St. Paul, MN 55105-1927
(651) 690-3320  Fax: same
Email: info@pangaea.org  Web: www.pangaea.org
**Editor**: Bonnie Hayskar
**ISBN prefix**: 0-9630180
**Average number of new titles published per year**: 3
**Number of titles in print**: 16
**Distributor**: publisher direct via website's shopping cart feature (books come through IndyBook.com) or by phone, fax, or postal mail (online order form available)
**Publication interests**: Anthropology, Bilingual, Conservation, Cultural Studies, Ecology/Environmentalism, Human Rights, Indigenous Peoples, Natural/Nature, Social Justice, Sociology, Third World
**Motto**: "Publisher for nature and peoples of the earth."

Founded in 1991, Pangaea is an independent publishing house focused on the natural history of the earth and on her people producing multilingual natural history and cultural works with an emphasis on the Americas. The Earth appeared differently 225 million years ago. All continental landmasses were joined into one supercontinent, later named Pangaea, surrounded by the Pan-thalassa Sea, a universal ocean. Named from the Greek, *pan* means "all" and *gaea* "Earth." Many of the books are bilingual in Spanish and English. Pan-gaea maintains the Street Children–Community Children Worldwide Re-source Library website, www.pangaea.org/street_children/kids.htm, with links to articles, organization, print and media resources, human rights treaties and documents, and other materials. The books on ecotourism and natural resources were developed in conjunction with in-country authorities on con-servation. Examples of titles include Daniel Cheng Yang's *Kakuma Turkana: dueling struggles: Africa's forgotten peoples*, documents the way of life of the indige-nous Turkana of Kenya, an ancient pastoralist people, and the over 81,000 refugees of civil war in East Africa, and Nancy Leigh Tierney's *Robbed of Hu-manity: lives of Guatemalan street children*, an analysis of the social conditions that send children, unprotected, to the streets and what they encounter.

## PARIS PRESS

P.O. Box 487
Ashfield, MA 01330
(413) 628-0051  Fax: same
Email: info@parispress.org  Web: www.parispress.org

**Editor**: Jan Freeman
**ISBN prefix**: 0-9638183, 1-930464
**Average number of new titles published per year**: 2-3
**Number of titles in print**: 11
**Other materials produced**: CDs
**Distributor**: publisher direct via website's shopping cart feature (payment through PayPal) or postal mail using the online order form; Consortium
**Publication interests**: Literary, Poetry, Reprints, Social Issues, Women's Issues/Studies
**Motto**: "Literature by women."

Founded in 1995, Paris Press publishes works by women that have been ne-glected or misrepresented by the literary world. The editor values works that are daring in style and in courage to speak truthfully about society, culture, history, and the human heart. Examples of titles include: Bryher's *Visa for Avalon*, a futuristic novel written over 40 years ago, yet still manages to speak directly to the politics of today warning against apathy and its effects on civil rights; Jan Freeman's *Autumn Sequence*, poems celebrating women's erotica; Adrian Oktenberg's *The Bosnia Elegies*, poems that confront the terrible human realities of the war in Bosnia; Virginia Woolf's *On Being Ill*, a discussion of taboos associated with illness and how it changes our relationship to the world around us; and Elizabeth Cady Stanton's *Solitude of Self*, a reflection on solitude and its integral relationship to self-reliance and equality.

## PATHFINDER PRESS
306 W. 37th St., 10th floor
New York, NY 10018
(212) 741-0690  Fax: (212) 727-0150
Email: pathfinder@pathfinderpress.com  Web: www.pathfinderpress.com

**Editor**: Mary-Alice Waters, President and senior editor
**ISBN prefix**: 0-87348, 0-913460
**Average number of new titles published per year**: 6-8
**Number of titles in print**: 390
**Other materials produced**: *New International: a magazine of Marxist politics and theory* and the *Education for Socialists* bulletin; also, posters, videos, pamphlets
**Distributor**: publisher direct via website's shopping cart feature, or by mail, P.O. Box 162767, Atlanta, GA 30321-2767
**Publication interests**: Economics, Globalization, History, Labor/Labor Studies, Politics, Reprints, Social Issues, Social Justice, Socialism/Marxism, Unions/Unionizing, Women's Issues/Studies
**Motto**: "Writings and speeches of revolutionary leaders from around the world."

Founded in 1970, Pathfinder Press is both a publisher and distributor of the works of the leaders of struggles by working people worldwide against exploitation and oppression. Authors include Karl Marx, Friedrich Engels, V. I. Lenin, Rosa Luxemburg, Leon Trotsky, Fidel Castro, Ernesto Che Guevara, and others. Some materials are available in Spanish, French and other languages. Examples of titles include: Jack Barnes' *Capitalism's World Disorder: working-class politics at the millennium*, argues that workers and farmers have the power to transform the world; *Malcolm X Talks to Young People*, four talks and an interview given to young people in the last months of Malcolm X's life; James Cannon's *History of American Trotskyism: report of a participant*, a series of 12 talks given in 1942 that recount a decisive period in the efforts to build a proletarian party in the U.S.; and Armando Hart's *Aldabonazo: inside the Cuban revolutionary underground, 1952-58*, a firsthand account of the men and women who led the urban underground in the fight against the U.S.-backed tyranny in the 1950s.

## PEMMICAN PUBLICATIONS
150 Henry Ave.
Winnipeg, Manitoba R3B 0J7 Canada
(204) 589-6346  Fax: (204) 589-2063
Email: pemmican@pemmican.mb.ca  Web: www.pemmican.mb.ca

**Editor**: Diane Ramsay, Managing Editor
**Associated with**: The Metis Culture and Heritage Resource Centre
**ISBN prefix**: 0-919143, 0-921827, 1-894717
**Average number of new titles published per year**: 6-8
**Number of titles in print**: 85
**Distributor**: publisher direct via website's downloadable order form that can
be faxed or emailed; Goodminds.com (Brantford, Ontario).
**Publication interests**: Adolescent, Children/Juvenile, Cultural Studies,
Indigenous Populations, Poetry
**Motto**: "Committed to the promotion of Metis culture and heritage."

Founded in 1980, Pemmican Publications is committed to publishing books
which depict Metis, First Nations and Aboriginal cultures and lifestyles in a
positive and accurate manner addressing historical, social and contemporary
issues. Pemmican was incorporated as a Metis publishing house for Metis and
Aboriginal people to tell their own stories from their own perspectives. The
publications depict traditional lifestyles, the art of oral storytelling, living in
harmony with nature and the environment, and the heritage of Metis and the
Providence of Manitoba. The press also publishes books by non-Aboriginal
writers whose works are related to Metis and Aboriginal issues. The press is a
leading publisher of Inuit literature and children's books. Examples of titles
include: Jane Chartrand's *How the Eagle Got His White Head*, an Algonquin legend, Lawrence J. Barkwell's *Metis Legacy*, a press bestseller, details the contributions of the Metis people to Canada, winner of the 2002 Saskatchewan
Book Award for Publishing in Education, and *La Laveng: Michif peekishkwewin,
The Heritage Language of the Canadian Metis, vol. 1 Language Practice, vol. 2 Language
Theory* (grades 9-12).

## THE PILGRIM PRESS
700 Prospect Ave.
Cleveland, OH 44115-1100
(216) 736-3764  Fax: (216) 736-2207
Email: pilgrim@ucc.org  Web: www.pilgrimpress.com

**Editor**: Timothy G. Staveteig
**Associated with**: Pilgrim Press is a division of the United Church for Homeland Ministries of the United Church of Christ
**ISBN prefix**: 0-8298
**Average number of new titles published per year**: 50
**Number of titles in print**: 450
**Distributor**: publisher direct via website's bookcart feature, or by phone (800) 537-3394 or fax (216) 736-2206
**Publication interests**: Ecology/Environmentalism, Ethics, Feminist, Globalization, Multiculturalism, Peace, Religion, Sexuality, Social Justice, Spirituality
**Motto**: "Addressing difficult and complex social issues in the context of faith."

Founded in 1621, Pilgrim Press, the oldest press in the United States, is devoted to giving the voiceless a voice, opposing injustice, and providing ethical insights to an increasingly fragile planet. A religious community fled Great Britain in 1608 to establish a religious community in the open intellectual atmosphere of Leyden, Netherlands. Having been excluded from the dominant religious culture, the press sought ways to lift up marginalized voices of conscience and encourage those who resisted practices of domination. Its publishing efforts so infuriated King James I that he instructed his ambassador to have the presses destroyed. The Pilgrims set sail, this time to establish Plymouth Colony, and there established the press. While many titles fall within the traditional areas of Christianity—confirmation, hymnals, ministry, etc., others continue the historical vision producing titles such as *Global Voice: for Gender Justice*, edited by Ana Maria Tepedino, Dwight Hopkins and Ramathate T.H. Dolamo, an anthology of essays written by theologians from Africa, Asia, Latin America, and U.S. minority groups; Mary E. Hobgood's *Dismantling Racism: an ethics of accountability*, identifies an ethical agenda for social elites and seeks to persuade them that an agenda of justice and an ethics of accountability will be of primary benefit to them; and The Earth Bible Series, edited by Norman C. Habel and Shirley Wurst, introduces in four titles a new understanding of the earth using six ecojustice principles, moving beyond identifying ecological themes in creation theology.

**PLAIN VIEW PRESS**
P.O. Box 42255
Austin, TX 78704
(512) 441-2452 Fax: same

Email: sbright1@austin.rr.com
Web: www.plainviewpress.net

**Editor**: Susan Bright
**ISBN prefix**: 0-911051, 1-891386
**Average number of new titles published per year**: 16
**Number of titles in print**: 50
**Distributor**: publisher direct via website's shopping cart feature. Newest titles books are available
through Ingram's print on demand fulfillment center, Lightning Source. Eventually all titles will be through Lightning Source.
**Publication interests**: Ecology/Environmentalism, Feminist, Gender Studies, Human Rights, Literary, Peace, Poetry, Social Justice, Women's Issues/Studies
**Motto**: "We find healing in existing reality."

Founded in 1975, Plain View Press grew out of the feminist movement and its books are authored by a far-flung community of activists who bring humanitarian enlightenment to individuals and communities grappling with major issues of our time—peace, justice, environment, education and gender. The books are issue-based, literary, and culture and gender diverse resulting from artistic collaboration between writers, artists and editors. The New Voices Series is a showcase for new American writers often in the form of an edited edition of writers. The Foundation Series, produced in collaboration with the Foundation for a Compassionate Society, presents the theoretical vision and activism that emerged from the World's Women's Movement at the end of the 20th century. Here are guiding principles for a new feminism for both activists and common women who have worked for freedom, justice, compassion, and respect for all people. A title example is *Feminist Family Values Forum*, edited by Susan Bright, containing poems by Gloria Steinem, Angela Davis, Maria Jimeniz, and Miliani Trask.

## PLUTO PRESS
345 Archway Road
London N6 5AA United Kingdom
+44(0) 208 348 2724  Fax: +44(0) 208 348 9133
Email: pluto@plutobooks.com  Web: www.plutobooks.com

**Editor**: Roger van Zwanenberg, Publisher, and Anne Beech, Editorial Director

**ISBN prefix**: 0-7453, 0-86104, 0-902818, 0-904383, 1-85305
**Average number of new titles published per year**: 60
**Number of titles in print**: 400+
**Distributor**: publisher direct via website's shopping cart feature; University of Michigan Press (800) 621-2736 or email custserv@press.uchicago.edu (USA); UBC Press, www.ubcpress.ca (Canada)
**Publication interests**: Anthropology, Black Studies, Critical Theory, Cultural Studies, Ecology/Environmentalism, Economics, Globalization, History, International Issues/Relations, Law/Legal Studies, Media Studies, Middle East Studies, Politics, Social Issues, Social Justice
**Motto**: "Independent progressive publishing."

Founded in 1970, Pluto Press, one of the leading progressive independent presses, is committed to publishing the best in critical writing across the social sciences and humanities. Authors include Pierre Bourdieu, Jean Baudrillard, Frantz Fanon, Susan George, Antonio Gramski, Manning Marable, and bell hooks. Examples of titles include: Andrew Simms' *Ecological Debt: the health of the planet and the wealth of nations*, explores the global wealth gap built on ecological debts which the world's poor are now having to pay for; Li Onesto's *Dispatches from the People's War in Nepal*, interviews of those involved in Nepal's Maoist revolution; and David Mosse's *Cultivating Development: an ethnography of aid policy and practice*, explains practical problems in development and examines the politics and ethics of engaging with development.

## POLYCHROME PUBLISHING COMPANY
4509 North Francisco
Chicago, IL 60625-3808
(773) 478-4455  Fax: (773) 478-0786
Email: info@polychromebooks.com  Web: www.polychromebooks.com

**ISBN prefix**: 1-879965
**Average number of new titles published per year**: 2
**Number of titles in print**: 17
**Distributor**: publisher direct via website's shopping cart feature or by phone or fax
**Publication interests**: Asian American, Children/Juvenile, Cultural Studies, Discrimination, Ethnic, Minorities, Multiculturalism, Poetry, Race/Race Relations
**Motto**: "Stories of color for a colorful world."

Founded in 1990, Polychrome Publishing is the only publisher in the country that specializes in producing Asian American children's books, pre-kindergarten through 8th grade. These books are meant to validate experiences common to Asian American children and educate others about the Asian American community, its needs, concerns and interests. The books offer children the tools to value their own experience as well as to understand the diverse cultural heritages of others. "Polychrome" means many colors, and the press produces children's books for a multicultural market, books that introduce characters and illustrate situations with which children of all colors can identify. The books are designed to promote racial, ethnic, cultural, and religious tolerance and understanding. The publications portray children of all colors as they see themselves and the world around them. Examples of titles include: *Children of Asian America*, compiled on behalf of the Asian American Coalition, an anthology of children's stories and poems about the experiences of being an Asian American child from ten different Asian ethnic communities; Sandra S. Yamate's *Ashok by Any Other Name*, about an Indian American boy who wishes he had a more "American" name; and Esther Chiu's *The Lobster and the Sea*, story of an Asian American child who must reconcile American values with Asian ones when her grandfather decides that it's time to return home.

## THE POST-APOLLO PRESS

35 Marie St.
Sausalito, CA 94965
(415) 332-1458  Fax: (415) 332-8045
Email: postapollo@earthlink.net  Web: www.postapollopress.com

**Editor**: Simone Fattal
**ISBN prefix**: 0-942996
**Average number of new titles published per year**: 3-4
**Number of titles in print**: 44
**Distributor**: publisher direct via website's printable pricelist and order form, or by phone, fax or email; Small Press Distribution
**Publication interests**: Feminist, Literary, Poetry, Translations, Women's Issues/Studies

Founded in 1982, The Post-Apollo Press specializes in writing mostly by women in quality paperback editions of fine literature, poetry and essays. Fattal founded the press in order to publish an English translation of *Sitt Marie-Rose*, a feminist novel on the Lebanese Civil War by Etel Adnan, a prominent poet, painter and essayist. Fattal went on to introduce other major foreign poets and writers to the U.S. The name refers to the Apollo space program that sent men to the moon and opened a new age and a "new dimension to our imagination." Authors include internationally-known poets Etel Adnan and Anne-Marie Albiach, and novelists Marguerite Duras and Ulla Berkewicz. Examples of titles include Marc Atherton's *Where the Rocks Started*, a journey into the chaos of Columbia, and Joanne Kyger's *Some Life*, poems about the deep attachment to nature and friendship. Iva de Vitray-Meyerovitch's *Rumi and Sufism*, translated from the French by Simone Fattal and illustrated with 45 photos is an important scholarly study on the great poet Rumi, his life and work, providing the American reader with a broader understanding of Islam and Sufism.

## THE PUSHCART PRESS
P.O. Box 380
Wainscott, NY 11975
(631) 324-9300

**Editor**: Bill Henderson
**ISBN prefix**: 0-916366, 1-888889
**Average number of new titles published per year**: 3
**Number of titles in print**: 75
**Distributor**: W.W. Norton (800) 233-4830; Penguin Books Canada (800) 399-6858
**Publication interests**: Anthologies, Literary, Poetry, Reference

Founded in 1972, The Pushcart Press encourages the noncommercial press and publishes important and unusual book manuscripts that have been over-looked by commercial firms. The press produces the distinguished Pushcart Prize, an annual anthology of best short stories, poems and essays from small press and literary magazines. *Pushcart Prize: the best of the small presses*, is a yearly anthology of fiction, essays and poetry from the small presses chosen by writers. The press also produces books for the writers, for example, *Writing for Your Life: today's outstanding authors talk about the art of writing and the job of publishing*, edited by Sybil S. Steinburg and Jonathan Bing, and Bill Henderson's *Publish It Yourself: literary tradition and how-to*. At the 2001 Small Press Book Fair in New York, Bill Henderson, founder and publisher, was honored with the Small Press Center's Poor Richard's Award (now called the Ben Award), marking an individual's outstanding contribution to publishing.

## THE RALPH J. BUNCHE CENTER FOR AFRICAN AMERICAN STUDIES

160 Haines Hall
P.O. Box 951545
Los Angeles, CA 90095-1545
(310) 825-7403 Fax: (310) 825-5019
Web: www.bunchecenter.ucla.edu

**Editor**: Darnell M. Hunt, Director
**Associated with**: University of California at Los Angeles
**ISBN prefix**: 0-934934
**Average number of new titles published per year**: 1-2
**Number of titles in print**: 11
**Other materials produced**: *Bunche Review* and the *Bunche Research Report*
**Distributor**: publisher direct via websites's order form or by phone (800) 206-2227
**Publication interests**: African American, Cultural Studies, Development Studies, Discrimination, Economics, Minorities, Political, Race/Race Relations, Social Issues, Social Justice, Urban Issues

Founded in 1970, The Ralph J. Bunche Center for African American Studies' mission is to disseminate new knowledge about people of African descent throughout the Diaspora. The publications illuminate the past and present social, economic and political conditions of African Americans and connect the struggles for social and economic justice in our own society with those of disenfranchised peoples of the world. There are four publication series: CAAS Afro-American Culture and Society, CAAS Urban Policy Series, CAAS Community Classics, and Minority Economic Development Series. Examples of titles include: St. Clair Drake's *Black Folk Here and There*, 2 vols, presents a wide range of theories that attempt to explain what happens when Black people and white people interact and why color prejudice may arise; Paul Von Blum's *Resistance, Dignity, and Pride: African American art in Los Angeles*, presents the lives and works of sixteen African American visual artists who have collectively made powerful contributions to African American art history; and Trevor Purcell's *Banana Fallout: class, color, and culture among West Indians in Costa Rica*.

## RED LETTER PRESS
4710 University Way NE, #100
Seattle, WA 98105
(206) 985-4621  Fax: (206) 985-8965
Email: redletterpress@juno.com  Web: redletterpress.org/index.html

**Editor**: Helen Gilbert
**Associated with**: Radical Women and the Freedom Socialist Party
**ISBN prefix**: 0-932323
Average number of new titles published per year: **2**
**Number of titles in print**: 30
**Other materials produced**: booklets, pamphlets, special supplements from the *Freedom Socialist Newspaper*
**Distributor**: publisher direct via website's printable order form; Small Press Distribution
**Publication interests**: Critical Theory, Feminist, Globalization, Human Rights, Minorities, Politics, Social Issues, Social Justice, Socialism/Marxism, Women's Issues/Studies
**Motto**: "Radical perspectives on history, politics, and world events."

Founded in 1995, Red Letter Press is a nonprofit corporation that produces socialist feminist literature that advances human rights and combats prejudice and poverty by publishing works that educate about civil liberties, inform on international issues, analyze social problems, explore progressive political theories, and encourage dialogue and critical thought. The writings are meant to educate about the ideas, experiences and history of women, people of color, sexual minorities, workers, immigrants, Jews, youth and elders, and disabled, social-issue activists, radicals, and others whose voices and viewpoints are generally ignored by commercial publishers. A number of titles are in Spanish, and the materials are made available to the general public at affordable prices. The Red Banner Reader Series are socialism/anti-capitalism booklets, for example, Susan Williams' *Capitalism's Brutal Comeback in China*. The Radical Women's Publications are pamphlet-like publications on women's issues, for example, *3 Asian American Writers Speak Out on Feminism*. Examples of other titles include Clara Fraser's and Richard Fraser's *Crisis and Leadership*, on how and why the Socialist Worker's Party abandoned its revolutionary program, and Richard Fraser's and Tom Boot's *Revolutionary Integration: a Marxist analysis of African American liberation*.

# RE/SEARCH PUBLICATIONS
20 Romolo, Suite B
San Francisco, CA 94133
(415) 362-1465  Fax: (415) 362-0742
Email: info@researchpubs.com   Web: researchpubs.com

**Editor**: V. Vale
**ISBN prefix**: 0-940642
**Average number of new titles published per year**: 1
**Number of titles in print**: 20
**Other materials produced**: RE/Search eNewsletter on the website; distributes music CDs
**Distributor**: publisher direct via website's order form, or by phone, fax, or mail
**Publication interests**: Alternative Culture, Music, Popular Culture, Punk, Sexuality, Zines

Founded in 1980, RE/Search Publications was inspired by the punk rock cultural revolution and seeks to demystify the "control process" that thwarts creativity, joy, pleasure and exercise of freedom. The press produces books on body modification, sexuality, and subversive acts that cover a range of cultural peculiarities and anti-corporate activism, from sadomasochism to sword swallowing to zine culture. The press has published recorded conversations with certain counterculture notables including beat author William Burroughs, rocker/poet/publisher Henry Rollins, and pain-performance artist Bob Flanagan, among others. The RE/Search series represent many of the publications, for example, the best selling RE/Search #12, *Modern Primitives, personal tatooing, multiple piercings, and ritual sacrification*. Other title examples include: *Real Conversations 1: Henry Rollins, Jello Biafra, Lawrence Ferlinghetti, Billy Childish, and others*, recorded conversations which discuss many issues relevant to every creative artist and thinker; *Modern Pagans: an investigation of contemporary pagan practices*, interviews with many pagans about wicca, witchcraft, sex, child raising and more; and *J.G. Ballard Conversations* and *J.G. Ballard Quotes* from the visionary thinker and writer.

## RETHINKING SCHOOLS
1001 E. Keefe Ave.
Milwaukee, WI 53212
(414) 964-9646  Fax: (414) 964-7220
Email: webrs@execpc.com  Web: www.rethinkingschools.org
**Editor**: Leon Lynn, Book Director
**ISBN prefix**: 0-942961
**Average number of new titles published per year**: 1
**Number of titles in print**: 15
**Other materials produced**: *Rethinking Schools*, a quarterly journal, and T-shirts
**Distributor**: publisher direct via website's order form, or by phone (800) 669-4192 or fax
**Publication interests**: Activism, Education, Multiculturalism, Race/Race Relations, Social Change, Social Justice
**Motto**: "Agenda for change."

Founded in 1986, Rethinking Schools is committed to equity and to the vision that public education is central to the creation of a humane, caring, multiracial democracy. The motivating vision behind the Rethinking Schools organization is the notion of "the common school." This vision includes the belief that schools are integral "not only to preparing all children to be full participants in society, but also to be full participants in this country's ever-tenuous experiment in democracy." The organization has been intimately involved with addressing such educational issues as standardized testing, textbook-dominated curricula, and problems facing urban schools, particularly issues of race. Some of the books come from expanded issues of *Rethinking Schools* magazine, an activist publication with articles written by and for teachers, parents and students addressing key policy issues, such as vouchers, marketplace-oriented reforms, funding equity, and school-to-work. Examples of titles include *Rethinking Mathematics: teaching social justice by the numbers*, edited by Eric Gutstein and Bob Peterson, proposes teaching math in a way to help make the world more equal and just, and *Why the Testing Craze Won't Fix Our Schools*, edited by Kathy Swope and Barbara Miner, a critique of standardized tests and alternate ways to access how well our children are learning.

## RISING TIDE PRESS
P.O. Box 30457
Tucson, AZ 85751
(520) 888-1140  Fax: (520) 888-1123

Email: milestonepress@earthlink.net  Web: www.risingtidepress.com (under construction)

**Editor**: Brenda Kazen and Debra Tobin
ISBN prefix: **1-883061, 0-9628938**
**Number of titles in print**: 29
**Distributor**: Bella Books Distribution (800) 553-1973 or www.bellabooks.com (search under Rising Tide).
**Publication interests**: Adventure, Fantasy, Lesbian, Mystery, Romance, Science Fiction
**Motto**: "Books to stir the imagination."

Founded in 1991, Rising Tide Press is a woman-owned publishing company providing fiction and nonfiction that portrays women as strong, dynamic, creative forces. Rising Tide is expanding into the young adult market, particularly with books that depict strong role models for young adult readers. The press sponsors the Alice B Award, Reader's Appreciation for Writers of Lesbian Fiction. A title example is Gwen Leonhard's *Feathering Your Nest: an interactive workbook and guide to a loving lesbian relationship*.

**SEAL PRESS**
1400 65th St., Suite 250
Emeryville, CA 94608
(510) 595-3664  Fax: (510) 595-4228
Web: www.sealpress.com

**Editor**: Faith Conlon
**Affiliated press name**: imprint of Avalon Publishing Group
**ISBN prefix**: 1-58005, 0-931188, 1-878067
**Average number of new titles published per year**: 15
**Number of titles in print**: 160
**Distributor**: publisher direct via website's link to Amazon.com; Publishers Group West (800) 788-3123; Publishers Group West Canada
**Publication interests**: Erotica, Feminist, Health, Lesbian, Literary, Parenting, Poetry, Popular Culture, Travel, Women's Issues/Studies
**Motto**: "By women. For women."

Founded in 1976, Seal Press provides a forum for women writers and feminist issues. The books represent the diverse voices and interests of women—their lives, literature, and concerns, and are eclectic in topical coverage including body image, mystery, popular culture, parenting, and recovery, as well as substantial number of women's outdoor and adventure titles. Seal's authors are radical and original thinkers, professionals with a distinct point-of-view, gutsy explorers, truth-tellers, and writers who engender laughter, tears, and rage. Seal was launched with a single volume of poetry, printed by hand and distributed to bookstores in the Pacific Northwest. Several years later, the company published *Getting Free*, a handbook for battered women that had been turned down by every major New York publisher. The book was an overnight success and is now in its fourth edition. Examples of titles include: *Sex and Single Girls*, edited by Lee Damsky, has over forty contributors covering everything from online sex to masturbation; Inga Muscio's *Cunt* was the first health book for Africa American women and her *Autobiography of a Blue-eyed Devil: my life and time in a racist, imperialist society* argues that the history we learn in school is no more than a brand, developed by white men who, often unjustly, won the right to spin their stories as hard facts; Miriam Peskowitz's *The Truth Behind the Mommy Wars: who decides what makes a good mother?* explores the new century collision between work and mothering concluding that parents want more options and less judgment; and Kristin Rowe-Finkbeiner's *The F Word: feminism in jeopardy: women, politics and the future* won the 2004 IPPY Award in the Women's Issues category.

## SECOND STORY PRESS
20 Maud St., Suite 401
Toronto, Ontario M5SV 2M5 Canada
(416) 537-7850  Fax: (416) 537-0588
Email: info@secondstorypress.ca
Web: www.secondstorypress.on.ca

Editor: **Margie Wolfe, Publisher**
ISBN prefix: **1-896764, 0-921299, 0-929005, 1-897187**
**Average number of new titles published per year**: 13
**Number of titles in print**: 114
**Distributor**: publisher direct via postal mail; University of Toronto Press (800) 565-9523 (Canada); Orca Book Publisher (800) 210-5277 (USA)
**Publication interests**: Children/Juvenile, Cookery, Disabilities, Feminist, Health, Judaica, Literary, Women's Issues/Studies, Young Adult
**Motto**: "Feminist publishers."

Founded in 1988, Second Story Press produces feminist titles for both adults, young adults and children, specializing in quality fiction and nonfiction that challenge, stimulate, delight and entertain. The Holocaust Remembrance Series for Young Readers has grown to six titles including Karen Levine's *Hana's Suitcase*, a multiple award winner, an ALA Notable Books Award, and a number one bestselling children's book in Canada. Examples of other titles include: *Hear Me Out! True stories of teens confronting homophobia* by Teens Educating and Confronting Homophobia, a project of Planned Parenthood; *A Princess, A Tiger, and Other Deaf Tales* by writers and illustrators who are deaf themselves, for readers under 8 years of age; *River of Hands*, stories for deaf children by deaf children; *Where's Mom's Hair?*, a picture book that helps youngsters understand a parent's chemotherapy, written by a cancer survivor and her two young sons; and *Consuming Passions: feminist approaches to weight preoccupation and eating disorders*, edited by Catrina Brown and Karin Jasper.

## SEE SHARP PRESS
P.O. Box 1731
Tucson, AZ 85702-1731
(520) 628-8270  Fax: same
Email: info@seesharppress.com  Web: www.seesharppress.com

**Editor**: Chaz Bufe
**ISBN prefix**: 0-9613289, 1-884365
**Average number of new titles published per year**: 2
**Number of titles in print**: 17
**Other materials produced**: pamphlets, bumper stickers
**Distributor**: publisher direct via website's shopping cart feature (payable through PayPal), or by mail using the website's printable order form, or by phone; Independent Publishers Group (IPG) (800) 888-4741
**Publication interests**: Anarchism, Atheism, Humor, Music, Reprints, Sexuality
**Motto**: "Rabble-rousing reading."

Founded in 1984, See Sharp Press publishes nonfiction on a wide variety of unusual and controversial topics in the areas of music, sex, anarchism, and atheism. In addition, the press is the only publisher in the U.S. specializing in deprogramming Alcoholics Anonymous, for example, Ken Ragge's *The Real AA: Behind the Myth of 12-step Recovery* and Stanton Peele's, Chaz Bufe's and Archie Brodsky's *Resisting 12-step Coercion: how to fight forced participation in AA, NA, or 12-step treatment*. Examples of other titles include: H.L. Mencken's *The Philosophy of Friedrich Nietzsche*; Frank Fernandez' *Cuban Anarchism: the history of a movement*, the story of the driving force behind Cuba's revolutionary and labor movements; Upton Sinclair's *The Jungle: the uncensored original edition* (1905); and Chaz Bufe's *An Understandable Guide to Music Theory: the most useful aspects of theory for rock, jazz, and blues musicians.*

## SERPENT'S TAIL
4 Blackstock Mews
London N4 2BT England
Email: info@serpentstail.com  Web: www.serpentstail.com

**Editor**: Pete Ayrton
**Affiliated press names**: Midnight Classics, Mask Noir, High Risk Books
**ISBN prefix**: 1-85242, 0-9631095
**Average number of new titles published per year**: 20
**Number of titles in print**: 250+
**Distributor**: publisher direct via website's shopping cart feature (can view prices in US dollars); Consortium
**Publication interests**: Alternative Culture, Avant-garde, Cultural Studies, Erotica, Film, Gay, Lesbian, Music, Mystery, Poetry, Popular Culture, Punk, Sexuality, Translations
**Motto**: "Committed to publishing extravagant, outlaw voices neglected by the mainstream."

Founded in 1986, Serpent's Tail produces challenging literature in well-designed, affordable paperback editions from writers whose voices do not normally have a venue in the mainstream press, for example, experimental writers, Blacks, Hispanics, and literature in translation. High Risk Books focuses on transgressive works of fiction and poetry. Midnight Classics reissues cult favorites. Mask Noir features the best of both new and established mystery writers. Music books include areas of rock, jazz and hip-hop. Other books showcase the work of America's and Britain's most important radical cultural communicators. Examples of titles include: John Godfrey's *Altered State: the story of ecstasy culture and acid house*, tracks the development of the Ecstasy culture; Erik Davis' *Tech Gnosis: myth, magic and mysticism in the age of information*; and *The Piano Teacher*, a haunting tale of morbid voyeurism and masochism, by Elfriede Jelinek, Austrian novelist, playwright and Nobel Prize winner in Literature in 2004.

## SEVEN STORIES PRESS
140 Watts St.
New York, NY 10013
(212) 226-8760  Fax: (212) 226-1411
Email: info@sevenstories.com  Web: www.sevenstories.com

**Editor**: Dan Simon, Publisher
**Affiliated press name**: Siete Cuentos, an imprint committed to publishing the fine works of literature and nonfiction titles for the Spanish speaking communities in the U.S. and beyond.
**ISBN prefix**: 1-58322, 1-888363
**Average number of new titles published per year**: 30
**Number of titles in print**: 150+
**Other materials produced**: *Autodafe*, the journal of the International Parliament of Writers
**Distributor**: publisher direct via the website's shopping cart feature or by phone (800) 596-7437; Consortium (800) 283-3572; Publishers Group Canada (800) 663-5714
**Publication interests**: Biography/Memoir, Health, Hispanic/Latino, History, Human Rights, International Issues/Relations, Latin American Studies, Literary, Media Studies, Poetry, Politics, Reprints, Translations

Founded in 1996, Seven Stories Press publishes works of the imagination together with political titles by voices of conscience. The press has consistently attracted many important voices away from the corporate publishing sector, including Noam Chomsky, Aung San Suu Kyi, Kurt Vonnegut, Angela Davis, and Howard Zinn. The press publishes reprints of classic works by noted authors, for example, Nelson Algren, Upton Sinclair and Anton Chekhov, and is an important publisher of works in translation, for example Jean Giono's *The Solitude of Compassion*, originally published in France 1932, a collection of short stories of small-town life. The press has published on First Amendment grounds, important books that were being refused the right to publish for political reasons, for example, Gary Webb's *Dark Alliance*, a book about the CIA-Contra-crack cocaine connection, Carol Felsonthal's biography of the Newhouse publishing family, *Citizen Newhouse*, and Mumia Abu-Jamal's censored essays in the award winning *All Things Censored*. The Open Media series, founded 1991, (brought to Seven Stories by senior editor Greg Ruggiero in 1997), has established itself as a leader in American peace and justice publishing, for example, Noam Chomsky's bestselling *9-11* and Ruggiero's *Microradio and Democracy: (Low) Power to the People*. Examples of other titles include Loretta Napoleoni's *Terror Incorporated: tracing the dollars behind the terror networks*, tracks the financiers behind global terrorism, and *The Future of Media: resistance and reform in the 21st century*, edited by Russell Newman, Ben Scott and Robert W. McChesney, about the state of media in the U.S. and what we can do about it.

## SIERRA CLUB BOOKS
85 Second St., 2nd floor
San Francisco, CA 94105
(415) 977-5500  Fax: (415) 977-5799
Email: information@sierraclub.org  Web: www.sierraclub.org/books

**Editor**: Helen Sweetland, Publisher
**Affiliated press names**: Sierra Club Books for Children
**ISBN prefix**: 0-375, 0-87156, 1-57805
**Average number of new titles published per year**: 12
**Number of titles in print**: 130
**Other materials produced**: *Sierra* magazine, calendars
**Distributor**: publisher direct via website's order for feature; University of California Press (800-777-4726, USA and Canada)
**Publication interests**: Children/Juvenile, Conservation, Development Studies, Education, Environment, Nature/Natural, Social Justice, Sustainable Development
**Motto**: "Explore, enjoy and protect the planet."

Founded in 1892, the Sierra Club is probably the most recognizable environmental organization in the United States. Know for its advocacy, the Sierra Club works on urgent campaigns to save threatened areas, and is concerned with problems associated with wilderness, forestry, clean air, coastal protection, energy conservation, population, international development lending, and land use. Most books fall in line with the club's advocacy efforts, but some titles are more mainstream, for example, the adventure guides and picture books. Examples of advocacy titles include: Daniel Imhoff's *Paper or Plastic: searching for solutions to an over packaged world*, addresses ways to counter the 300 pounds annually that each person produces in packaging waste; Carl Rope's and Paul Rauber's *Strategic Ignorance: why the Bush Administration is recklessly destroying a century of environmental progress*; Robert D. Bullard's *The Quest for Environmental Justice: human rights and the politics of pollution*; and Michael K. Stone's and Zenobia Barlow's *Ecological Literacy: educating our children for a sustainable world*.

## SISTER VISION PRESS

P.O. Box 217, Station E
Toronto, Ontario M6H 4E2 Canada
(416) 533-9353  Fax: (416) 533-9676
Email: sisvis@web.net

**Editor**: Makeda Silvera and Stephanie Martin
**Affiliated press names**: also referred to as Sister Vision: Black Women
and Women of Color Press
**ISBN prefix**: 0-920813, 1-896705
**Average number of new titles published per year**: recent publishing
activity could not be confirmed, but a backlist of titles is still available.
**Number of books in print**: 50
**Distributor**: University of Toronto Press (800) 565-9523
**Publishing interests**: Ethnic/Ethnic Studies, Indigenous Populations, Lesbian, Literary, Minorities, Poetry, Race/Race Relations, Women's Issues/Studies

Founded in 1985, Sister Vision Press gives voice through its publications to
Caribbean , Asian, First Nations, African and mixed-race women on many
themes and issues including those which have traditionally been silenced such
as lesbianism, bisexualism, and oppression. The press was founded by two
women from Jamaica (sistahs) who had a "vision" of publishing innovative,
challenging and provocative works by Canadian women of color. Examples of
titles include: Connie Fife's *The Colour of Resistance: a contemporary collection of
writing by aboriginal women*; Stephanie Martin's and Makeda Silvera's *Sapodilla:
the Sister Vision book of poetry*; Afua Cooper's *Utterances and Incantations: women,
poetry and dub*.

## SOFT SKULL PRESS

55 Washington St., Suite 804
Brooklyn, NY 11201
(718) 643-1599  Fax: (866) 881-4997
Email: richard@softskull.com  Web: www.softskull.com

**Editor**: Richard Eoin Nash, Publisher, Sarah Groff-Palermo, Managing Editor
**ISBN prefix**: 1-887128, 1-932360, 1-933368
**Average number of new titles published per year**: 6
**Number of titles in print**: 120+

**Distributor**: publisher direct via website's shopping cart feature, or by phone (888) 876-6622; Publishers Group West
**Publication interests**: Alternative Culture, Art, Biography/Memoir, Comics/Comix, Erotica, Gay, History, Lesbian, Music, Poetry, Politics, Punk
**Motto**: "Provocative food for the brain."

Founded in 1992, Soft Skull Press, spawned in the punk music and left political scene, publishes books that resist the defensive conformity of contemporary America. Soft Skull reprinted the controversial biography of George W. Bush, *Fortunate Son* (now in its 3rd edition) by J.H. Hatfield after St. Martin's Press recalled the book claiming that the "author's credibility has come into question." Example of titles include: Yvonne Bynoe's *Stand and Deliver: political activism, leadership and hip hop culture*, a critical analysis of the social and cultural issues related to the Hip Hop generation as it seeks to develop as a political movement; Jerome Sala's *Look Slimmer Instantly*, a poetic critique of the commercialism and shallowness of American media and culture; and J. Dee Hill's *Freaks and Fire: the underground reinvention of circus*, profiles of low-budget, seedy traveling shows.

## SOUTH END PRESS
7 Brookline St., #1
Cambridge, MA 02139-4146
(617) 547-4002  Fax: (617) 547-1333
Email: info@southendpress.org  Web: www.southendpress.org

**Editor**: as a worker's collective, everyone is an editor
**Associated with**: Institute for Social and Cultural Change (also includes *Z Magazine*, Znet, Alternative Radio, and Speak Out)
**ISBN prefix**: 0-89608
**Average number of new titles published per year**: 10-12
**Number of titles in print**: 200+
**Distributor**: publisher direct via website's shopping cart feature, or by phone (800) 533-8478, fax, or mail (with check or money order); Consortium (800) 283-3572 (U.S. and Canada)
**Publication interests**: African-American, American Indian, Asian American, Cultural Studies, Ecology/Environmentalism, Economics, Feminist, Gay, Globalization, Hispanic/Latino, International Issues/Relations, Lesbian, Media Studies, Middle East Studies, Political, Social Change, Social Issues, Social Justice, Sociology, Women's Issues/Studies
**Motto**: "Books to help you change your world."

Founded in 1977, South End Press is a nonprofit, collectively run book publisher that tries to meet the needs of readers who are exploring, or already committed to, the politics of radical social change. The press publishes books that encourage critical thinking and constructive action on the key political, cultural, social, economic, and ecological issues shaping life in the U.S. and in the world. The books are meant to give expression to a wide diversity of democratic social movements and to provide an alternative to the products of corporate publishing. Prominent authors include bell hooks, David Barsamian, Winona LaDuke, Arundhati Roy, and Noam Chomsky. Examples of book titles include: Andrea Smith's *Conquest: sexual violence and American Indian genocide*, a powerful analysis of sexual violence that reaches far beyond conventional understandings; Vanessa Tait's *Poor Workers' Unions: rebuilding labor from below*, introduces community/labor partnerships, workers' centers, and independent caucuses that are revitalizing labor for the 21st century; and Jael Silliman et al., *Undivided Rights: women of color organize for reproductive justice*, case studies of women minorities' fight for jurisdiction over their own bodies and reproductive destinies.

## SPINIFEX PRESS

504 Queensbury St., P.O. Box 212
North Melbourne, Victoria 3051 Australia
Email: women@spinifexpress.com.au  Web: www.spinifexpress.com.au
+61 (0)3 9329 6088  Fax: +61 (0)3 9329 9238

**Editor**: Susan Hawthorne and Renate Klein
**ISBN prefix**: 1-875559, 1-876756
**Average number of new titles published per year**: 6-7
**Number of titles in print**: 165
**Distributor**: publisher direct via website's shopping cart feature (US and Canadian dollar costs available); Independent Publishers Group (USA) (800) 888-4741; Fernwood Books (Canada)
**Publication interests**: Anthologies, Art/The Arts, Feminist, Gender Studies, Health, Lesbian, Literary, Poetry, Politics, Reprints, Sexuality, Social Justice, Women's Issues Studies
**Motto:** "An independent feminist press."

Founded in 1991, Spinifex Press is one of Australia's leading feminist presses publishing innovative and controversial fiction and nonfiction by Australian and international authors. Spinifex's Feminist Classics reprints noteworthy titles, for example, Kerryn Higgs' *All That False Instruction*, a 1975 prize winning novel that explores women's relationships. Title examples include: Jennifer Kelly's *Zest for Life: lesbian's experiences of menopause*, highlights how lesbians are invisible in society at large and that menopause need not be a time of despair; Zillah Eisenstein's *Against Empire: feminisims, racism and the West*, a critique of neoliberal globalization and instead looks to a global anti-war movement to counter U.S. power; Sandy Jeffs' *Wings of Angels: a memoir of madness*, the author's journey into madness; and *Not for Sale: feminists resist prostitution and pornography*, edited by Christine Stark and Rebecca Whisnaut.

## SPINSTERS INK
P.O. Box 242
Midway, FL 32343
(800) 301-6860  Fax: (850) 576-3498
Email: info@spinstersink.com  Web: www.spinstersink.com

**Editor**: Linda Hall
**Affiliated press name**: Shares production, marketing and distribution resources with Bella Books
**ISBN prefix**: 1-883523
**Average number of new titles published per year**: 12
**Number of titles in print**: 50
**Distributor**: publisher direct via website (requests link directly to Bella Books); Bella Distribution Services (800) 533-1973
**Publication interests**: Feminist, Lesbian, Literary, Women's Issues/Studies
**Motto**: the press's logo, the spinning wheel, represents the act of producing yarns or stories to share with readers.

Founded in 1978, Spinsters Ink is committed to giving voice to women writers from every walk of life. The press's mission is to publish fiction and nonfiction that deals with significant issues in women's lives, from a feminist perspective. Following reorganization and under new ownership, Spinster's Ink books are once again available. Linda Hall, Spinsters Ink editor and vice president and COO of Bella Books, is part of a small group that acquired the remaindered inventory of the defunct Spinsters Ink. She plans continue the venerable legacy of the publishing house, but keeping it separate from Bella Books. An example of a current title is Jennifer L. Jordon's *Commitment to Die*, a Lambda Literary Award finalist. Jordon is author of the Kristin Ashe Mystery series with further titles forthcoming.

## SUMACH PRESS

1415 Bathurst St., Suite 202
Toronto, Ontario M5R 3H8 Canada
(416) 531-6250  Fax: (416) 531-3892
Email: sumachpress@on.aibn.com  Web: www.sumachpress.com

**Editor**: Beth McAuley, Lois Pike and Liz Martin
**Affiliated press name**: Milieu Press
**ISBN prefix**: 1-894549, 0-929005
**Average number of new titles published per year**: 11
**Number of titles in print**: 84
**Distributor**: University of Toronto Press (U.S. and Canada); ORCA Book
Publishers (800) 210-5277 (U.S.—young adult books only). Order online from
www.womensbookstore.com
**Publication interests**: Feminist, Health, History, Literary, Politics, Sexuality, Social Issues, Women's Issues/Studies
**Motto**: "Dynamic feminist writing with a critical perspective."

Founded in 2000, Sumach Press is a woman-owned, woman-operated publisher of thought-provoking books on issues of concern to women. The editors support works that challenge the complacency of contemporary life, particularly issues that touch on the lives of Canadian women. The press publishes writing that explores grassroots activism as well as informed scholarly critiques, and is committed to promoting a diversity of voices and opinion through a variety of genres, from serious studies to literary works. The press's Women's Issues Publishing Program promotes feminist titles that explore the contours of a more humane and equitable society on issues of race, gender and class, for example, Ann Bathwaite's et al., *Troubling Women's Studies: pasts, presents, and possibilities*, four essays on what is at stake in "passing on" the institutional project of women's studies at this historic moment. Examples of other titles include: *Weaving Connections: educating for peace, social and environmental justice*, edited by Tara Goldstein and Daniel Selby; *Women Working the NAFTA Food Chain*, edited by Deborah Brandt, a book about how the North American Free Trade Agreement is affecting the food system and its women workers; and Ilona Flutstein-Gruda's *When Grownups Play at War*, a translated memoir of refugee life in Uzbekistan in the 1940s.

**TSAR PUBLICATIONS**
P.O. Box 6996, Station A
Toronto, Ontario M5W 1X7 Canada
(416)483-7191  Fax: (416) 486-0706
Email: inquiries@tsarbooks.com  Web: www.tsarbooks.com

**Editor**: Nurjehan Aziz, publisher
**ISBN prefix**: 0-920661, 1-894770
**Average number of new titles published per year**: 6-8
**Number of titles in print**: 70
**Other materials produced**: *The Toronto Review of Contemporary Writing Abroad*, a literary magazine of new writing
Distributor: **publisher direct via phone, fax or email; Small Press Distribution (800) 869-7753; LitDistCo (800) 591-6250 (Canada)**
**Publication interests**: Africa/African Studies, Asia/Asian Studies, Asian American, Caribbean, Children/Juvenile, Cultural Studies, History, India, Literary, Multiculturalism, Poetry, Race/Race Relations, Women's Studies/Issues
**Motto**: "Canada and the world."

Founded in 1981, TSAR Publications publish new Canadian and American authors that reflect the diversity of the rapidly globalizing world, particularly in Canada and the U.S. The focus is on works that can be termed "multicultural" and particularly those that pertain to Asia and Africa. By 1985, *The Toronto South Asian Review* magazine became so successful that book publishing became a natural venture. Authors include the poetry of Rienzi Crusz considered the best Sri Lankan poet writing in English today, short stories by Caribbean writer Raywat Deonandan, and Nigerian writer Frunso Aiyejina. Examples of titles include: Frunso Aiyejina's *The Legend of Rockhills and Other Stories*, treats the political and cultural life of Nigeria with biting satire; *Floating the Borders*, edited by Nurjehan Aziz and M.G. Vassanji, new trends and writers who have transformed the face of Canadian literature in the last 30 years; Lien Chao's *Maples and the Stream: a narrative poem*, a bilingual Chinese and English poetry collection; and Cyril Dabydeen's *Drums of My Flesh*, a novel from an immigrant from Guyana (South America) who explores his past in the company of his young Canadian-born daughter.

## THEYTUS BOOKS

Green Mountain Rd., Lot 45 Site 50, Comp. 8 RR2
Penticon, British Columbia V2A 6J7 Canada
(250) 493-7181, ext.33  Fax: (250) 493-5302
Email: theytusbooks@vip.net  Web: www.theytusbooks.ca

**Editor**: Anita Large
**Associated with**: En'owkin Center, an Indigenous cultural, educational, ecological and creative arts post-secondary institution
**ISBN prefix**: 0-919441, 1-894778
**Average number of new titles published per year**: 2-3
**Titles in print**: 53
**Other materials produced**: *Gatherings: The En'owkin Journal of First North American People* (annual)
**Distributor**: Orca Book Publishers (USA) (800) 210-5277; University of Toronto Press (Canada except BC and Alberta) (800) 565-9523
**Publication interests**: Aboriginal Studies, Anthologies, Children/Juvenile, Cultural Studies, Indigenous Populations, Literary, Poetry
**Motto**: "First and foremost in Aboriginal writing."

Founded in 1980, Theytus Books is the first publisher in Canada to be under Aboriginal ownership and control. The press has a mandate to produce quality literature presented from an Aboriginal perspective. Theytus seeks to work in partnership with Aboriginal authors to ensure that the Aboriginal voice is expressed in the highest possible level of cultural authenticity. Theytus is a Salishan word which means preserving for the sake of handing down, and was chosen to symbolize the goal of documenting Aboriginal cultures and worldviews through books. Titles include fiction, non-fiction, anthologies, poetry, and children's books. Examples of titles include: Chris Bose's *Somewhere in This Inferno*, a narrative journey of a young Native man traveling the world attempting to find his place and make sense of the societies around him; *(Ad)dressing Our Words: Aboriginal perspectives on Aboriginal literatures*, edited by Armand Ruffo, a critical anthology; and *Crisp Blue Edges: Indigenous creative nonfiction*, edited by Rasunah Marsden.

## THIRD WOMAN PRESS

Email: nalarcon@berkeley.edu
Web: www.thirdwomanpress.com (under construction)

**Editor**: Norma Alarcon

**ISBN prefix**: 0-943219
**Average number of new titles published per year**: currently inactive
**Number of titles in print**: 13
**Distributor**: Small Press Distribution
**Publication interests**: Feminist, Gender Studies, Hispanic (Latina), Lesbian, Literary, Minorities, Race/Race Relations, Sexuality, Women's Issues/Studies

Founded in 1989, Third Woman Press provides a forum for the written and visual expressions of women of color. The press grew from early efforts by the editor to establish a space for Latina self-invention, self-definition and self-representation. *Third Woman*, a Latina journal of Chicana feminist writing, was in existence from 1984-89. The press is currently inactive, but still distributes its titles through Small Press Distribution (search by publisher name in "Advanced" search feature). Examples of titles include: Carla Trujillo's *Chicana Lesbians: the girls our mothers warned us about*, winner of the Lambda Literary Award for Best Anthology and Outwrite's Vanguard Award; Elain Kim's and Norma Alarcon's *Writing Self Writing Nation*, five Asian American women celebrate their rediscovery; and *The Sexuality of Latinas*, edited by Norma Alarcon, Ana Castillo and Cherrie Moraga, a book that has gone through several reprintings.

## THIRD WORLD PRESS

7822 S. Dobson Ave.
P.O. Box 19730
Chicago, IL 60619
(773) 651-0700  Fax: (773) 651-7286
Email: twp3@aol.com  Web: www.thirdworldpressinc.com

**Editor**: Haki R. Madhubuti and Gwendolyn Mitchell
**ISBN prefix**: 0-88378
**Average number of new titles published per year**: 6
**Number of titles in print**: 110
**Distributor**: publisher direct via website's shopping cart feature or order form for use by mail or fax; also, orders taken by phone.
**Publication interests**: Africa/African Studies, African American, History, Literary, Men's Issues/Studies, Minorities, Poetry, Politics, Race/Race Relations, Social Issues, Third World, Women's Issues/Studies

Founded in 1967, Third World Press is the nation's oldest, continuously running, black-owned press that publishes books in all genres. The books focus on issues, themes and critique related to an African American public and spur critical debate over issues of race, culture, politics and social health. The press is a beacon for Black writers who have founded its nurturing environment more conducive to creative success than larger, market-driven, mainstream publishers. A number of books are by notable authors including Gwendolyn Brooks and Sonja Sanchez. Examples of titles include Tony Medina's *Committed to Breathing*, poems that concerns itself with using language as a liberating tool and a launching pad for dismantling myths of a culture and dominating social structure, and Regina Jennings' *Race, Rage and Roses*, poems of victories over guile, brutality, loneliness, misunderstandings, and oppression.
**Motto**: "Progressive Black publishing."

## TIA CHUCHA PRESS
12737 Glenoaks Blvd., #22
Sylmar, CA 91342
(818) 754-2402  Fax: (818) 362-7102
Email: info@tiachucha.com  Web: www.tiachucha.com

**Editor**: Luis Rodriguez
**ISBN prefix**: 1-882688, 0-9624287
**Associated with**: Centro Cultural and Café Cultural, Los Angeles, a nonprofit learning and cultural arts center
**Average number of new titles published per year**: 3
**Number of titles in print**: 38
**Other materials produced**: chapbooks
**Distributor**: Northwestern University Press (800) 621-2736
**Publication interests**: Anthologies, Art/The Arts, Bilingual, Ethnic/Ethnic Studies, Literary, Poetry, Popular Culture
**Motto**: "Where art and minds meet–for a change."

Founded in 1989, Tia Chucha Press serves as a forum for literary crosscultural expression producing works often neglected by most mainstream media and publishing. Tia Chucha was formerly associated with the Guild Complex in Chicago, a multi-arts organization. In 2004, the press relocated to Los Angeles and is associated with Centro Cultural, a center providing space for people to create, imagine, and express themselves in an effort to improve the quality of life in the surrounding community. Authors are of Mexican, African, Puerto Rican, Jamaican, Japanese, Italian and Anglo decent. They are women, men, gay and straight. Examples of titles include: *Power Lines: a decade of poetry from Chicago's Guild Complex;* Astellas DeLuiz' *Shards of Light*, a bilingual anthology of 21 poets; *Open First: an anthology of young Illinois poets*, edited by Anne Schultz; and Luis J. Rodriguez' *My Nature is Hunger: new and selected poems*.

## UCLA AMERICAN INDIAN STUDIES CENTER
3220 Campbell Hall
P.O. Box 951548
Los Angeles, CA 90095-1548
(310) 825-7315  Fax: (310) 206-7060
Email: aisc@ucla.edu  Web: aisc.ucla.edu

**Associated with**: University of California at Los Angeles
**ISBN prefix**: 0-935626
**Average number of new titles published per year**: 2
**Number of titles in print**: 27
**Other materials produced**: *American Indian Culture and Research Journal* (quarterly), videos, audiotapes of music and dance, conference proceedings
**Distributor**: publisher direct via website's printable order form for use by mail or fax, by email at sales@aisc.ucla.edu, or by phone (310) 206-7060; Small Press Distribution
**Publication interests**: American Indian, Art/The Arts, Cultural Studies, Discrimination, Minorities, Politics, Reference, Social Justice

Founded in 1970, the UCLA American Indian Studies Center press is devoted to scholarship by and about Indian people, including policy and politics, cultural issues, political issues, urban Indian experience, Federal Indian policy, economic development, land tenure, and issues within tribal communities. Underlying the mission is an acknowledgement that the indigenous peoples of North America are generally poorly understood and have distinct social, cultural, economic, political, and legal needs by virtue of their status as indigenous nations colonized by a major world power. The center serves as the educational and cultural needs of the American Indian students at UCLA and the Los Angeles American Indian communities. Examples of titles include: *Indian Gaming: who wins?* edited by Angela Mullis and David Kamper; *American Indian Theater in Performance: a reader*, edited by Hanay Geiogamah and Jaye T. Darby, presents the views of leading playwrights, directors, scholars and educators in contemporary Native theater; Duane Champagne's and Abu Sa'ad's *The Future of Indigenous Peoples: strategies for survival and development*; and *Through Indian Eyes: the native experience in books for children*, edited by Beverly Slapin and Doris Seale.

## UCLA ASIAN AMERICAN STUDIES CENTER
3230 Campbell Hall
405 Hilgard Ave.
Los Angeles, CA 90095-1546
(310) 825-2974  Fax: (310) 206-9844
Email: rleong@ucla.edu  Web: www.sscnet.ucla.edu/aasc

**Editor**: Don Nakanishi, Director and Russell Leong, Editor
**Associated with**: University of California at Los Angeles
**ISBN prefix**: 0-934052
**Average number of new titles published per year**: 1-2
**Number of titles in print**: 25
**Other material produced**: *Amerasia Journal* and *AAPI Nexus: Asian Americans and Pacific Islanders Policy, Practice and Community*
**Distributor**: publisher direct via website's order form; Small Press Distribution
**Publication interests**: Art/The Arts, Asian American, Biography/Memoir, Discrimination, History, Literary, Media Studies, Politics, Reference

Founded in 1969, the UCLA Asian American Studies Center's mission is to interpret, define, and forage the separate collective identities of Americans of Asian and Pacific Island heritage, and to integrate multi-disciplinary approaches to the understanding of significant historical and contemporary Asian and Asian Pacific issues. The press jointly publishes the Intersections: Asian and Pacific American Transcultural Studies series with the University of Hawaii Press, and the Asian American Public Policy Research series with the Leadership Education for Asian Pacifics (LEAP) organization. Examples of titles include: *The New Fact of Asian Pacific America: numbers, diversity and change*, edited by Eric Lai and Dennis Arguelles, a comprehensive analysis of the significant demographic and cultural changes of Asian Pacific America; Yuri Kochiyama's *Passing It On: a memoir*, an account of an extraordinary Asian American woman who spoke out and fought for human rights; *Asian Americans on War and Peace*, edited by Russell C. Leong and Don T. Nakanishi, addresses the parallels between recent world events and the legacy of war, xenophobia, and resistance in Asian American history.

## UCLA CHICANO STUDIES RESEARCH CENTER
193 Haines Hall
P.O. Box 951544
Los Angeles, CA 90095-1544
(310) 825-2642  Fax: (310) 206-1784
Email: press@chicano.ucla.edu  Web: www.chicano.ucla.edu/press

**Editor**: Chon A. Noreiga, Director and Wendy Belcher, publications coordinator
**Associated with**: University of California at Los Angeles
**ISBN prefix**: 0-89551
**Average number of new titles published per year**: 1-2
**Number of titles in print**: 23
**Other materials produced**: *Aztlan: A Journal of Chicano Studies*, Latino Policy and Issues Brief series, CRSC Research Report series, and DVDs in the Chicano Cinema and Media Arts series
**Distributor**: publisher direct via website's order form for mail or fax; also, orders taken by phone; Small Press Distribution
**Publication interests**: Cultural Studies, Discrimination, Hispanic/Latino, History, Minorities, Politics, Reference, Religion, Social Issues, Social Justice

Founded in 1969, the UCLA Chicano Studies Research Center promotes the study and dissemination of knowledge on the experience of the people of Mexican descent and other Latinos in the U.S. Emphasis is on interdisciplinary and collaborative research that analyzes and articulates issues critical to the knowledge of Chicano and Latino communities in the U.S. The center produced the first Zapotec-English dictionary. Examples of other titles include: *I am Aztlan: the personnel essay in Chicano studies*, edited by Chon A. Noriega and Wendy Belcher, twelve essays reflecting on the role of the "I" in Chicano and Latino culture, and the diverse ways in which personal voice and experience inform their research and *The Chicano Studies Reader: an anthology of Aztlan scholarship, 1970-2000*, edited by Chon A. Noriega et al., significant articles from *Aztlan: A Journal of Chicano Studies*.

## THE VEGETARIAN RESOURCE GROUP
P.O. Box 1463
Baltimore, MD 21203
(410) 366-8343  Fax: (410) 366-8804
Email: vrg@vrg.org  Web: www.vrg.org/catalog/index.htm

**Editor**: depends on the project.
**Associated with**: distributes vegan/vegetarian books from other presses
**ISBN prefix**: 0-931411
**Average number of new titles published per year**: 1-2
**Number of titles in print**: 15
**Other materials produced**: *Vegetarian Journal*, pamphlets, article reprints
**Distributor**: publisher direct via website's order form or printable order form for mail or fax; also, orders taken by phone or email. **Publication interests**: Cookery, Ecology/Environmentalism, Ethics, Health, Hunger, Nutrition, Vegetarianism

Founded in 1982, The Vegetarian Resource Group is a non-profit organization dedicated to educating the public on vegetarianism and the interrelated issues of health, nutrition, ecology, ethics, and world hunger. The organization's health professionals, activists, and educators work with businesses and individuals to bring about healthy changes in schools, workplaces, and communities. Best sellers include *Simply Vegan* and *Meatless Meals for Working People*. Examples of other titles include: Davida Gypsy Breier's *Vegan and Vegetarian FAQ*, helps non-vegetarians and new vegetarians understand some of the issues and ingredients that concern vegetarians; Debra Wasserman's and Reed Mangels' *Vegan Handbook*, information on meal planning, nutrition, leather alternatives, vegetarian history, online resources, and business ethics and the environment; and Vonnie Winslow Crist's *Leprechaun Cake and Other Tales: a vegetarian story cookbook*, about a leprechaun in the kitchen, baby dragon down the block, friendly forest deer from South America, and the Snow Queen's Unicorn teach children, and the adults who love them, about friendship, caring, and healthy cooking

## VERSO

6 Meard St.                                    180 Varick St., 10th floor
London W1F 0EG                        New York, NY 10014-4606
England                                         (212) 807-9680
                                                       Fax: (212) 807-9152
Email: versony@versobooks.com  Web: www.versobooks.com

**Affiliated press names**: originally called New Left Books
**ISBN prefix**: 1-85984, 0-86091, 0-902308
**Average number of new titles published per year**: 60
**Number of titles in print**: 350+

**Distributor**: publisher direct (800) 223-4830 (USA) or (800) 399-6858 (Canada); W.W. Norton (USA) (800) 458-6515, Penguin Books Canada (416) 925-2249
**Publication interests**: Critical Theory, Cultural Studies, Globalization, History, International Issues/Relations, Latin American Studies, Literary Criticism, Middle East Studies, Philosophy, Political, Reprints, Social Change, Social Justice, Socialism/Marxism, Sociology, Third World, Translations
**Motto**: "Books with a critical edge."

Founded in 1970, Verso can justifiably claim to be the largest radical publisher in the English-language world, and is a leading radical publisher presenting an alternative point of view. The press was founded by the London-based *New Left Review*, a journal of left-wing theory. The press developed an early reputation as a translator of classic works of European literature and politics by authors such as Jean Paul Sartre, Louis Althusser, and Ernest Mandel. Translations include the work of Guy Debord, Carlo Ginzburg, Jurgen Habermas, and Gabriel Garcia Marquez. The press retained U.S. rights, and U.S. editors have contracted with authors such as Noam Chomsky, Andrew Kopkind, Manning Marable, and Edward Said. Examples of titles include: Tariq Ali's *The Dictatorship of Capital*, analyzes capitalism's queasy relationship to democracy; Benedict Anderson's *Under Three Flags: anarchism and the anti-colonial imagination*, traces the origin of nationalism and anti-globalization; Mike Davis' *Planet of Slums*, raises the lid on the effects of a global explosion of disenfranchised slum-dwellers; and Rigoberta Menchu's *Crossing Borders: an autobiography*, the press's best-selling title, was awarded the Nobel Peace Prize in 1992.

## VOLCANO PRESS, INC.
21496 National St., P.O. Box 270
Volcano, CA 95689-0270
(209) 296-4991  Fax: (209) 296-4995
Email: sales@volcanopress.com  Web: www.volcanopress.com

**Editor**: Ruth Gottstein
**Affiliated press names**: Mother Lode Books
**ISBN prefix**: 0-912078, 1-884244
**Average number of new titles published per year**: 6
**Number of titles in print**: 85
**Other materials produced**: posters, videos

**Distributor**: publisher direct via website's shopping cart feature, or by fax, mail, or phone (800) 879-9636
**Publication interests**: Children/Juvenile, Domestic Violence, Gender Issues, Health, Sexuality, Women's Issues/Studies, Young Adult
**Motto**: "Resources on family violence and women's health."

Founded in 1973, Volcano Press has a goal of diminishing the life span of abuse through heightened consciousness, prevention and education. Family violence is defined as the life span of abuse that extends from infancy to old age. The press produces counselor guides, anger workbooks, and other tools for implementing treatment on abuse and domestic violence. Examples of titles include: Elaine Weiss' *Surviving Domestic Violence: voices of women who broke free*; Paul Kivel's *I Can Make My World a Safer Place*, a kid's cartoon book about stopping violence; and Helen M. Eigenberg's *Women Battering in the United States*, an overview that frames the issues and reviews major debates in the literature.

## WEST END PRESS
P.O. Box 27334
Albuquerque, NM 87125
(505) 345-5729 Fax: same
Email: jcrawfor@unm.edu

**Editor**: John Crawford
**ISBN prefix**: 0 931122, 0-9705344, 0-9753486
**Average number of new titles published per year**: 4
**Number of titles in print**: 43
**Distributor**: publisher direct (catalog available upon request); University of New Mexico Press (800) 249-7737, Small Press Distribution
**Publication interests**: Ethnic/Ethnic Studies, Feminist, Literary, Minorities, Poetry, Political, Social Justice
**Motto**: "Don't mourn—organize."

Founded in 1977, West End Press is literary and progressive with an orientation toward working-class and multicultural writers producing many works with political and social themes. Most titles are books of poetry. In 1976, founder John Crawford met Meridel Le Sueur, a 76-year-old novelist from Minnesota who was a strong feminist before her time who wrote on political themes. Meridel introduced Crawford to some younger writers, and as a result, he started the press. A majority of the writers are women, including five titles by Meridel. Other authors include Navaho poet Lucy Tapahonso, Chicano poet and playwright, Cherrie Moraga, Hopi poet Wendy Rose, Laguana Pueblo poet Paula Gunn Allen, Asian poet Nellie Wong, Chicano poet E.A. Mares, Paiute poet Adrian Louis, and Black poet Michelle T. Clinton. Examples of titles include Joseph Bruchac's *Ndakinna = Our Land: new and selected poems* and two plays by Cherrie Moraga, *The Hungary Woman: a Mexican medea* and *Heart of the Earth: a Popul Vuh story.*

## WHITE PINE PRESS

P.O. Box 236
Buffalo, NY 14201-0236
(716) 627-4665 Fax: same
Email: wpine@whitepine.org Web: www.whitepine.org

**Editor**: Dennis Maloney
**ISBN prefix**: 0-934834, 1-877727, 1-893996
**Average number of new titles published per year**: 9
**Number of titles in print**: 125+
**Distributor**: publisher direct via website's order form; Small Press Distribution, Consortium
**Publication interests**: American Indian, Essays, Ethnic/Ethnic Studies, Latin American Studies, Literary, Multiculturalism, Poetry, Short Stories, Translations
**Motto**: "A world of voices."

Founded in 1973, White Pine Press is a nonprofit, literary press dedicated to discovering, producing and marketing exceptional works of poetry, fiction and nonfiction from around the world, and making this work accessible to a diverse public. The press produces four series: Secret Weavers Series, voices of Latin American women; Dispatches Series, bringing fine fiction from around the world; Human Rights Series, for example, Marjorie Agosin's *An Absence of Shadows*, haunting poems of the victims of human rights abuses in Latin America; and New American Voices Series, first novels by American writers. The press has published Nobel Prize laureates William Golding, Juan Ramon Jimenez, Gabriela Mistral and Pablo Neruda. Maurice Kenny's *Stories for a Winter's Night: fiction by Native American writers* was winner of the 2001 Skipping Stones Honor Award for upper grades. Other examples of titles include: *These are Not Sweet Girls: Latin American women poets*, edited by Marjorie Agosin; *Afterwards: Slovenian Writings, 1945-1995*, edited by Andrew Zawacki; and *Stories in the Stepmother Tongue*, edited by Josip Novakovich and Robert Shapard, stories written in English by writers who emigrated to the U.S.

## WOMEN'S PRESS
180 Bloor St. West, Suite 801
Toronto, Ontario M5S 2V6 Canada
(800) 463-1988 (U.S. office) (416) 929-2774  Fax: (416) 929-1926
Email: ruthbsc@cspi.org  Web: www.womenspress.ca

**Editor**: Althea Prince, Managing Editor
**Affiliated press names**: imprint of Canadian Scholars' Press
**ISBN prefix**: 0-88961
**Average number of new titles published per year**: 7
**Number of titles in print**: 150+
**Distributor**: publisher direct via website's order feature, by phone (866) 870-2774 (worldwide), or by fax (905) 873-6170
**Publication interests**: Biography/Memoirs, Children/Juvenile, Feminist, Health, Lesbian, Literary, Poetry, Politics, Race/Race Relations, Sexuality, Women's Issues/Studies
**Motto**: "Canada's oldest English-language feminist publisher."

Founded in 1972, Women's Press is devoted to the circulation of the ideas and the experiences of women, especially women who have not always been heard or who have faced discriminatory barriers because of race, class, origins, or sexual orientation. Originally founded with collective ownership, the Women's Press has been managed since 2000 by Canadian Scholars' Press, a press established in 1986 to overcome the problems found in assembling appropriate teaching materials for post-secondary classes. Canadian Scholars Press plans to continue the anti-oppression and feminist themes of the press. Examples of titles include: Elly Danica's *Don't: a woman's word* and *Beyond Don't: dreaming past the dark*, best-selling titles from a survivor of child abuse; Mairuth Sarsfield's *No Crystal Stair*, explores an increasingly difficult contemporary reality–functioning as white though surviving as black; and *Feminisms and Womanisms: a women's studies reader*, edited by Althea Prince and Susan Silva-Wayne.

## THE WOMEN'S PRESS
27 Goodge St.
London W1T 2LD England
+44 (0)20 7636 3992  Fax +44 (0)20 7637 1866
Email: sales@the-womens-press.com  Web: www.the-womens-press.com

**ISBN prefix**: 0-704338, 0-704328, 0-912670, 0-704344, 0-704347
**Average number of new titles published per year**: 15
**Number of titles in print**: 108
**Distributors**: publisher direct via website's order feature (through Plymbridge distribution); Trafalgar Square, North Pomfret, VT, (800) 423-4525 (USA); Codasat (Canada), harful@bc.sympatico.com
**Publication interests**: Adolescents, Biography/Memoir, Feminist, Health, Literary, Psychology, Reprints, Social Issues, Women's Issues/Studies
**Motto**: "Great writing by great women."

Founded in 1978, The Women's Press is dedicated to publishing incisive feminist fiction and non-fiction by outstanding women writers from all around the world. The press reprints feminist classics such as Jane Austin's *Love and Friendship*, Angela Y. Davis' *Women, Race and Class*, and Alice Walker's *The Color Purple*. The press's Livewire list is a series of up-front, contemporary, issue-driven works of fiction and non-fiction for young women. Other examples of titles include: Shelley Bovey's *Sizeable Reflections: big women leading full lives*; Mary Daly's *Gyn/Ecology*, radical feminist theory; Andrea Dworkin's *Pornography*, a study of the damaging effects of pornography and its ramifications on society; and Joni Seager's *The Atlas of Women*, a vivid portrait of the status of women at the beginning of the 21st century.

## WORLDWATCH INSTITUTE
1776 Massachusetts Ave., NW
Washington, DC 20036-1904
(202) 452-1999  Fax: (202) 296-7365
Email: worldwatch@worldwatch.org  Web: www.worldwatch.org

**Editor**: Christopher Flavin, President
**ISBN prefix**: 0-393
**Average number of new titles published per year**: 3
**Number of titles in print**: 17
**Other materials produced**: *World Watch* magazine, World Watch Paper series
**Distributor**: publisher direct by phone (888) 544-2303, by email wwpub@worldwatch.org, or by fax (570) 320-2079
**Publication interests**: Ecology/Environmentalism, Energy, Globalization, International Issues/Relations, Politics, Population Studies, Social Change, Sustainable Development

**Motto**: "Independent research for an environmentally sustainable and socially just society."

Founded in 1974, Worldwatch Institute is dedicated to fostering the evolution of an environmentally sustainable society, one in which human needs are met in ways that do not threaten the health of the natural environment or the prospects of future generations. Only a global approach to issues such as climate change, depletion of the stratospheric ozone layer, the loss of biological diversity, degradation of oceans, and population growth can be effective. The institute believes in the power of information and provides publications that inform readers on how to build a sustainable society. Examples of titles include Hilary French's *Vanishing Borders: protecting the planet in the age of globalization*, a plan of action for ensuring environmental stability in the wake of globalization, and Brian Halweil's *Eat Here: reclaiming homegrown pleasures in a global supermarket*, readers discover why eating local food is one of the most significant choices they can make for the planet and themselves. The two annual flagship publications are *State of the World*, reports on progress toward a sustainable society, and *Vital Signs*, reports on environmental trends that are shaping our future.

## WRITERS CORPS BOOKS
25 Van Ness, Suite 240
San Francisco, CA 94102
(415) 252-4655 Fax: (415) 252-2595
Email: Ayesa.Rockwell@sfgov.org
Web: www.sfartscommission.org/WC

**Editor**: Janet Heller, Project Manager
**Associated with**: San Francisco Arts Commission
**ISBN prefix**: 1-888048
**Average number of new titles published per year**: 1
**Number of titles in print**: 11
**Distributor**: publisher direct via website's link to Small Press Distribution
**Publication interests**: Adolescents, Anthologies, Discrimination, Literary, Minorities, Poetry, Poverty
**Motto**: "Works to transform and strengthen individuals and communities through the written and spoken word."

Founded in 1994, Writers Corps increases community awareness and understanding of the lives of youth through the program's publications and special events. The program places writers in low-income community settings to teach creative writing to at-risk youth 6 to 21 years of age with the stated objective of improving the learning attitude, ability and self-sufficiency. Writers Corps programs are allied with WritersCorps programs in Bronx, NY and Washington, DC. Primary publications are the annual anthologies of poetry and prose by the youth, including *Same Difference: young writers on race* (1998), *What It Took for Me to Get Here* (1999), *Smart Mouth* (2000), *Jump* (2001), *Believe Me, I Know* (2002), *Paint Me Like I Am: teen poems from WritersCorps* (2003), Introduction by nikki giovanni and published by HarperCollins, *City of One: young writers speak to the world* (2004), Introduction by Isabelle Allende and published by Aunt Lute Books, and *Where Were You: poetry and images from WritersCorps* (2005). Also, teacher's guides, for example, *Lessons Along the Way: creative writing exercises from WritersCorps.*

## ZED BOOKS
7 Cynthia St.
London N1 9JF England
+44 (0)207 837 4014  Fax: +44 (0)207 833 3960
Email: zedbooks@zedbooks.demon.co.uk  Web: www.zedbooks.co.uk

**Editor**: Dr. Anna Hardman, Senior Editor
**ISBN prefix**: 0-86232, 0-905762, 1-85649, 1-84277
**Average number of new titles published per year**: 70
**Number of titles in print**: 1167
**Distributor**: publisher direct via website's shopping cart feature ($ prices available); Palgrave (USA) (800) 221-7945; Fernwood Books (Canada)
**Publication interests**: Africa/African Studies, Asia/Asian Studies, Cultural Studies, Development Studies, Ecology/Environmentalism, Economics, Feminist, Globalization, Human Rights, International Issues/Relations, Middle East, Politics, Sociology, Women's Issues/Studies
**Motto**: "Books that matter."

Founded in 1977, Zed Books is dedicated to contributing to a deeper understanding of the issues, conditions of life, oppressive structures, and dominant ideologies which confront ordinary people when drawing attention to the human struggles, and to innovative ideas that hold out some hope for an improvement in the human condition. The press is managed cooperatively by its worker directors with the purpose of publishing and distributing, North and South, books that make a positive difference in the real world of both social action and intellectual ideas. Many books are published in association with a wide variety of other organizations. Authors include intellectuals, writers, and activists such as Nawal el Sadaawi, Vandana Shiva, Samir Amin, Maria Mies, Wolfgang Sachs, and others. About half of the authors are from the South. Example of titles include: *Feminism in India*, edited by Maitrayee Chandhuri, an overview of the rich history of feminism in India; Tony Shelly's *Oil: politics, poverty and the planet*, highlights political and social issues in the global energy sector; and Roger Burbach's and Jim Tarbell's *Imperial Overstretch: George W. Bush and the hubris of empire*, how the neoconservatives and the petro-military complex have hijacked US foreign policy.

# ALTERNATIVE PUBLISHERS OF BOOKS:
# A BIBLIOGRAPHY, 1996-2005

Byron Anderson
  **Alternative Publishers of Books in North America, 6ᵗʰ ed.**

**Adams, Kate. Built Out of Books. Lesbian Energy and Feminist Ideology in Alternative**
      **Publishing.** *Journal of Homosexuality* 34, 3-4 (November-December 1998): 113-141.

**Albert, Michael. What Makes Alternative Media Alternative?**
*Z Magazine* (February 24, 2003).     Also online at
http://www.zmag.org/whatmakesalti.htm.

**Anderson, Byron. The Other 90 Percent: What Your MLS**
      **Didn't Teach You.** *Counterpoise* 3, 3/4 (July/October 1999):
      11-13. Republished online, Library Juice May 3, 2000:
      http://libr.org/Juice/issues/vol3/LJ_3.17.html#18.

_____. **Pursuing Small, Independent Book Publishers.**
      *Counterpoise*, 4, 3 (July 2000): 17-19.

_____. **Reference Works from Selected Small Alternative Presses.** *Reference Services Review* 25, 2 (Summer 1997):
      65-72.

**Atton, Chris. Alternative Media.** Thousand Oaks, CA: Sage,
      2002.

_____. **A Re-assessment of the Alternative Press.** *Media,
      Culture and Society* 21, 1 (January 1999): 51-76.

**Angel, Karen. Independent-Bookstore Presses Keep Alternative Voice Alive.** *Publisher's Weekly* 244, 16 (April 21, 1997):
      24-27, 30.

_____. **The Small Presses: Getting in the Door.** *Publisher's
      Weekly* 244, 47 (November 17, 1997): 32-34.

**Bagdikian, Ben H. The New Media Monopoly.** Boston, MA:
      Beacon Books, 2004.

**Barbato, Joseph. The Rise and Rise of the Small Press: How
      the Independent Publishers Created a World--and
      Market--of Their Own.** *Publisher's Weekly* 244, 31 (July
      1997--Special Anniversary Issue): 39-48.

**Barnes, Jim. New England's Patriots of Publishing**. *Independent Publisher* 17, 5 (September/October 1999): 20-23+.

**Barsamian, David. The Business of Books: An Interview with Andre Schiffrin**. *Z Magazine* (September 2003).

**Chomsky, Noam. What Makes Mainstream Media Mainstream?** *Z Magazine* (June 1997).

**Clay, Steven and Rodney Phillips. A Secret Location on the East Side: Adventures in Writing 1960-1980**. New York: New York Public Library and Granary Books, 1998.

**Cooper, Amy. A Voice for the Voiceless: Orbis Books Amplifies the Best in Third World Theology**. *Small Press* 15, 1 (January/February 1997): 26-27,65.

**Copper Canyon Press and Small Press Destiny**. *ForeWord* 2, 8 (August 1999): 13.

**Dilevko, Juris and Keren Dali. Reviews of Independent Press Books in "Counterpoise" and Other Publications**. *College & Research Libraries* 65, 1 (January 2004): 56-77.

**Directory of Ethnic & Multicultural Publishers, Distributors & Resource Organizations, 4th edition. Compiled and Edited by Vladimir F. Wertsman** for the American Library Association's Ethnic Material Information Exchange Round Table. New York: D. Cohen, 1999.

**Duncombe, Stephen. What's Alternative?** *Passages* 33 (Winter 2002): 5-7.

**Evans, Alice. Seal Press: Fishing Theaters**. *Poets and Writers Magazine* 25, 1 (January 1, 1997): 62-71.

**Gold, Jerome. Publishing Lives: Interviews with Independent Book Publishers in the Pacific Northwest and British Columbia**, vol. 1. Seattle, WA: Black Heron Press, 1996.

_____. **Obscure in the Shade of Giants: Publishing Lives**, vol 2. Seattle, WA: Black Heron Press, 2001.

**Herdeck, Donald. Appreciating the Difference: The Autobiography of Three Continents Press, 1993-1997**. Pueblo, CO: Passeggiata Press, 1998.

**Herman, Edward S. All the Book Reviews Fit to Print: Tolerance of the Conservatively Correct**. *Z Magazine* 12, 4 (April 1999): 40-45. Also, online: http://www.zmag.org/Zmag/articles/april99herman.

Kauka, Kanani. A Life's Work: An Interview with Firebrand Books Publisher Nancy Bereano. *Lambda Book Report* 5, 11 (1997): 1.

Keyes, Heather. Can you Tell Me Where Stony River Is? *Feminist Voices* 10, 3 (July 17, 1997): 5.

Kranich, Nancy. A Question of Balance: the Role of Libraries in Providing Alternatives to the Mainstream Media. *Collection Building* 19, 3 (2000): 85-90. Also online at http://libr.org/Juice/issues/vol3/LJ_3.18.html#12.

Kruse, Ginny Moore, Kathleen T. Horning and Megan Schliesman. Multicultural Literature for Children and Young Adults: A Selected Listing of Books By and About People of Color, volume two, 1991-1996. Madison, WI: Cooperative Children's Book Center, 1997.

LaMattina, Elaine. Literature: Culture's Most Valuable Resource. *Counterpoise* 1, 1 (January 1997): 5-6.

Marinko, R. A. and K. H. Gerhard. Representations of Alternative Press in Academic Library Collections. *College & Research Libraries* 59, 4 (July 1998): 363-377.

Martin, Justin. Black Sparrow Press: Bukowski Was Just the First. *Poets & Writers Magazine* 27, 3 (May/June 1999): 40-43.

McChesney, Robert W. The Big Media Game Has Fewer Players. *The Progressive* 63 (November 1999): 20+.

_____. Media Rich, Democracy Poor. Urbana, IL: University of Illinois Press, 1999.

Miller, Mark Crispin. The Crushing Power of Big Publishing. *The Nation* 264, 10 (March 27, 1997): 11-21,29.

Nardini, Bob. A Library Bookseller Looks at the Alternative Press. *Counterpoise* 3, 1 (January 1999): 15+.

Noll, Elizabeth. An Extraordinary Edition: Literary Leader Emile Buchwald Retires [Milkweed Editions]. *Minnesota Women's Press* 19, 7 (June 18-July 1, 2003).

The New Press Guide to Multicultural Resources for Young Readers. Daphne Muse, editor. New York: The New Press, 1997.

Odelius, Kristy. Whole Culture, Whole People, Whole Books [Third World Press]. *ForeWord* 1,7 (December 1998): 34-36.

Project Censored. The Progressive Guide to Alternative Media and Activism. Open Media Pamphlet Series. New York: Seven Stories Press, 1999.

**Quinn, Judy. Seven Stories: Taking on Bigger Publishers'
    "Discomfort" Books.** *Publisher's Weekly* 245, 18 (May 4,
    1998): 11, 22.

**Reid, Calvin. The New Press: Five Years 'In the Public Inter-
est'.** *Publisher's Weekly* 244, 45        (November 3, 1997): 14.

**Ruff, Allen. 'We Called Each Other Comrade': Charles H.
    Kerr & Company, Radical Publishers.** Champaign, IL:
    University of Illinois Press, 1997.

**Samek, Toni. Intellectual Freedom and Social Responsibility
    in American Librarianship, 1967-1974.** Jefferson, NC:
    McFarland, 2001.

_____. **Intellectual Freedom Within the Profession. A
    Look Back at Freedom of Expression and the Alterna-
    tive Library Press.** *Counterpoise* 4, 1/2 (January/April 2000):
    10-16. Also online at
    http://www.libr.org/Juice/issues/vol6/LJ_6.6.html.

**Scheinmann, Vivian J. Editor and Author Barbara Smith:
    The Reader's Companion Changes Women's His-
    tory.** *The Women's Times* 5, 6 (March 31, 1998): 32.

**Schiffrin, Andre. Bucking the Monoliths: Publishing with a
    Mission.** *American Libraries* 30, 5 (May 1999): 44-46.

_____. **The Business of Books: How the International
    Conglomerates Took Over Publishing and Changed
    the Way We Read.** London: Verso; New York: W. W. Nor-
    ton, 2000.

_____. **Random Acts of Consolidation.** *The Nation* 269, 1
    (July 5, 1999): 10.

**Lee, Sunyoung. Kaya** [publishing house]. *Counterpoise* 5, 1 (January
    2001): 15-16.

**Stevens, Jen. Arte Publico.** *Counterpoise* 6, 1/2 (January/April 2002):
    23-25.

**Stewart, Sean. An Analysis of Reviews in Alternative Press
    Journals and Public Library Holdings of Alternative
    Press Books.** *Counterpoise* 6,4 (October 2002) 12-18.

**Streitmatter, Rodger. Voices of Revolution: The Dissident
    Press in America.** New York: Columbia University Press,
    2001.

**Tan, Cecilia. Pride and Perseverance: Independent Publish-
    ers Reflect the Growth and Changing Tastes of Les-**

**bian and Gay Communities**. *Publisher's Weekly* 246, 18 (May 3, 1999): 43-46.

**Valentine, Victoria. Big Fish in a Little Sea: A Black Publishing House Net Best-Selling Author Walter Mosley**. *Emerge* 8, 4 (February 1997): 84-88.

**Wehr, Margaret. The Culture of Everyday Venality: or a Life in the Book Industry**. *The Review of Contemporary Fiction* 17, 1 (Spring 1997): 159-167.

**Willett, Charles. Consider the Source: A Case Against Outsourcing Materials Selection in Academic Libraries**. *Collection Building* 17, 2 (1998): 91-95.

_____. **The State of Alternative Publishing in America: Issues and Implications for Libraries**. *Counterpoise* 3, 1 (January 1999): 14-16.

# PRESSES, including imprints

AK Press
Advocado Press, The
Advocate Books *see*: Alyson Publications
Africa World Press
African American Images
Afro-Bets Kids *see*: Just Us Books
Akashic Books
Alice James Books
Alice Street Editions *see*: Harrington Park Press
Alyson Publications
Alyson Wonderland *see*: Alyson Publications
Amnesty International (USA)
Annick Press
Apex Press, The
Arbeiter Ring Publishing
Arsenal Pulp Press
Arte Pubico Press
Asia American Writers Workshop
Atrium Society
Aunt Lute Books
Autonomedia
Beacon Press
Bebob Books *see*: Lee & Low Books
Bella Books
Between the Lines
Bilingual Review/Press
Black & Red
Black Classic Press
Black Ice Books *see*: Fiction Collective Two
Black Rose Books
Black Swan Press/Surrealist Editions
Book Publishing Company
Bootstrap Press *see*: Apex Press
Caddo Gap Press
Calaca Press
CALYX Books
Canadian Centre for Policy Alternatives, The
Canadian Committee on Labour History

Carolina Wren Press
Charles H. Kerr Publishing Company
Chelsea Green Publishing Company
Chicory Blue Press
Children's Book Press
Chusma House Publications
Cinco Puntos Press
City Lights Books
Clarity Press
Clasicos Chicanos/Chicano Classics *see*: Bilingual Review/Press
Cleis Press
Coffee House Press
Common Courage Press
Copper Canyon Press
Creation Books
Crocodile Books *see*: Interlink Publishing
Cultural Survival
Curbstone Press
Dalkey Archive Press
Dollars & Sense
Down There Press
DuForcelf *see*: Black Classic Press
Earthscan Publications
Eros Comix *see*: Fantagraphics Books
Fantagraphics Books
Feminist Press at the City University of New York
Feral House
Fernwood Publishing
Fiction Collective Two (FC2)
Firebrand Books *see*: Fiction Collective Two
Floricanto Press
Food First Books
Freedom Press
Freedom Voices Publications
Frog Books *see*: Kumarian Press
Gabriel Dumont Institute
Garamond Press
Gay Sunshine Press/Leyland Publications
Graywolf Press
Green Candy Press

Green Dragon Press
Green Print *see*: Merlin Press
Greenfield Review Press, The
Hanging Loose Press
Harrington Park Press
Haymarket Books
High Risk Books *see*: Serpent's Tail
Holy Cow! Press
Human Rights First
Human Rights Watch
ITDG Publishing
Inform, Inc.
Institute for Local Self-Reliance, The
Interlink Publishing
International Labor Office
International Publishers Company
International Relations Center
Ishmael Reed Publishing Company
Island Press
Just Us Books
Kage-an Books *see*: Copper Canyon Books
Kaya
Kegedonce Press
Kelsey Street Press
Kumarian Press
Lantern Books
Latin American Bureau
Latin American Literary Review Press
Last Gasp
Lawrence Hill Books
Lee & Low Books
Lollipop Power Books *see*: Carolina Wren Press
Loompanics Unlimited
Lotus Press
MEP Publications
Maissonneuve Press
Manic D Press
Mask Noir *see*: Serpent's Tail
Mehring Books
Meiklejohn Civil Liberties Institute

Mercury House
Merlin Press
Midnight Editions *see*: Cleis Press
Midnight Classics *see*: Serpent's Tail
Milieu Press *see*: Sumach Press
Milkweed Editions
Monthly Review Press
Morning Glory Press
Nation Books
New Clarion Press
New Press, The
New Society Publishers
New Victoria Publishers
Nordic Africa Institute/Nodiska Afrikanstitutet, The
Ocean Press
Olive Branch Books *see*: Interlink Publishing
Onlywomen Press
Open Hand Publishing
Orbis Books
Orion Society
Oxfam
Pact Publications
Pangaea
Paris Press
Pathfinder Press
Pemmican Publications
Pilgrim Press, The
Pinata Press *see*: Arte Publico Press
Plain View Press
Pluto Press
Polychrome Publishing Company
Post-Apollo Press, The
Punk Planet Books *see*: Akashic Books
Pushcart Press, The
RDV Books *see*: Akashic Books
Ralph J. Bunche Center for African American Studies, The
Red Letter Press
Red Sea Press, The *see*: Africa World Press
Re/Search Publications
Rethinking Schools

Rising Tide Press
Santofa Books *see*: Just Us Books
Seal Press
Second Story Press
See Sharp Press
Serpent's Tail
Seven Stories Press
Shearwater Books *see*: Island Press
Sierra Club Books
Sister Vision Press
Soft Skull Press
South End Press
Southern Tier Editions *see*: Harrington Park Editions
Spinifex Press
Spinsters Ink
Sumach Press
TSAR Publications
TallMountain Circle Books *see*: Freedom Voices Publications
Theytus Books
Third Woman Press
Third World Press
Tia Chucha Press
UCLA American Indian Studies Center
UCLA Asian American Studies Center
UCLA Chicano Studies Research Center
Vegetarian Resource Group, The
Verso
Volcano Press
West End Press
White Pine Press
Women's Press (Toronto)
Women's Press, The (London)
Worldwatch Institute
Writers Corps Books
Yes Press *see*: Down There Press
Zed Books

# SUBJECT INDEX

Book Publishing Company, Children's Book Press, Greenfield Review
Press, Holy Cow! Press, Lee & Low Books, New Press, South End
Press, UCLA American Indian Studies Center, White Pine Press
**Animal Rights**
Between the Lines, Lantern Books
**Anarchism**
AK Press, Arbeiter Ring Publishing, Autonomedia, Black Rose Books,
Black Swan Press/Surrealist Editions, Charles H. Kerr Publishing,
Freedom Press, Haymarket Books, Last Gasp, Loompanics Unlimited,
See Sharp Press
**Anthologies**
Arsenal Pulp Press, Asian American Writers' Workshop, Bilingual Re-
view/Press, CALYX Books, Chicory Blue Press, Children's Book Press,
Copper Canyon Press, Dollars & Sense, Fantagraphics Books, Graywolf
Press, Greenfield Review Press, Hanging Loose Press, Holy Cow! Press,
Kegedonce Press, Manic D Press, Pushcart Press, Spinifex Press, They-
tus Books, Tia Chucha Press, Writers Corps Books
**Anthropology**
African World Press, Pangaea, Pluto Press
**Architecture**
Chelsea Green Publishing, New Society Publishers
**Art/The Arts**
African World Press, Autonomedia, Beacon Press, Bilingual Re-
view/Press, CALYX Books, Cleis Press, Creation Books, Curbstone
Press, Fantagraphics Books, Feral House, Interlink Publishing, Kaya,
Kelsey Street Press, Last Gasp, Soft Skull Press, Spinifex Press, Tia
Chucha Press, UCLA American Indian Studies Center, UCLA Asian
American Studies Center
**Asia/Asian Studies**
Amnesty International, Kaya, TSAR Publications, Zed Books
**Asian American**
Asian American Writers' Workshop, Children's Book Press, Firebrand
Books, Greenfield Review Press, Human Rights Watch, Kaya, Lee &
Low Books, New Press, Polychrome Publishing, South End Press,
TSAR Publications, UCLA Asian American Studies Center
**Avant-garde**
Fiction Collective Two, Last Gasp, Serpent's Tail
**Bilingual** see also: **Multiculturalism**
Arte Publico Press, Bilingual Review/Press, Calaca Press, Carolina
Wren Press, Children's Book Press, Cinco Puntos Press, Copper Can-

yon Press, Floricanto Press, Latin American Literary Review Press,
Ocean Press, Pangaea, Tia Chucha Press

**Biography/Memoir**
African American Images, Alyson Publications, Arsenal Pulp Press,
Arte Publico Press, Aunt Lute Books, Bilingual Review/Press, Charles
H. Kerr Publishing, Chicory Blue Press, City Lights Books, Cleis Press,
Feminist Press at the City University of New York, Feral House, Fire-
brand Books, Floricanto Press, Graywolf Press, Harrington Park Press,
Holy Cow! Press, Just Us, Books, Lawrence Hill Books, Lee & Low
Books, Ocean Press, Open Hand Publishing, Seven Stories Press, Soft
Skull Press, UCLA Asian American Studies Center, Women's Press
(Toronto), Women's Press (London)

**Black/Black Studies** see: **African American**

**Children/Juvenile**
African World Press, Alyson Publications, Annick Press, Arte Publico
Press, Atrium Society, Beacon Press, Book Publishing Company, Caro-
lina Wren Press, Children's Book Press, Cinco Puntos Press, Down
There Press, Feminist Press at the City University of New York, Flori-
canto Press, Gabriel Dumont Institute, Interlink Publishing, Just Us
Books, Lee & Low Books, Milkweed Editions, Morning Glory Press,
Open Hand Publishing, Polychrome Publishing, Second Story Press,
Sierra Club Books, TSAR Publications, Theytus Books, Volcano Press,
Women's Press (Toronto)

**Civil Liberties** see also: **Human Rights**
Advocado Press, Arte Publico Press, Curbstone Press, Human Rights
First, Lawrence Hill Books, Lee & Low Books, Loompanics Unlimited,
MEP Publications, Meiklejohn Civil Liberties Institute, New Clarion
Press

**Comics/Comix**
Cleis Press, Fantagraphics Books, Feral House, Freedom Press, Gay
Sunshine Press/Leyland Publications, Green Candy Press, Last Gasp,
Manic D Press, Soft Skull Press

**Communism** see: **Socialism/Marxism**

**Conflict Resolution** see also: **Peace/Non-voilence**
Atrium Society, Kumarian Press

**Conservation** see also: **Ecology/Environmentalism, Natu-
ral/Nature**
Chelsea Green Publishing, Earthscan Publications, ITDG Publishing,
Institute for Local Self-Reliance, Island Press, Orion Society, Oxfam,
Pangaea, Sierra Club Books

**Cookery** see also: **Vegetarianism**
Arsenal Pulp Press, Book Publishing Company, Interlink Publishing,
Second Story Press, Vegetarian Resource Group
**Counterculture** see: **Alternative Culture**
**Critical Theory**
AK Press, Fernwood Publishing, Merlin Press, Pluto Press, Red Letter
Press, Verso
**Cultural Studies**
AK Press, African World Press, Annick Press, Arbeiter Ring Publishing,
Arsenal Pulp Press, Arte Publico Press, Aunt Lute Books, Autonomedia,
Between the Lines, Black Rose Books, Cinco Puntos Press, Cultural
Survival, Curbstone Press, Feminist Press at the City University of New
York, Feral House, Fernwood Publishing, Freedom Press, Gay Sun-
shine Press/Leyland Publications, Graywolf Press, Maissoneuve Press,
Mercury House, Nation Books, New Press, Pangaea, Pluto Press, Poly-
chrome Publishing, Ralph J. Bunche Center for African American
Studies, Serpent's Tail, South End Press, TSAR Publications, Theytus
Books, UCLA American Indian Studies Center, UCLA Chicano Stud-
ies Research Center, Verso, Zed Books
**Developing Countries** see: **Third World**
**Development Studies**
African World Press, Clarity Press, Cultural Survival, Earthscan Publi-
cations, Garamond Press, ITDG Publishing, Inform, Inc., Institute for
Local Self-Reliance, International Labour Office, Island Press,
Kumarian Press, Latin American Bureau, Maissoneuve Press, Monthly
Press Review, Nordic Africa Institute, Pact Publications, Ralph J.
Bunche Center for African American Studies, Sierra Club Books, Zed
Books
**Discrimination** see also: **Race/Race Relations**
Advocado Press, African American Images, Green Dragon Press, Poly-
chrome Publishing, Ralph J. Bunche Center for African American
Studies, UCLA American Indian Studies Center, UCLA Chicano
Studies Research Center, Writers Corps Books
**Disabilities**
Advocado Press, Second Story Press
**Domestic Violence**
Morning Glory Press, Volcano Press
**Ecology/Environmentalism** see also: **Conservation, Natu-
ral/Nature, Sustainable Development**

Apex Press, Beacon Press, Between the Lines, Black Rose Books, Book
Publishing Company, Chelsea Green Publishing, Common Courage
Press, Cultural Survival, Dollars & Sense, Earthscan Publications,
Fernwood Publishing, Food First Books, Garamond Press, ITDG Pub-
lishing, Inform, Inc., Institute for Local Self-Reliance, International
Relations Center, Island Press, Kumarian Press, Lantern Books, Mais-
soneuve Press, Mercury House, Merlin Press, Milkweed Editions,
Monthly Press Review, New Society Publishers, Orion Society, Oxfam,
Pangaea, Pilgrim Press, Plain View Press, Pluto Press, South End Press,
Vegetarian Resource Group, Worldwatch Institute, Zed Books
**Economics**
African World Press, African American Images, Apex Press, Arbeiter
Ring Publishing, Between the Lines, Black Rose Books, Canadian Cen-
tre for Policy Alternatives, Charles H. Kerr Publishing, Chelsea Green
Publishing, Clarity Press, Common Courage Press, Cultural Survival,
Dollars & Sense, Earthscan Publications, Freedom Press, Garamond
Press, Haymarket Books, Human Rights Watch, Inform, Inc., Institute
for Local Self-Reliance, International Labour Office, International
Publishers Company, International Relations Center, Island Press,
Kumarian Press, Latin American Bureau, MEP Publications, Mais-
soneuve Press, Monthly Press Review, Nation Books, New Press, Nor-
dic Africa Institute, Oxfam, Pluto Press, Ralph J. Bunche Center for
African American Studies, South End Press, Zed Books
**Education**
African American Images, Apex Press, Beacon Press, Between the
Lines, Caddo Gap Press, Canadian Centre for Policy Alternatives,
Cinco Puntos Press, Food First Books, Freedom Voices Publications,
Gabriel Dumont Institute, Inform, Inc., Institute for Local Self-
Reliance, Just Us. Books, Latin American Bureau, Morning Glory
Press, New Press, New Society Publishers, Orion Society, Pact Publica-
tions, Rethinking Schools, Sierra Club Books
**Energy** see also: **Sustainable Development**
Canadian Centre for Policy Alternatives, ITDG Publishing, Institute
for Local Self-Reliance, Island Press, New Society Publishers, World-
watch Institute
**Erotica** see also: **Sexuality**
Alyson Publications, Arsenal Pulp Press, Bella Books, Cleis Press, Crea-
tion Books, Down There Press, Fantagraphics Books, Feral House,
Firebrand Books, Gay Sunshine Press/Leyland Publications, Green

Candy Press, Last Gasp, Loompanics Unlimited, Manic D Press, Seal
Press, Serpent's Tail, Soft Skull Press
**Ethics**
Orion Society, Pilgrim Press, Vegetarian Resource Group
**Ethnic/Ethnic Studies** see also: **Minorities**
Children's Book Press, Floricanto Press, Greenfield Review Press, Har-
rington Park Press, Human Rights Watch, Open Hand Publishing,
Polychrome Publishing, Sister Vision Press, Tia Chucha Press, West
End Press, White Pine Press
**Fantasy**
Bella Books, Fantagraphics Books, Rising Tide Press
**Feminism/Feminist** see also: **Women's Issues/Studies**
Arsenal Pulp Press, Aunt Lute Books, Beacon Press, Bella Books, CA-
LYX Books, Carolina Wren Press, Chicory Blue Press, City Lights
Books, Common Courage Press, Feminist Press at the City University
of New York, Firebrand Books, Floricanto Press, Harrington Park
Press, Nation Books, Onlywomen Press, Pilgrim Press, Plain View
Press, Post-Apollo Press, Red Letter Press, Seal Press, Second Story
Press, South End Press, Spinifex Press, Spinsters Ink, Sumach Press,
Third Woman Press, West End Press, Women's Press (Toronto),
Women's Press (London), Zed Books
**Film**
Arbeiter Ring Publications, Creation Books, Feral House, Serpent's
Tail
**First Nations/Peoples** see: **Indigenous Populations**
**Folklore/Folk Tales**
Children's Book Press, Cinco Puntos Press, Greenfield Review Press
**Gay** see also: **Gender Studies**
Akashic Books, Alyson Publications, Arsenal Pulp Press, Beacon Press,
Carolina Wren Press, City Lights Books, Cleis Press, Gay Sunshine
Press/Leyland Publications, Graywolf Press, Green Candy Press, Har-
rington Park Press, Last Gasp, Manic D Press, New Press, Serpent's
Tail, Soft Skull Press, South End Press
**Gender Studies**
Arsenal Pulp Press, Beacon Press, Black Rose Books, Cleis Press,
Common Courage Press, Fernwood Publishing, Firebrand Books,
Garamond Press, Green Dragon Press, Harrington Park Press, Interna-
tional Labour Office, Kumarian Press, Latin American Bureau, Manic
D Press, Nation Books, Plain View Press, Spinifex Press, Third Woman
Press, Volcano Press

**Globalization** see also: **International Issues/Relations**
Amnesty International, Apex Press, Arbeiter Ring Publishing, Aunt
Lute Books, Beacon Press, Between the Lines, Black Rose Books, Ca-
nadian Centre for Policy Alternatives, Clarity Press, Common Courage
Press, Cultural Survival, Dollars & Sense, Earthscan Publications,
Fernwood Publishing, Food First Books, Garamond Press, Haymarket
Books, Human Rights Watch, ITDG Publishing, International Labour
Office, International Relations Center, Island Press, Kumarian Press,
Latin American Bureau, MEP Publications, Maissoneuve Press, Me-
hring Books, Merlin Press, Monthly Press Review, Nation Books, New
Press, New Society Publishers, Nordic Africa Institute, Ocean Press,
Orbis Books, Oxfam, Pilgrim Press, Pluto Press, Red Letter Press,
South End Press, Verso, Worldwatch Institute, Zed Books
**Health**
African World Press, Between the Lines, Book Publishing Company,
Canadian Centre for Policy Alternatives, Chelsea Green Publishing,
Common Courage Press, Down There Press, Fernwood Publishing,
ITDG Publishing, Inform, Inc., Interlink Publishing, Island Press,
Kumarian Press, Lantern Books, Morning Glory Press, Nordic Africa
Institute, Oxfam, Seal Press, Second Story Press, Seven Stories Press,
Spinifex Press, Sumach Press, Vegetarian Resource Group, Volcano
Press, Women's Press (Toronto), Women's Press (London)
**Hispanic/Latino**
**Annick Press, Arte Publico Press, Bilingual Review/Press,
Calaca Press, Carolina Wren Press, Children's Book Press,
Chusma House Publications, Cinco Puntos Press, Cleis
Press, Curbstone Press, Floricanto Press, Greenfield Review
Press, Lee & Low Books, New Press, Seven Stories Press,
South End Press, Third Woman Press, UCLA Chicano Stud-
ies Research Center**
**History**
African World Press, Autonomedia, Beacon Press, Between the Lines,
Black & Red, Black Classic Press, Black Rose Books, Canadian Com-
mittee on Labour History, Charles H. Kerr Publishing, Curbstone
Press, Fernwood Publishing, Floricanto Press, Gabriel Dumont Insti-
tute, Green Dragon Press, Haymarket Books, Interlink Publishing, In-
ternational Publishers Company, Just Us Books, Lawrence Hill Books,
MEP Publications, Maissoneuve Press, Mehring Books, Merlin Press,
Monthly Press Review, Nation Books, New Clarion Press, New Press,
Nordic Africa Institute, Ocean Press, Open Hand Publishing, Pluto

Press, Seven Stories Press, Soft Skull Press, Sumach Press, TSAR Publications, Third World Press, UCLA Asian American Studies Center, UCLA Chicano Studies Research Center, Verso

**Human Rights** see also: **Civil Liberties**
African World Press, Amnesty International, Apex Press, Calaca Press, Clarity Press, Cleis Press, Cultural Survival, Curbstone Press, Food First Books, Human Rights First, Human Rights Watch, International Labour Office, Kumarian Press, Latin American Bureau, MEP Publications, Meiklejohn Civil Liberties Institute, Nation Books, New Press, Nordic Africa Institute, Orbis Books, Oxfam, Pact Publications, Pangaea, Plain View Press, Red Letter Press, Seven Stories Press, Zed Books

**Humor**
New Victoria Publishers, See Sharp Press

**Hunger**
Food First Books, Human Rights Watch, Nordic Africa Institute, Orbis Books, Oxfam, Vegetarian Resource Group

**Immigration** see also: **Refugees**
Amnesty International, Cinco Puntos Press, New Press

**Indigenous Populations** see also: **Alaska Native**, **American Indian**
Arbeiter Ring Publications, Clarity Press, Common Courage Press, Cultural Survival, Fernwood Publishing, Food First Books, Gabriel Dumont Institute, Greenfield Review Press, ITDG Publishing, Kegedonce Press, Pangaea, Sister Vision Press, Theytus Books

**International Issues/Relations** see also: **Globalization**
AK Press, Amnesty International, Apex Press, Between the Lines, Black Rose Books, Clarity Press, Common Courage Press, Cultural Survival, Dollars & Sense, Feminist Press at the City University of New York, Fernwood Publishing, Food First Books, Haymarket Books, Human Rights First, Human Rights Watch, ITDG Publishing, Inform, Inc., International Labour Office, International Publishers Company, International Relations Center, Kumarian Press, MEP Publications, Maissoneuve Press, Mehring Books, Merlin Press, Monthly Press Review, Nation Books, New Press, Nordic Africa Institute, Ocean Press, Oxfam, Pluto Press, Seven Stories Press, South End Press, Verso, Worldwatch Institute, Zed Books

**Labor/Labor Studies** see also: **Unions/Unionizing**
Apex Press, Arbeiter Ring Publishing, Between the Lines, Black & Red, Canadian Centre for Policy Alternatives, Canadian Committee on La-

bour History, Charles H. Kerr Publishing, Common Courage Press, Garamond Press, Haymarket Books, International Labour Office, International Publishers Company, International Relations Center, MEP Publications, Mehring Books, Merlin Press, Monthly Press Review, New Press

**Latin American Studies**

African World Press, Amnesty International, Arte Publico Press, Bilingual Review/Press, Cinco Puntos Press, Curbstone Press, Floricanto Press, Haymarket Books, Human Rights Watch, Latin American Bureau, Monthly Press Review, Ocean Press, Seven Stories Press, Verso, White Pine Press,

**Law/Legal Studies**

Advocado Press, Human Rights First, Human Rights Watch, Island Press, Meiklejohn Civil Liberties Institute, New Press, Pluto Press

**Lesbian** see also: **Gender Studies**

Akashic Books, Alyson Publications, Arsenal Pulp Press, Aunt Lute Books, Beacon Press, CALYX Books, Carolina Wren Press, City Lights Books, Cleis Press, Firebrand Books, Graywolf Press, Green Candy Press, Harrington Park Press, Last Gasp, Manic D Press, New Press, New Victoria Publishers, Onlywomen Press, Rising Tide Press, Seal Press, Serpent's Tail, Sister Vision Press, Soft Skull Press, South End Press, Spinifex Press, Spinsters Ink, Third Woman Press, Women's Press (Toronto)

**Literary** see also: **Anthologies, Poetry, Short Stories**

African World Press, Akashic Books, Alice James Books, Arsenal Pulp Press, Arte Publico Press, Asian American Writers' Workshop, Aunt Lute Books, Autonomedia, Beacon Press, Bella Books, Bilingual Review/Press, Black Classic Press, Black Swan Press/Surrealist Editions, Calaca Press, CALYX Books, Carolina Wren Press, Chicory Blue Press, Chusma House Publications, Cinco Puntos Press, City Lights Books, Cleis Press, Coffee House Press, Curbstone Press, Dalkey Archive Press, Feminist Press at the City University of New York, Fiction Collective Two, Firebrand Books, Gay Sunshine Press/Leyland Publications, Graywolf Press, Greenfield Review Press, Hanging Loose Press, Harrington Park Press, Holy Cow! Press, Interlink Publishing, Ismael Reed Publishing, Kaya, Kegedonce Press, Kelsey Street Press, Latin American Literary Review Press, Mercury House, Milkweed Editions, New Victoria Publishers, Open Hand Publishing, Paris Press, Pathfinder Press, Plain View Press, Post-Apollo Press, Pushcart Press, Seal Press, Second Story Press, Seven Stories Press, Sister Vision Press,

Spinifex Press, Spinsters Ink, Sumach Press, TSAR Publications, Theytus Books, Third Woman Press, Third World Press, Tia Chucha Press, UCLA Asian American Studies Center, West End Press, White Pine Press, Women's Press (Toronto), Women's Press (London), Writers Corps Books

**Marajuana**
Green Candy Press

**Media Studies**
Autonomedia, Between the Lines, Black Rose Books, Common Courage Press, Fernwood Publishing, Haymarket Books, Latin American Bureau, New Press, Pluto Press, Seven Stories Press, UCLA Asian American Studies Center

**Men's Issues/Studies**
African American Images, Harrington Park Press, South End Press, Third World Press

**Middle East Studies**
Amnesty International, Haymarket Books, Human Rights Watch, Pluto Press, South End Press, Verso, Zed Books

**Minorities** see also: **Alaska Native, African American, American Indian, Asian American, Discrimination, Ethnic/Ethnic Studies, Hispanic/Latino, Indigenous Populations, Race/Race Relations**
African American Images, Annick Press, Arte Publico Press, Asian American Writers' Workshop, Aunt Lute Books, Black Rose Books, Calaca Press, CALYX Books, Carolina Wren Press, Chicory Blue Press, Children's Book Press, Chusma House Publications, Cinco Puntos Press, Clarity Press, Curbstone Press, Floricanto Press, Food First Books, Freedom Voices Publications, Greenfield Review Press, Ismael Reed Publishing, Kaya, Lawrence Hill Books, Lee & Low Books, Milkweed Editions, New Press, Open Hand Publishing, Polychrome Publishing, Ralph J. Bunche Center for African American Studies, Red Letter Press, Sister Vision Press, Third Woman Press, Third World Press, UCLA American Indian Studies Center, UCLA Chicano Studies Research Center, West End Press, Writers Corps Books

**Multiculturalism** see also: **Bilingual**
Annick Press, Arsenal Pulp Press, Aunt Lute Books, Caddo Gap Press, Carolina Wren Press, Children's Book Press, Greenfield Review Press, Interlink Publishing, Lee & Low Books, Open Hand Publishing, Pilgrim Press, Polychrome Publishing, Rethinking Schools, TSAR Publications, White Pine Press

**Music** see also: **Punk**
AK Press, Akashic Books, Arsenal Pulp Press, Creation Books, Feral House, Interlink Publishing, Latin American Literary Review Press, Re/Search Publications, See Sharp Press, Serpent's Tail, Soft Skull Press
**Mystery**
Alyson Publications, Bella Books, New Victoria Publishers, Onlywomen Press, Rising Tide Press, Serpent's Tail
**Natural/Nature** see also: **Conservation**
Book Publishing Company, Chelsea Green Publishing, Earthscan Publications, Island Press, Lantern Books, Mercury House, Milkweed Editions, New Society Publishers, Orion Society, Pangaea, Sierra Club Books
**Parenting**
Carolina Wren Press, Morning Glory Press, Seal Press
**Peace/Non-violence** see also: **Conflict Resolution, Social Justice**
Atrium Society, Black Rose Books, International Relations Center, Kumarian Press, Meiklejohn Civil Liberties Institute, New Society Publishers, Orbis Books, Oxfam, Pact Publications, Pilgrim Press
**Philosophy**
Black Rose Books, Book Publishing Company, International Publishers Company, MEP Publications, Mehring Books, Verso
**Poetry** see also: **Literary**
African World Press, Alice James Books, Arsenal Pulp Press, Arte Publico Press, Asian American Writers' Workshop, Aunt Lute Books, Bilingual Review/Press, Black Classic Press, Black Swan Press/Surrealist Editions, Calaca Press, CALYX Books, Carolina Wren Press, Charles H. Kerr Publishing, Chicory Blue Press, Children's Book Press, Chusma House Publications, Cinco Puntos Press, City Lights Books, Cleis Press, Coffee House Press, Copper Canyon Press, Curbstone Press, Dalkey Archive Press, Freedom Voices Publications, Graywolf Press, Greenfield Review Press, Hanging Loose Press, Holy Cow! Press, Ismael Reed Publishing, Kaya, Kegedonce Press, Kelsey Street Press, Latin American Literary Review Press, Lotus Press, Maissoneuve Press, Manic D Press, Mercury House, Milkweed Editions, Open Hand Publishing, Paris Press, Pathfinder Press, Plain View Press, Polychrome Publishing, Post-Apollo Press, Pushcart Press, Seal Press, Serpent's Tail, Seven Stories Press, Sister Vision Press, Soft Skull Press, Spinifex Press, TSAR Publications, Theytus Books, Third World Press, Tia Chucha

Press, West End Press, White Pine Press, Women's Press (Toronto), Writers Corps Books

**Political/Politics**

AK Press, African World Press, Akashic Books, Amnesty International, Apex Press, Aunt Lute Books, Black Rose Books, Black Swan Press/Surrealist Editions, Canadian Centre for Policy Alternatives, Canadian Committee on Labour History, Charles H. Kerr Publishing, Chelsea Green Publishing, Cinco Puntos Press, City Lights Books, Clarity Press, Common Courage Press, Cultural Survival, Curbstone Press, Dollars & Sense, Earthscan Publications, Feminist Press at the City University of New York, Feral House, Fernwood Publishing, Fiction Collective Two, Food First Books, Freedom Press, Garamond Press, Gay Sunshine Press/Leyland Publications, Haymarket Books, Human Rights Watch, ITDG Publishing, Inform, Inc., Institute for Local Self-Reliance, Interlink Publishing, International Labour Office, International Publishers Company, International Relations Center, Ismael Reed Publishing, Island Press, Kumarian Press, Lantern Books, Latin American Bureau, Lawrence Hill Books, MEP Publications, Maissoneuve Press, Mehring Books, Merlin Press, Monthly Press Review, Nation Books, New Clarion Press, New Press, New Society Publishers, Nordic Africa Institute, Ocean Press, Open Hand Publishing, Pluto Press, Ralph J. Bunche Center for African American Studies, Red Letter Press, Seven Stories Press, Soft Skull Press, South End Press, Spinifex Press, Sumach Press, Third World Press, UCLA American Indian Studies Center, UCLA Asian American Studies Center, UCLA Chicano Studies Research Center, Verso, West End Press, Women's Press (Toronto), Worldwatch Institute, Zed Books

**Popular Culture** see also: **Alternative Culture**

Arsenal Pulp Press, Autonomedia, Beacon Press, Between the Lines, Black & Red, Black Classic Press, Fantagraphics Books, Feral House, Orbis Books, Orion Society, Oxfam, Re/Search Publications, Seal Press, Serpent's Tail, Tia Chucha Press

**Poor/Poverty** see also: **Race/Race Relations**, **Third World**

Between the Lines, Clarity Press, Curbstone Press, Freedom Voices Publications, ITDG Publishing, MEP Publications, Orbis Books, Oxfam, Pact Publications, Writers Corps Books

**Prison/Prisoners**

Amnesty International, Greenfield Review Press, Human Rights Watch, New Clarion Press

**Psychology**

Floricanto Press, Women's Press (London)
**Punk** see also: **Alternative Culture, Music**
AK Press, Akashic Books, Last Gasp, Manic D Press, Re/Search Publications, Serpent's Tail, Soft Skull Press
**Race/Race Relations** see also: **Discrimination**
African World Press, African American Images, Beacon Press, Children's Book Press, Common Courage Press, Fernwood Publishing, Garamond Press, Haymarket Books, Lawrence Hill Books, MEP Publications, Nation Books, New Press, Open Hand Publishing, Polychrome Publishing, Ralph J. Bunche Center for African American Studies, Rethinking Schools, Sister Vision Press, TSAR Publications, Third Woman Press, Third World Press, Women's Press (Toronto)
**Reference**
Arte Publico Press, Chelsea Green Publishing, Floricanto Press, Gabriel Dumont Institute, Green Dragon Press, Meiklejohn Civil Liberties Institute, Pushcart Press, UCLA American Indian Studies Center, UCLA Asian American Studies Center, UCLA Chicano Studies Research Center
**Refugees**
Amnesty International, Human Rights First, Human Rights Watch, Orbis Books, Oxfam
**Religion** see also: **Spirituality**
African World Press, African American Images, Amnesty International, Beacon Press, Interlink Publishing, Lantern Books, Orbis Books, Pilgrim Press, UCLA Chicano Studies Research Center,
**Reprints**
Bilingual Review/Press, Black & Red, Black Classic Press, Black Rose Books, Charles H. Kerr Publishing, Copper Canyon Press, Dalkey Archive Press, Fantagraphics Books, Feminist Press at the City University of New York, Freedom Press, Haymarket Books, International Publishers Company, Lawrence Hill Books, Merlin Press, Paris Press, Pathfinder Press, See Sharp Press, Seven Stories Press, Spinifex Press, Verso, Women's Press (London)
**Romance**
Alyson Publications, Bella Books, New Victoria Publishers, Onlywomen Press, Rising Tide Press
**Science Fiction**
Bella Books, Rising Tide Press
**Sexuality** see also: **Erotica**

Alyson Publications, Bella Books, Cleis Press, Creation Books, Down
There Press, Fantagraphics Books, Feral House, Firebrand Books, Gay
Sunshine Press/Leyland Publications, Green Candy Press, Harrington
Park Press, Last Gasp, Manic D Press, Morning Glory Press, Pilgrim
Press, Re/Search Publications, See Sharp Press, Serpent's Tail,
Spinifex Press, Sumach Press, Third Woman Press, Volcano Press,
Women's Press (Toronto)

**Short Stories**

Bilingual Review/Press, Coffee House Press, Graywolf Press, Holy
Cow! Press, Onlywomen Press, White Pine Press

**Social Change**

Apex Press, Arbeiter Ring Publishing, Aunt Lute Books, Beacon Press,
Book Publishing Company, Charles H. Kerr Publishing Company,
Children's Book Press, Curbstone Press, Earthscan Publications, Food
First Books, Garamond Press, ITDG Publishing, Institute for Local
Self-Reliance, International Labour Office, International Relations
Center, Island Press, Kumarian Press, Meiklejohn Civil Liberties Insti-
tute, Milkweed Editions, New Society Publishers, Nordic Africa Insti-
tute, Ocean Press, Open Hand Publishing, Pact Publications, Rethink-
ing Schools, South End Press, Verso, Worldwatch Institute

**Social Issues**

Advocado Press, Arbeiter Ring Publishing, Arte Publico Press, Between
the Lines, Chelsea Green Publishing, Earthscan Publications, Food
First Books, Freedom Voices Publications, Green Dragon Press, Inter-
national Labour Office, Lantern Books, Monthly Press Review, New
Press, New Society Publishers, Nordic Africa Institute, Orbis Books,
Paris Press, Pathfinder Press, Pluto Press, Ralph J. Bunche Center for
African American Studies, Red Letter Press, South End Press, Sumach
Press, Third World Press, UCLA Chicano Studies Research Center,
Women's Press (London)

**Social Justice** see also: **Peace/Non-violence**

AK Press, Amnesty International, Social Justice, Arbeiter Ring Publishing, Arte Publico Press, Beacon Press, Between the Lines, Bilingual
Review/Press, Black Rose Books, Calaca Press, CALYX Books, Canadian Centre for Policy Alternatives, Chusma House Publications, Clarity Press, Common Courage Press, Cultural Survival, Curbstone Press,
Food First Books, Freedom Voices Publications, Garamond Press, Harrington Park Press, Haymarket Books, Human Rights First, Human
Rights Watch, International Labour Office, International Relations
Center, Kumarian Press, Latin American Bureau, Lawrence Hill

Books, Meiklejohn Civil Liberties Institute, Monthly Press Review, Nation Books, New Press, New Society Publishers, Ocean Press, Orbis Books, Oxfam, Pact Publications, Pangaea, Pilgrim Press, Plain View Press, Pluto Press, Ralph J. Bunche Center for African American Studies, Red Letter Press, Rethinking Schools, Sierra Club Books, South End Press, Spinifex Press, UCLA American Indian Studies Center, UCLA Chicano Studies Research Center, Verso, West End Press

**Socialism/Marxism**

Arbeiter Ring Publishing, Black & Red, Canadian Committee on Labour History, Charles H. Kerr Publishing, Freedom Press, Haymarket Books, International Publishers Company, MEP Publications, Mehring Books, Merlin Press, Monthly Press Review, New Clarion Press, Red Letter Press, Verso

**Sociology**

African World Press, Arsenal Pulp Press, Black Rose Books, Pangaea, South End Press, Verso, Zed Books

**Spirituality** see also: **Religion**

Beacon Press, Lantern Books, Orbis Books, Pilgrim Press

**Surrealism**

AK Press, Black Swan Press/Surrealist Editions, Creation Books, Last Gasp

**Sustainable Development** see also: **Conservation, Ecology/Environmentalism**

Apex Press, Book Publishing Company, Chelsea Green Publishing, Clarity Press, Cultural Survival, Earthscan Publications, Food First Books, ITDG Publishing, Inform, Inc., Institute for Local Self-Reliance, International Labour Office, International Relations Center, Island Press, New Society Publishers, Sierra Club Books, Worldwatch Institute

**Third World** see also: **Globalization**

African World Press, Amnesty International, Apex Press, Aunt Lute Books, Between the Lines, Clarity Press, Cultural Survival, Curbstone Press, Earthscan Publications, Feminist Press at the City University of New York, Garamond Press, Human Rights Watch, ITDG Publishing, International Labour Office, Ismael Reed Publishing, Kaya, Kumarian Press, Monthly Press Review, Nordic Africa Institute, Orbis Books, Oxfam, Pangaea, Third World Press, Verso

**Translations**

Black & Red, Charles H. Kerr Publishing, Cinco Puntos Press, City Lights Books, Copper Canyon Press, Curbstone Press, Dalkey Archive

Press, Gay Sunshine Press/Leyland Publications, Graywolf Press, Hanging Loose Press, Holy Cow! Press, Interlink Publishing, Latin American Literary Review Press, Mehring Books, Mercury House, Post-Apollo Press, Serpent's Tail, Seven Stories Press, Verso, White Pine Press

**Travel**
Alyson Publications, Seal Press

**Unions/Unionizing** see also: **Labor/Labor Studies**
Charles H. Kerr Publishing, International Labour Office, International Publishers Company

**Urban Issues**
Black Rose Books, Dollars & Sense, Institute for Local Self-Reliance, Nordic Africa Institute, Ralph J. Bunche Center for African American Studies

**Vegetarianism**
Book Publishing Company, Interlink Publishing, Lantern Books, Vegetarian Resource Group

**Women's Issues/Studies** see also: **Feminism/Feminist**
African World Press, African American Images, Amnesty International, Arsenal Pulp Press, Arte Publico Press, Aunt Lute Books, Beacon Press, Black Rose Books, CALYX Books, Carolina Wren Press, Cleis Press, Cultural Survival, Curbstone Press, Feminist Press at the City University of New York, Fernwood Publishing, Firebrand Books, Floricanto Press, Green Dragon Press, Harrington Park Press, Haymarket Books, Human Rights Watch, ITDG Publishing, Interlink Publishing, International Labour Office, Kelsey Street Press, Kumarian Press, Latin American Literary Review Press, Manic D Press, Monthly Press Review, Morning Glory Press, New Press, Nordic Africa Institute, Open Hand Publishing, Oxfam, Paris Press, Pathfinder Press, Plain View Press, Post-Apollo Press, Red Letter Press, Seal Press, Second Story Press, Sister Vision Press, South End Press, Spinifex Press, Spinsters Ink, Sumach Press, TSAR Publications, Third Woman Press, Third World Press, Volcano Press, Women's Press (Toronto), Women's Press (London), Zed Books

**Zine Culture**
Re/Search Publications

**Byron Anderson** is Professor and Head of Reference at Northern Illinois University Libraries, DeKalb, Illinois. His research interests are in the areas of independent presses, media consolidation, and intellectual freedom. He is a long-time member of the Alternatives in Publication Task Force, a component part of the American Library Association's Social Responsibilities Round Table. He has served as complier and editor of the Alternative Publishers of Books in North America since its inception, 1994, and has authored both articles and bibliographies on the alternative press. He has been a speaker at a number of sessions discussing the alternative press.

**The Alternatives in Publication Task Force** is a part of the American Library Association's Social Responsibilities Round Table that promotes the acquisition and use of alternative information resources in libraries. Members of the task force feel that protecting access to a wide range of information resources, even in the face of partisan and doctrinal objection or economic indifference, is a major responsibility of librarians today. Librarians are obliged to serve the public rather than the information industry.

Printed in the United States
60545LVS00002B/19-21